STRONGER

STRONGER

GARETH THOMAS

EBURY
PRESS

1

Ebury Press, an imprint of Ebury Publishing
20 Vauxhall Bridge Road
London SW1V 2SA

Ebury Press is part of the Penguin Random House group of
companies whose addresses can be found at
global.penguinrandomhouse.com

Penguin
Random House
UK

First published by Ebury Press in 2021

www.penguin.co.uk

A CIP catalogue record for this book is available from
the British Library

ISBN 9781529107753

Typeset in 11.25/19 pt ITC Galliard Std
by Integra Software Services Pvt. Ltd, Pondicherry

Printed and bound in Great Britain by Clays Ltd, Elcograf S.p.A.

The authorised representative in the EEA is Penguin Random House Ireland,
Morrison Chambers, 32 Nassau Street, Dublin D02 YH68.

MIX
Paper from
responsible sources
FSC
www.fsc.org FSC® C018179

Penguin Random House is committed to a sustainable
future for our business, our readers and our planet. This
book is made from Forest Stewardship Council® certified
paper.

INTRODUCTION
THE END

It's a standard sexual health check. I enter the clinic, do a finger prick test where they take a small amount of blood and sit in my car while I wait for the results. I have gone through this routine several times before. Nothing to see here. Just a normal occurrence. Twenty minutes later my phone rings. Time to go back in. No problem. Barely worth thinking about. Like drinking a cup of tea, having a slice of toast.

The medic's expression is exactly the same. She is not downcast, nor does she seem nervous. It appears just an everyday moment. I am already thinking about the rest of the day. In fact, in my head, I am halfway home.

And then she says it.

'Your test has shown you are HIV positive.'

With a shocking, vivid clarity, I feel my world has completely ended. I am convinced, I do not question, that HIV is a death sentence. And now it is my death sentence. I am a dead man walking. I slump into the nearest chair and sob uncontrollably. Emotions – confusion, fear, revulsion, disbelief – fly around my skull before gathering one by one and solidifying into a single block of grief. I cry because I am sad, I cry because I have HIV and I cry because I am going to die. I think of my family and my friends; my loved ones whose lives I will once again plunge into chaos and despair. I am being engulfed by a giant wave and they are a long way away, watching me from the beach, helpless as I flounder. Just at the point when finally I am getting my life back on track I have ruined everything in the most awful of ways. I say the words in my head: 'You are crying for somebody who is already dead.'

I look up at the doctor. 'How long have I got left to live?' It strikes me in that moment as a question you only ever hear on medical dramas. Except this is real life. The end credits are my own.

It is then that she realises my knowledge of the virus is as flimsy as the tissue on which I am wiping my eyes. She begins to console me, telling me not to worry, while at the same time ringing Cardiff Royal Infirmary, which, she tells me, has a specialist team equipped for just this kind of scenario. They will explain exactly what the diagnosis means.

'Don't wait,' she tells me, 'go now.'

I can see she's right. Walking out of there with nowhere to go but the darkest recesses of my mind is a terrible idea – although thoughts of suicide, which have plagued me in the past, are, at this stage at least, absent. I don't feel the need to kill myself. I have the HIV to do it for me.

The doctor tells the infirmary team to expect me in about forty minutes. It is the most brutal drive of my life. I am a condemned man. This, as far as I'm concerned, is AIDS. There might as well be someone in the passenger seat holding a gun to my head. I have no doubt they are going to pull the trigger. There are only two things I am going to find out when I get there. How much longer I have to live and how awful will be my demise. I drive on autopilot as the same two questions sting the back of my eyes: How long? How bad? And then a third question enters my head. How am I going to tell my mum and dad I am going to die?

Dazed, punch-drunk, I park up and head for the unit. I am welcomed by expert medics who sit me down and give me the truth. 'You have nothing to worry about,' they tell me. 'All things being equal, your life expectancy won't be compromised. You are going to be OK.'

Great! Except none of it goes in, not a word.

All I hear is white noise, as if someone has turned up the volume on an untuned radio to full. I am genuinely just not of this world. I have heard 'HIV positive', decided I am dead, and that is the end of it. I don't hear what the doctors say and I don't want to hear. What does it matter? Death is just around the corner. For a few seconds I am transported back to my twelve-year-old self, sitting in front of the TV, the grey granite tombstone with AIDS carved into it in massive white letters with its equally blaring message underneath: 'DON'T DIE OF IGNORANCE.' When I was growing up in the 1980s, the equation was very simple and written starkly in huge letters – HIV equals AIDS; plague equals death. It's what I believe and nobody is going to tell me any different. Any soothing, comforting words I do pick up are dismissed by a single thought: 'Well, you would say that, wouldn't you? Of course you're going to tell me I'm OK. That's what everybody says when someone is terminally ill – "Don't worry. You'll be fine. We'll get through this."'

Unfortunately my brain isn't quite so adept at blocking out the physical element of the appointment. My last scrap of dignity vanishes as I lie on a hospital bed and endure a number of highly invasive procedures testing for any other sexually transmitted diseases. I curl up into a foetal position and weep as various swabs are applied to my body.

'How much worse can this get?' I think. 'I've just been told I have HIV, that I'm going to die, and now I'm being exposed in the most humiliating of ways.'

When the ordeal finishes, I numbly clean myself up, slump into the car and drive home.

I am living at my mum and dad's. I take a deep breath, open the front door, and walk in.

'All right, Gareth?' shouts my mum.

'Yes, Mum, everything's fine.'

How can I bring this weight of hurt into their lives? I can't put them through that pain. Nothing can ever be more important than pretending everything is OK.

I head upstairs to my old bedroom. Wherever I am in life all roads seem to lead back here. I start Googling 'HIV', trying to find out more about it but I am blind to any real information. All I want to see is negativity, awful stories of the virus and its effects. I don't want to understand, I just want to confirm the stereotypes and prejudices in my head, reasons that prove I am right rather than reasons that prove I am wrong. I am definitely dying and want to know how it is going to happen.

'Countries where you can go to die', I type. I need to find out if there is anywhere I can go to slip away quietly. That way I can just tell my mum and dad I am moving away for a while and go through the process in private without them knowing. I can't bear the thought of them ever knowing the truth, that they will be burdened with witnessing their son's death.

While I don't want to die, it's not something I'm afraid of. I truly believe there have been times already when I've been dead. I have been so close to taking my own life that I feel like I actually did it. I have coped with my own death and accepted it, so the act of dying holds no fear for me. It is what I will leave behind. How Mum and Dad will become not the parents of Gareth Thomas, the rugby player, but the parents of 'that guy who ran away and died of AIDS' – because I know wherever I die the truth, or a version of it, will inevitably come out.

The next day, and the day after, I outwardly carry on as normal while inside a volcano of anxiety rages. Here I am again, captive in my own head with a dirty little secret. It feels like I've never been away. Those few years of relative peace after coming out as gay were nothing more than a blip. I have relaxed and the result is I've been put squarely back in that same space. It's confirmation of what I have always known. Wherever I go I am nothing but trouble.

CHAPTER 1

REBORN

I am so grateful for that blood test. So grateful for everything that happened that day. I don't want anyone to read about my experience, my reaction, and conclude that care for those with HIV is somehow lacking. The medical staff who helped me, then and now, are incredible. They care and, like so many in our health service, they are up against it.

Like any sexually active person, I was following the NHS advice to be tested regularly. Had I not been diagnosed that day another six months would have passed before the next test. In that time the virus would have further encircled me and, because of its stealth, I would barely have noticed. I had felt well, I thought. It hadn't occurred to me there was anything wrong. But eventually, I would have suffered irreversible damage. I don't know how near I was to that point. I don't ever want to know. But I am so happy that I went to the clinic. And I am so happy that eventually the white noise faded just enough to allow me to start listening, to realise that being diagnosed with HIV wasn't the end of my life, it was just the start of the rest of it.

I started on medication more or less straight away. Only when I started taking the pills did I realise I hadn't been feeling OK at all. The drugs work efficiently, with the virus quickly becoming undetectable, at which point I understood how unwell I had actually been. Pre-diagnosis, I had been training as hard as ever, lifting weights, eating healthily, but, looking back now, I could see there was a sluggishness about me, as if I was shrouded by a thick clinging fog, or wearing a heavy backpack. As the drugs suppressed the virus, I began to experience what it was to feel normal again, as if my internal organs were being released from a tight grip. The more I analysed it, the more I started to feel like there was something invisible inside me, like a cage, cracking open. The burden lifted, the fog disappeared. I was free and I was living. You know that moment when you get your first pair of glasses? You put them on and suddenly – 'Wow!' Well, times that by a thousand. That is the power of the pill I take. As long as I have that drug, I cannot pass on HIV and I cannot get AIDS. The reassurance is massive but the virus's silent ability, if left unchecked, to eat away at me remains very, very frightening. It makes me realise just how much of a killer it can be. That is not something you can ever stick calmly away at the back of your mind.

I stand in front of the bathroom mirror and take my medication at 6am every day. At weekends, I give myself a treat and hit the snooze button until 6.30. It's not about thirty minutes extra sleep, it's about not having to get up to reality. I appreciate the miracle of medicine: that this minuscule pill, barely visible in the ruts, scars and gnarls of my palm, keeps me alive and maintains the safety of those around me. But each time I free one from its tiny foil bubble I am hit with a giant reminder of what I am living with. I want it to be the most irrelevant necessity in my life but I can't forget that this drug, Genvoya, is my life support, preventing the virus, one of the most intelligent there is, multiplying in my body. Miss taking that pill and I risk weakening my body's ability to suppress it. The possibility then arises of the virus releasing itself, at which point it can mutate and find a new form with which to fight the medicine. The hard work would be undone. The reason I face that unpalatable moment every day, watching as my reflection takes his pill, is to make sure my body never loosens its grip, to make sure I can carry on living my version of normality. Every day the pill tells me I have the virus and every day I listen. That's why I take it at 6am. It can have its little say, its little word in my ear, and then that's the end of it. Done. I can get on with my day. If I took it at six in the evening, I'd spend the whole day looking at the clock, waiting for that one-way discussion to start all over again.

Accepting the presence of HIV is one thing, being at peace with it to the point where I take my medication as routinely as I might a vitamin tablet is entirely another. Even though I live with HIV and know it doesn't restrict me, doesn't limit me and is by no means a measure of my capabilities, I still wish I didn't have it. If I had a pill that would get rid of it I wouldn't hesitate.

I don't want HIV. It's been the reason for years of living through hell. I have reached a point of understanding of its impact on me but that doesn't mean I can make peace with it.

I refused counselling. Only once, several years later, compelled by a need to clarify my thinking before coming out publicly about my diagnosis, did I speak to a counsellor. I knew I could survive whatever came at me from past experience but felt it would be useful to talk to somebody who really understood my mental state. However, all the experience did was highlight what I already knew – the only person who can provide the way forward is me. I trusted from previous times of crisis that, in the end, I would find the answers in myself. I'm not saying that should be the approach of everyone. Clearly it shouldn't. Many people will experience great benefit from counselling – maybe even myself one day – but, for now at least, I 'll deal with the hurdles placed in front of me in my own way.

As my stock of tablets gets lower and lower I start to feel bleak. Each time I swallow one, I am one step closer to having to go back to the clinic. I now maintain my dignity by doing the rectal and urethral swabs, both medical indicators, myself but every six months I go back to the clinic for a check-up and to get more pills. These appointments always prompt the memory of the moment I found out. Even something as minor as a blood test becomes massive if you have HIV because blood is somehow what it's all about. Vital for life; a source of death also. Living with HIV means that there are moments that drag me back, away from my otherwise lucky and happy life, moments I wish I didn't have to endure – giving blood or a urine sample, taking swabs. That six-monthly test is when I am forced, in the starkest of ways, via blood being syringed from my body, to meet my HIV head on. Unsurprising then that I find it so traumatic.

It's important to note, though, that from wherever HIV stigma stems, be it something we impose on ourselves or that comes from the ignorance of others, there is precisely zero among health professionals. To them, HIV is nothing to be embarrassed about. The last thing they want anyone worried about HIV to be is reticent, and anyone who carries a nervousness that the healthcare environment itself is judgemental should be reassured that it very much isn't.

Clearly, HIV is a virus of the mental, not just the physical. It means you encounter hurdles, each of which seem impossibly high but which must be overcome. Unless you want to live the rest of your life in isolation, telling others of your status is one such hurdle. In your mind it might well be the biggest of them all but my experience early on showed me that actually people – most people – are precisely the opposite of the judgemental back-turners of your imagination.

A few months after I'd been diagnosed, I started seeing someone. The second time we met, I told him my situation. It wasn't a discussion I was looking forward to, it felt like a huge and significant step to take, but he was well informed about the virus and was fine about it from the start. His reaction mirrored that of previous partners I'd called to inform once I knew I had the virus. Making those calls is by no means easy. They are calls with potential consequences, but I found the self-stigma I carried about HIV wasn't necessarily shared by others. Everyone is different. A person might have been in a relationship with someone with HIV before, they might have friends with the virus or they might just have been better educated than I was. In that case, an ex-partner telling them they have HIV is not as big a thing as I had imagined. I felt ashamed so I assumed everybody else felt the same. The reality was they didn't. They understood HIV on a broader level.

A further two-and-a-half years passed before I told anyone else close to me. In that time, I still hadn't come close to reconciling the situation with myself. My mental policy was one of avoidance. I only ever confronted my HIV when I had to, in the company of doctors or other medical professionals who I was unlikely to see in normal life. The first people I chose to tell were my old rugby pal Compo Greenslade, an incredible man who has been a guardian angel to me since we shared our first changing room at Bridgend, and his wife Kath.

I would often go to their house for a bite to eat and a couple of drinks and end up staying over. Over time, I became more and more conscious of having my HIV medication with me. What if I left my tablets in the bathroom or they fell out of my bag? It was simple paranoia. Neither of those things was likely to happen, and even if they did it was hardly likely the purpose of the tablets would be identified. But it felt important to me not to be in possession of a secret in such close and trusted company.

We sat around the kitchen table. I revealed my secret, explained the key points, and Compo and Kath sat and listened. Just as I knew they would be, they were totally understanding. They were no different with me at the end of that ten minutes than they had been at the start. I felt empowered by their reaction. In my head, it felt like I was owning up to doing something wrong.

To tell Compo and Kath and see their reaction was a big step in terms of allowing myself a degree of normalisation. If dealing with my HIV diagnosis was like flying a hot-air balloon, I had just discarded several very weighty sandbags over the side. We all need people we can trust. When we find them, we need to understand that they would actually 100 per cent welcome our unburdening, just as we would welcome theirs. We spend too much of our lives shackled by silence and fear when there are those who, whether they are old friends, part of a support group, a health professional, or on the end of a helpline, will deliver absolute support and understanding. To understand how to empower yourself, first of all you have to understand and accept your vulnerability.

I am a person who believes wholeheartedly in trust, because without it, how do any of us forge meaningful relationships? I'm not massive on mantras but I've always had a philosophy of 'trust people first – it's then up to them to do something to break it'. Unless I can see just cause, I don't go into any situation thinking, 'I don't trust this person.' I don't want to live a life where I'm suspicious of everyone I pass in the street. If anything, I want to be exactly the opposite. I want to believe that if I entrust my inner thoughts with someone, they will feel respected that I have allowed them in.

Sadly, there will always be those who take your optimism, your belief in common humanity, in togetherness of spirit, and throw it violently back in your face.

CHAPTER 2

BLACKMAIL

'Give me £250,000 or I will make it public.'

I couldn't believe what I was hearing. The words pushed me, with the force of ten men, into a corner. I fell to my knees, head in hands. When finally I looked up, I saw only the four walls closing in around me.

I found myself in this darkest of spaces for one reason only – I trusted someone, a person I once considered a friend, with my diagnosis. They then took that trust and twisted and mangled it to put themselves into a situation of power. They saw my trust as a way to make their life better. They were blackmailing me. They said it again: 'Give me £250,000 or I will make it public.'

I trusted someone and their first thought was not my welfare, but profit. It was the biggest of betrayals.

Being in the grip of someone who knows they can hurt you, dominate you, reduce you to nothing, is debilitating in the extreme. When somebody has that hold, you don't live by how you feel when you wake up, you live by how they feel when they wake up. If that happens to be 'I feel like shit', then you are in trouble. Their antidote to that feeling is simple – 'I will make you feel even worse than me.'

I know there will be many people reading this who have lived, perhaps are living, precisely that experience. They might be in abusive relationships, experiencing bullying, or trapped in dysfunctional families. It is an awful situation to be in, one of total helplessness, and one which can be deeply damaging if left to rot away at the soul. It is a power game with only one player. The aim is to deny someone else a voice. Success is measured by how much better, stronger, more valuable, more relevant, more needed, they feel at the end of the game than when they started. Bonus points for how much they can grind you down.

People don't understand how hard it can be to escape from control. They will ask, 'Why didn't you tell someone? Why didn't you just walk away?' But it's a million miles away from being as simple as that. Whatever the situation, there will be so many elements involved – psychological, physical, financial, emotional, to name but a few. It isn't a question of walking out of a door. It's a question of walking through a minefield, with what appears little or zero hope of reaching the other side.

At that stage, even several years in, I was still coming to terms with my HIV diagnosis and I had still only told ex-partners, my then partner and husband-to-be Stephen, and my friends Compo and Kath. It's not like being told you've got a bit of a sniffle. HIV was something I thought about every day, same as I do now. It weighed on me, a secret I was determined to keep for so many reasons. I was still chained to the negative tropes that so often accompany the virus. That people who have HIV are promiscuous; that they are transmitters of illness; that HIV came about because gay people can't help sleeping around. The stigma of that perceived promiscuity, the shame that I would be thought of as being HIV positive because of some sordid bed-hopping existence – 'You know why he's got HIV? Because he's been with loads and loads of people' – kept me silent. Feelings of shame were pushing me downwards. I could already hear in my head the questions I imagined would come my way. People would be unforgiving.

'Been putting it about a bit, have you?' 'When did you catch it?' 'Who have you been sleeping with?'

Strange, isn't it? If someone tells you they've got lung cancer, the first thing you say isn't, 'How many fags have you smoked in the last twenty years?' If someone tells you they have diabetes, you don't start banging on about their diet. And yet when it comes to HIV, people feel like they can assume whatever they want, even if – because there is so much disinformation and lack of knowledge out there – most of it has no relevance whatsoever. I didn't want an inquisition. I wasn't ready to be treated like the accused in a morality trial.

Of course, those who cared for me would never even think about 'fault'. But I didn't have the capacity for rational thought, to the extent I was thinking about my brother and how he would feel when I cuddled his daughter, my niece. Would he be afraid of me being close to her? That I might pass it on to her? Of course he wouldn't, not in a million years, but fear distorts the mind. With HIV, I would no longer be a fun uncle enjoying time with his brother's kids. I wouldn't even get through the door. And what would people who didn't know me be like? I had visions of walking into a bar or a café and everyone making a bolt for the door. They wouldn't want to breathe the same air as me, let alone risk using a cup that had been near my mouth, touching the door handle in the toilet. I'd be a leper.

I was desperate also not to burden my family, my mum and dad especially, with more worry. I had already put them through the whole messy process of coming out as gay. It might have been more than ten years ago but I could never forget how desperate those times were, how hard it was for them to witness the collapse of my marriage, to see me wracked with guilt about how so much of my life had been based around a lie and hear how close I had come to taking my own life. How do I thank them for their endless devotion, their loyalty? By showering them with the ignominy that comes from society's ignorance about HIV. I could imagine only too well the sneering remarks they might overhear in a shop or a pub. 'First he comes out as gay, and now guess what? He's got HIV. What a surprise. Then again, he's a bender so what do you expect. Dirty bastard.'

Even if people didn't use my HIV to feed their homophobia, even if my being gay was seen as a matter of absolute insignificance, I still felt HIV would be a step too far for the majority of people. It was something I could have prevented. So how could I expect people to reach again into their reserves of understanding and empathy for something I had brought on myself?

Any time I tried to open my mind, I was sent flying by an influx of fear and negativity. I would imagine the reactions of family, friends, those I knew, those I didn't know, until my mind was a runaway train speeding helplessly towards utter desolation and rejection.

Not for the first time, I looked for a way to shut out forever the nightmare existence being played out in my head. People describe suicide as the most selfish of acts but I saw it as exactly the opposite. Not only was it my way out of a life of hell, it was actually a way of stopping my parents, my family, my friends, from going through a life of hell as well. In complex emotional situations, selfishness is not part of the conversation. We need to remember that before we rush to judge.

In my case, suicidal thoughts have always come from a belief that taking my life would make everyone else's better. Whenever I've been confronted with circumstances which have led me to that bleak point, I have been consumed by one thought: 'What's the one thing that joins all the dots together to create the chaos in my life?' The answer has always been the same – me. Take away the dots and that chaos is gone. After the HIV diagnosis, time and again I'd go to bed at night and think it would be so much easier if I didn't wake up in the morning.

Suicide was never about me being OK with what was happening in my life, it was about others not being OK with it. For me, life without other people – my husband Stephen, my family, friends – was not worth living. The flipside of that, in my head at least, was that life for them with me would not be worth living. At that point, death really does seem like the easiest thing to do to stop the pain for everyone.

The less someone thinks about death, the more comfortable and settled their life, the less suicide makes any sense. But, in a place of mental strife, killing yourself appears so, so easy. In the aftermath of my HIV diagnosis, more than any other situation where I've had suicidal thoughts or attempted to kill myself, I felt like every scenario was an opportunity to take the easy way out. I use the word 'easy' in the context of the mental process that some experience at such personally devastating times. Such is the nightmare existence being played out in your head that your troubled mind keeps reminding you that there is a way to shut it all out forever. A simple thing like driving to the shops became six or seven opportunities to get rid of the demons. A bridge to drive off. A wall to slam into. Do it and the things that kept me awake, gave me stress all day, would be gone, to the extent it was easier to turn the wheel in the direction of death than it was to make myself stop. At one point, I was sat in my car outside a shop. In the distance I spotted a truck heading down the road. I had a huge mental flash. 'All I need to do is put my foot on the accelerator, hit this truck head on, and then it's done.' I managed to pull myself back from the brink. At various other times, I wanted to drive off a cliff and swerve off a mountain pass. When life puts you in a desperate position, when your head is absolutely fucked, you see a potential way out in everything. A different option, an easy option, one you can take and then you will be out of it. Gone.

I don't know if I really wanted to die but what I do know for a fact is I wanted to close my eyes and not open them again. I hated the world in front of me and didn't want to see it anymore. I didn't want to live. I didn't want to die. I just wanted to close my eyes and not see the mess I had created.

My having HIV shouldn't in any way affect who I am or what I can do. It shouldn't affect those around me. But at that point, across all those areas, I was totally unconvinced that would be the case. I found public knowledge of my HIV impossible to even think about. My life since coming out as gay had been about breaking stigma, and I was happy and pleased that I felt I had done this. But now I could see only widescale derision if people were to find out about this second revelation. The last thing I wanted was to subject my family to that, the same as I didn't want to be responsible for heaping more negativity on gay people and those with HIV. I knew for sure there were people who would use the revelation to bolster their prejudiced views of homosexuals as weak, reckless and plague-ridden. I could see it panning out one way and one way only – people using this information as a way of getting to me and my family, rejecting me, distorting my way of life. They would take great delight in stripping me of all positivity, everything I had worked so hard for since coming out as gay.

Shame descended on me like permanent drizzle. If I had to go to the clinic, I would essentially wear a disguise – baseball cap with peak pulled down to my nose, coat zipped up to my chin. I so feared being seen, someone wondering what I was doing there, maybe putting two and two together and figuring out my secret. My diagnosis would be the talk of South Wales by teatime.

I can see now that, subconsciously, I was also hiding from myself. I didn't want to admit that I was in this situation. Outwardly, I was going for a check-up, like thousands of people do for thousands of reasons every day. Inwardly, I wanted to hose myself down. I felt grubby, as if I had been rolling in dirt and accrued layer after layer.

This is of course a privilege not granted to others, but thankfully my appointments were always outside regular hours. The hospital, realising my anonymity, after being an international sportsman, was unusually compromised, would also let me in through a side entrance. I appreciated the comfort of invisibility but there was no avoiding the hammer blow of reality.

I was being blackmailed, for God's sake. Didn't that say everything? There was no way anyone would or could blackmail me if I wasn't dealing with something that was absolutely a matter of shame. If you are being blackmailed then you have done something terrible that others must never know about. This is your punishment, to be tied to the end of a string, a puppet dangled above a stage on which you will do anything not to appear. Your destiny and, by association, that of your loved ones is, quite literally, in the hands of another. You have lost control of your life because you have done something terrible.

I needed total control over the information, who should have it and how they should find out. Instead, in the wrong hands, as I had always feared, the contents of my mental safe had been rifled and become something powerful with which to crush me. My blackmailer had weaponised my HIV and was now aiming it straight at me. I would do anything to deflect those bullets. Maybe – and this shows how scrambled my mind was – a quarter of a million pounds was worth it.

'OK,' I thought, 'two-hundred-and-fifty grand – if I sell the house then I can get that money together. At least then my parents won't know. At least then they can live their lives and I can try to move on with my HIV back in its box.'

To even consider giving into blackmail may sound odd but any time in my life when people I have trusted have decided to use something against me, my first instinct has been to ask, 'What can I do to make this quiet? What can I do to make it go away? What can I do that will mean I can go to bed tonight and be able to sleep?'

Deep down, though, I knew also that such an attitude leads to a single destination – problem after problem after problem. If there was a guarantee that if I paid the money it would be the end of the matter, maybe I would have done it. But I've watched the cop shows, seen the movies. What do blackmailers do? They come back for more. The very fact they are blackmailers shows exactly what kind of people they are. Blackmail is rarely about money, it's about taking over your mind. That's what the blackmailer is really getting off on. They are like an old-style highwayman waiting unseen to catch you unawares, except for one difference. 'Your money or your life?' They want both.

Being blackmailed only added to and compounded a fear, a loss of control, which I already felt keenly. I would mull the same question over and over in my head – 'Why? Why would anybody use this against me?' I could perhaps have understood it just a little if this was someone trying to blackmail me emotionally. When people experience emotional overload they can act irrationally. But to actually use it for financial gain? That was on another level completely. It felt so clinical to put a figure on my HIV, my life. I would lie awake at night thinking, 'Where does that figure come from? Is that what my life is worth to someone?'

It made me even more afraid of what my blackmailer was capable of. When someone starts off that low, what might going even lower entail? At the very least, with a word in the ear of a tabloid journalist, he seemed able to destroy my entire world. What else was he planning? What other vile tricks did he have up his sleeve?

I knew ultimately that to make him go away I would have to wrestle back control. If not, I would never have another night where I could sleep easy. I would be waiting, waiting, always waiting, for the next demand, the next threat. It was then that I started recording his calls. As I clicked the button on my mobile, so I pressed the button on a whole new mindset.

'Right,' I thought, 'no more. You want to take me on? Well, this is how I play my game. You think being vulnerable makes me weak. Actually, my vulnerability gives me strength.' It was the moment of me initiating the fightback.

I didn't know exactly what I would do with those recordings. I knew that sometimes the best way to fight people who are in the gutter is to get in the gutter yourself but I didn't want to stoop to the level of my tormentor. I could have gone to the police but I found the thought of being caught up in the wheels of justice, potentially a big court case, in which my secret would no doubt come out and be smeared in a sensationalist and scandalous way all over the papers, overwhelming and distressing. But the recordings gave me something, the start of me being able to analyse with precision what was happening, to take the emotion out of it and formulate a plan of action.

Recording the calls became the catalyst for starting the mental process of clawing back my self-belief to the point where I no longer cared what he was capable of. If I didn't care, then he had no power.

I refused to pay. I refused to give up my freedom.

'Do what you want. I've had enough. I'm not engaging with this anymore.' In one single act, I had reduced him to nothing.

That regaining of control came with a new and totally liberating thought. 'If I can get up tomorrow feeling good, then I can stay feeling good.'

But if a blackmailer can't get what they want one way, they will try another. My tormentor believed his knowledge had value. And so, I believe, denied one windfall, he went to the dregs of the newspaper industry in search of another.

CHAPTER 3

KICKED TO THE GUTTER

It's 5.15am when I see him.

My dad pulls out the drive. And there he is, standing in the middle of the road. Immediately I am concerned. It is such an odd, potentially unpredictable, even dangerous, situation.

'Just ignore him,' I implore Dad. 'It'll be a drunk or a junkie. Just drive. Don't stop.' I have a train to catch – I've stayed at my parents overnight so dad can give me a lift to the station.

My dad, though, is one of life's good blokes. 'No,' he replies. 'We've got to stop. We've got to find out what's wrong.'

He brakes. 'Don't open your window,' I tell him. If we do have to engage with this stranger, I want him to come to my side of the car, then if he does try something I can clock him.

I wind down my window. The man needs no invitation. He sticks his head through, right in front of my face but speaking directly to my dad. He introduces himself as a reporter from the

Sun – and then he says it. 'Do you want to comment on the fact that your son is living with HIV and could die of AIDS?'

He withdraws his head, at which point my father hits the accelerator and we drive off.

There then descends the most excruciating silence.

'What on earth do I say to that?' I think. I am pretty sure my dad is thinking exactly the same thing.

In the end I speak up. 'Look, Dad,' I say, 'just forget that happened. It's all right, don't worry, it's just journalists being journalists.' I'm trying to downplay what the reporter has said while also closing any avenues of conversation. It works in so much as neither of us mentions it again.

Dad drops me at the station and drives off. By the time I slump into my seat on the train my head is totally fried. I have to go to London – I have a meeting about a potentially massive work opportunity – but all I can think about is my dad, what he must be thinking about me and what is happening at home. Has he told Mum? If so, what the hell kind of state must they both be in?

I find out just as my train pulls into Paddington. My mum rings. She doesn't even say hello. 'What's happening?' she cries. 'Are you dying?' She is in tears, absolutely petrified, screaming. 'What's this all about?'

It turns out Dad had gone back to the house and not said anything to my mum. The journalist, however, remained in his car outside. He let a couple of hours pass before walking up the path and knocking on the door. My dad answered, spotting straight away that the uninvited caller had a recording device in his hand. My mum then appeared a couple of seconds later. Dad again asked the reporter what he wanted. He said those exact same words again.

'Do you want to make a comment on the fact that your son is living with HIV and could die of AIDS?' Dad shut the door on him, but the damage was done.

My mind is screeching, like the wheels of the train as it bustles across the points towards the platform. 'Mum,' I plead, 'just let me get to where I need to be, do what I have to do, and then I'll be on the first train home.' I might as well be on the moon so far from Sarn do I feel at that time.

The meeting is a blur. All I can think about is what is unfolding at home, the sound of my mum crying, the no doubt hidden anguish of my dad. I picture them sat there in the living room, cups of tea going cold in their hands, Mum glancing through teary eyes at the tall glass-fronted cabinet of proud and treasured memories of her youngest son, trying to make some kind of sense of what the reporter has told them. They have opened their front door – and had a grenade thrown into their lives.

The second the meeting finishes, I get up, run out the building and leap on the train. I have to ring Mum and Dad but I don't want anyone to hear and so here I am, in the rattling, grimy emptiness between carriages – passengers, pushchairs, kids coming past – trying to explain to my parents that I'm not going to die.

I feel sick. Physically sick. Almost retching sick. My HIV diagnosis should always have been my information to tell my parents. If I was ever going to share my secret then it had to be at a time that was right, not for me, but for them. Maybe there would have been something in the news, a film, or on TV that could have created an opening for me to start a discussion, assess whether they were in the right frame of mind to understand and absorb it, rather than be floored by the shock of a sucker punch from a *Sun* reporter. Journalists can sensationalise a story in a newspaper but equally they can sensationalise it when they break their skewed version of events to those involved. For my parents, what he's said on their doorstep is no different to them walking past a newsagents and seeing 'GARETH THOMAS WILL DIE OF AIDS' on the stand outside.

If ever this moment was going to happen, then it should have been the three of us sat around the kitchen table. I would have thought about it so carefully – the right words, the calming tone, the reassuring information – instantly accessible and leading hopefully to a place of comfort and understanding. It would have been a measured discussion, bonded by three people's intimate understanding of and love for one another. But the reporter has taken that potential, that opportunity, away. Instead of them slowly taking on board the subtleties of the situation, he has charged into Mum and Dad's world and taken a chainsaw to their emotions. His actions truly feel like a violent assault on my family. He might as well have kicked the door down and spray-painted 'Your son has AIDS and is going to die' on the living-room wall. How can a newspaper believe they have a right to act in that manner?

The *Sun* has stripped me of my rightful choice of whether to share my most intimate medical information with anyone. They have denied me the chance to tell my own parents that their son has HIV. They have robbed me of it to make themselves money. In their skewed world, a family in tatters equals a plus on the balance sheet. They have forced a man to stand in a cramped, dirty space between two train carriages and try to have one of the most vital and personal conversations of his life with a mum and dad who have been terrified half to death. What a way to make a living.

I clasp my mobile to my ear and speak as quietly as I can. 'Look,' I tell Mum and Dad, 'it is true – I have HIV. But nothing they have said about me dying from AIDS is correct. I am going to be all right.'

I keep repeating it – 'I am going to be all right.'

But they need to see me for it to do any good. As it is, my words of reassurance are lost in the air that rushes past the carriage. I carry on trying my best to keep them as calm as possible, but again and again, at the most poignant of moments, the train goes through a tunnel, the connection is lost, and I'm left feverishly stabbing the redial button, seeking desperately to get them back again.

How has it come to this?

Eventually, I get back to their house. I hug my mum, who is still in absolute bits, as I walk through the door.

'I'm not going to die.' I hold her as I say it over and over again. 'I am not going to die.'

We sit down. I can suddenly feel myself shaking. My legs won't keep still. I have to get the words out. 'I don't have AIDS,' I splutter. 'I have HIV and because I am on medication I will have the same life expectancy as I would if I didn't. I am not at risk of transmitting it to anybody else. It just cannot happen. I am OK. There is absolutely nothing to worry about.'

I am giving them all the correct information but understandably they are still in aftershock from the journalist's pummelling. The brass neck of the bloke is such that he has even left his business card, detailing how to contact him to make a comment. I look at the card with disgust. I don't even want to touch it.

Everything it represents is repulsive.

CHAPTER 4

NO SAFE PLACE

What I saw before me that day, two bewildered, frightened people, was the exact reason I had carried my burden of knowledge alone. I knew I would have got so much back from them. I knew they would have been totally amazing and supportive but I thought it was best to keep them out of it. I put my own emotional needs to one side when I made that choice. There was no need for them to be weighed down. This wasn't like my sexuality. It wasn't like I was ever going to turn up at their door hand-in-hand with HIV. It was something that was always going to be invisible to everyone. It was never, or so I thought, going to spring from a jack-in-a-box in front of them. Once I'd understood what the diagnosis meant, that I was not going to get ill and die, I made a conscious decision that they didn't need to know, didn't need to plunge deep into the same abyss I was experiencing. And that, without an absolute shadow of a doubt, would still be the situation now if that reporter hadn't turned up in their street that day.

Of course, just as I suspected, my life has been massively enhanced by them knowing, because they are such incredible people who will never do less than support their children 100 per cent. But I feel equally sure their lives have not been enhanced in any way at all. It doesn't matter whether children are four or forty-five, parents feel their pain acutely. When I told them everything I had been through, including the blackmail attempt, they took it all in with a mixture of anguish, anger and bemusement that anybody should have to tolerate so much. They were devastated that my world, just as it had settled into something resembling peace and normality, had been turned upside down again. They had a weight on their shoulders that had been non-existent at 5.14am that morning.

Understandably, they also felt hurt that I hadn't told them about my HIV, that I had chosen to take this journey on my own. As with my sexuality, they felt that the reason I had held back was because I feared their reaction. 'What did you think we'd say? Did you think we would cast you aside because of it?'

Eventually, their shock morphed into a better understanding of the reality and we began to talk about how we would deal with the situation.

'Do we sit back and hope the newspaper goes away? That the blackmailer won't come back?'

One of their greatest strengths has always been to take on board information, however hard that might be, grab a cup of tea, sit down and say, 'Right, what are we going to do about it?' They will also completely respect the decision of the person at the heart of the issue. But none of us felt qualified to form a strategy against one of the most powerful media organisations in the land, one that had laid out its stall early as willing to ride roughshod over anything even slightly resembling morals or decency, and to take a machete to privacy.

All we knew for sure was the *Sun* had their quarry and so I went up to London to meet David Sherborne, a leading privacy lawyer, whose client list down the years includes Meghan Markle, Princess Diana, Tony Blair, Michael Douglas and Kate Moss. If these were the lengths the *Sun* was prepared to go to in order to print the story, then I needed the very best on the case. David was exactly that.

When I explained the situation – a newspaper seeking to out someone for having HIV – his view from the start was they would never run it. They might threaten to but it would never happen. Such an intrusion could not be justified in any circumstances. But when it's you in the firing line of these vast media organisations, even a small element of doubt is too much. I didn't know the ins and outs of this insane world I'd been thrust into. Also, I had seen some of the stories the *Sun* had printed in the past. Holding back didn't seem their style. Why should I be any different?

David told me that if the unthinkable did happen and the story was slated to appear in the *Sun on Sunday*, which apparently was the plan – the tabloids save their biggest 'scoops' for a

Sunday (perhaps I should have been honoured!) – then it is most likely they would ask us for a comment by 6pm on the preceding Friday. Each week at that exact time I would sit by the phone waiting for David to call to tell me if he had heard from them. Thumbs up, thumbs down. I was like a captive awaiting his fate in the Colosseum. Fear, the thing I had vowed to banish from my life when I came out as gay, had avalanched back into my life. Somewhere at the bottom of a thirty-foot drift of blinding white despair I was struggling to breathe. For most people, a newspaper is something they pick up in a tea break and toss to one side once their fifteen minutes is up. For me, it was something that, on any given day, could bring an increasingly fragile existence crashing down. Let me make this clear: I was scared like I had never been scared ever in my life before.

One minute past six on Friday – it was all I cared about. Once the clock had ticked past the vertical and David had called I knew my HIV secret was safe – well, for another seven days at least. The relief was as profound as it was short-lived. As Monday arrived, so the countdown, and the worrying, would start all over again. I would feel the slow build-up of anxiety, at that point a nagging nausea, a rising bile, in the pit of my stomach. By Wednesday, I would be pacing, restless, barely able to think or eat, my appetite and my concentration vanishing into a black hole of 'what ifs'.

By Friday, I might as well have woken in a dungeon, so dark was my outlook. I would spend the day immersed in a thick fog of panic. If David did ring with bad news, I would have twenty-four hours to tell everybody I cared about I was living with HIV before it was on the front of the biggest-selling newspaper in Britain. The spectre of informing so many people in such a short space of time was overwhelming. Being told I was HIV positive scared me like shit and now I was even more scared when I thought about other people finding out and the spite it might unleash.

As the hours wore past, my mind would be increasingly mashed, until it was little more than a jelly. Who was to say the HIV story wasn't just the tip of the iceberg of what the newspapers had in store for me? Who was to say that beneath the water didn't lurk even more grief and anxiety?

I had faced these waters before when I was trying to reconcile how people would react to me coming out as a gay man. But this situation somehow felt more uncontrollable and more sensational than anything I had faced back then. Friday afternoons were horrific.

Until that point, I had always thought of panic attacks as trivial. You just told whoever was having a bit of a turn to get a grip and everything would be OK. I was about to learn a very important lesson. One week, I was waiting by the upstairs phone in my parents' house. As the clock crawled in slow motion towards six, I was becoming more and more worked up. This was going to be the week David rang with bad news, I could just feel it. The more I thought about it, the more I became convinced. And then the ceiling began to fall in around me. I was trapped, no escape. I could feel a straitjacket being forced on to me, an invisible presence pulling the straps so tight I could barely breathe. I was gasping and with every useless heave of my chest I was sinking more and more into a state of abject panic. One was feeding the other, starving me of oxygen. My mum walked into the room to find me quite literally going blue. She managed not to panic. Instead she got hold of me by the shoulders and looked me square in the face.

'You've got to calm down!'

Her eyes, her voice, were the only things on the planet that could have had any effect at that time. She sat with me and gradually I managed to get my breathing under some kind of control. I felt exhausted, more so than I had ever been on a rugby field. It was as if the entire world and everything in it had a rough edge. There was nowhere I could relax.

At 6pm, David told me the *Sun* hadn't been in touch. Not that it mattered, my mind was already switching to next week – 'I'll bet that's when it will happen.' With seven days to go, already I was convinced that next week David would call with confirmation the newspaper had decided to print and we would either have to brace ourselves for the inevitable or seek the intervention of the courts. I, the subject of this hidden battle, the lad from Sarn, who happened to be good at rugby, would be a bystander as legal types slung courtroom terminology around like black confetti. David might have insisted that the *Sun* hadn't got a leg to stand on, but when it's your life on the line it's not so easy to put your faith in a stranger in a horsehair wig.

If I was to avoid ending up in a heap on the floor every week, I had to find a way to head off panic attacks. I didn't try to avoid them. Instead, when they were coming on, I learned how to calm myself down, keep breathing and figure a way of getting through to the end. After a few weeks, we agreed that if there was nothing to report David wouldn't ring. It somehow made 6pm on Friday a little less dramatic. I could breathe out. 'OK, he's not rung. We must be all right.' The panic eased a little as no longer did I have that awful moment of lifting the receiver and wondering what he was going to say.

As the weeks went on, and the prospect of publication receded, my anxiety became less and less. But even when David said there was no need to think about it anymore, for two or three months afterwards I found it impossible to stop looking at the clock on a Friday. I trusted David implicitly but I had become conditioned to think that 6.01pm was a place of safety, one that allowed me to lift the burden of potential exposure for forty-eight hours.

I knew for sure that David's honesty and certainty had saved me an even more intensely damaging experience. Right from the start I saw he wasn't a person who was going to bite his tongue and tell me what I wanted to hear.

'When I talk to you,' he told me at our first meeting, 'you can trust me. When I tell you what will happen, I'll do so because that's what I believe. Not to make you feel better.'

His job is about protecting people's privacy from a rabid press. I can't help thinking that shouldn't even be a job.

CHAPTER 5

BAIT

To this day my dad remains angry with the journalist from the *Sun*. I understand why. His standards are on a different plane from the uninvited visitor on his doorstep. He was neither going to argue with him in public nor have it captured on a recording. This is a man who has worked hard for his retirement so he and my mum can have some quieter years enjoying each other's company. And then a journalist goes and does that. Whatever that journalist or those above him thought, there can be absolutely no justification for behaving so callously. Mum and Dad lived that moment. They can still see his face, hear his words, feel their every internal organ fall through the floor. Don't give me the 'only following orders' routine. This is not a war. A decision like that comes down to personal choice. If you don't want to do that job, leave and do something else.

I, however, am not angry. Being angry gives that journalist relevance. He is nothing to me. I'm not angry with him any more than I'm happy with him. I only want to move forward with life. That's not to say I don't understand my dad's anger at the way he and my mum were treated that day. It's just that I have learned not to let anger dominate me. Anger is negative, eats away at you, saps your strength and leaves you feeling helpless and exhausted. It is reactive, not proactive. It holds you back and keeps you mentally tethered to one place. For that reason, I would willingly forgive that journalist if he asked. I genuinely would accept his apology.

'You know what, mate?' I'd tell him. 'I hope you have learned something from it and moved on. If you haven't, then maybe you should. You are a better person than you showed that day.'

I know as well, however, that the harassment goes on. If one in ten men are gay, we can be sure that within the Premier League, for example, there are players in the closet. Those statistics suggest there would be at least two gay participants in every game. Chances are, there will be teammates who know about them, and, via the grapevine, people in the media. That's why we see so many 'Prem Star To Come Out As Gay' headlines. Newspapers are digging a sharp stick into that person's back. 'We know – wouldn't it be better just to come out and tell us? Or would you prefer that, with typical understatement and charm, we told everyone on your behalf?' As much as they are testing that person's nerve, they are also fishing. Maybe a reader will guess who the mystery man is and have the picture or private message that – whoopee! – completes the jigsaw.

Thing is, I like journalists. I know lots of fantastic writers and reporters who do some remarkable work and are motivated by a desire to expose injustice and make a difference. But the ones who do the sneaky, underhand stuff can, sadly, be feral. Real journalism done well is a brilliant tool. Some, though, would rather use their pen to slash at people and leave them barely breathing. That kind of journalism is horrific and ruins people's lives.

I would love to understand the mindset of the person who felt it was OK to tell my parents that their son was going to die – because that is effectively what he did. I would love to understand how he could have gone home that night, maybe to his family, maybe to read a story to his kids and kiss them goodnight, then gone to bed, got up the next day and done it all over again. I don't know if it's just me, but I really can't fathom how someone can do what they did to my parents and reconcile it as just part of their job, just a way to earn money to put food on the table. Morally, it is indefensible. There is no place for that kind of journalism or journalist. They don't have the right to share the same job title as those good and committed journalists whose writing effects change and rights wrongs. I feel for decent journalists who are tarred with the same brush as those who want to rifle through dustbins and peep through windows at those on the edge, those trying desperately to hold things together, so they can put it on the front of a newspaper and crash their lives. Perhaps more sickening is the fact there is somebody above that person who has given them the green light to do so.

'I want you to leave your morals on the doorstep because – guess what? – if you don't I'll get rid of you and get someone else in here to do the same thing.'

Why do they do it, ultimately? Clickbait. That is all. Something that will drive advertising to create more money for the business. Just a tiny insignificant cog in the steamroller machine of sensationalism; a headline on a phone that someone absent-mindedly clicks and in so doing feeds the people who run this seedy life-wrecking business. Maybe when the journalist who turned up in Sarn that morning sits back and considers what happened that day, he will see that he too was nothing more than a pawn in a bigger commercial game, one that puts sensation over celebration, shock over normalisation. The result of the mire of sensationalised language and headlines is that those considering coming out are further discouraged from doing so.

We only evolve through learning, understanding how people are and how they live their lives. What makes them feel good? What makes them feel isolated? What makes them feel despair? Where are the points of reference in the *Sun*'s pages for anyone who sees themselves as outside the newspaper's bank of stereotypes? For decades, differences have been highlighted in the manner of a circus freak show. Newspaper proprietors will argue that they are giving readers what they want. There is, sadly, some truth in that statement. Be it rugby, basketball, tennis or whatever, it seems people are intrigued by sex and sexuality. On any level, sex does indeed sell. The prurient interest in my life never stopped after I came out as gay. Some years ago, a newspaper rang me and said they were running a front-page story that I was going to become a porn star. I couldn't believe what I was hearing.

'You what?'

'No point in denying it. We know. You've been in Germany doing auditions.'

In the end I had to prove I was in the UK at the relevant time so they wouldn't print the story. Some random person imagines some bollocks and gives it to the press and I'm the one scrabbling around for evidence to show it's not true. A porn star? Imagine my mother and father reading that over their corn flakes.

Press abuse bothers me a lot. There are simply no limits for certain elements of the media. I have spoken to the family of Captain Tom Moore, the centenarian ex-army officer who raised more than £30 million for NHS charities in the early days of the coronavirus pandemic by walking up and down his garden. A hero in anyone's book. And yet photographers had been seen near the house while journalists had been contacting friends and neighbours to try to find any cracks in the family.

It's an awful feeling to think that people are actively trying to destroy you, that they will seize on and distort anything to bring your world crashing down. For proof you need look no further than Caroline Flack, the *Love Island* presenter who took her own life amid a media feeding frenzy over her private life and impending court case. When I turned on the television and saw that she had died I felt pain for her and her family.

Social media, and its potential to drive readers to click on stories, has brought out the worst in certain newspapers. More clicks means more advertising revenue and the easiest way to make that happen is a sensationalist headline, all too often leading to an entirely benign story that in no way justifies such treatment. As consumers, we scroll on to the next story without a second thought about how disastrous that headline, that grotesque distortion, might be for the person concerned.

Don't be fooled into thinking negative and damaging media attention is something that happens only to those who are famous. Anyone deemed to have a story that will get clicks is seen as fair prey – the clickbait world is increasingly mainstream. Recently I saw an article on a newspaper website about a rugby player I knew, a really good prop, who had been released by his team and told he needed to lose weight. I felt the headline they used, suitably gratuitous to get more clicks, was fat-shaming him. Immediately, I sent the newspaper a message saying it was disgusting, they should take it down and make a public apology. I argued that if the article had been about a woman with a weight issue then it would (at least I hoped, possibly naively) never have been couched in those terms. That it was about a man shouldn't make a difference and they should feel ashamed to have written it. On the end of every piece of clickbait is a human being with emotions just the same as the rest of us.

We are now in a desperate time where the media and social media have formed an incestuous and parasitic relationship. Media organisations find their news on social media, and social media reports that news. Who actually is who anymore? Certainly neither will ever take responsibility for their actions. Like the part they played in the tragedy of Caroline Flack's death. As soon as they could, they washed their hands of her and moved on to their next victim. But I can't and won't forget the way that certain elements behaved after her death – for example, the way newspapers tried to clean up their past in terms of what they had written about her, articles suddenly vanishing from their websites. Those on social media were no different, presenting wholly different opinions to the ones they'd been spouting just days previously.

We can't simply blame the media, the paparazzi. Keep visiting those websites, buying those papers, and we are all part of the problem one way or another. None of us is perfect. We can, though, keep dusting off our moral compass, keep checking we are moving in the right direction. At some point, the excesses of the press will be so off kilter with modern feelings, modern emotions, that, like me waiting for my weekly call from David, they too will be denied oxygen. At that point, they can either moderate or they can die. Perhaps then those seeking to deal privately with grief, misfortune or a world turned upside down can do so without wondering who is lurking at the end of the drive.

For now, however, some things never change. The *Sun* still refers to me as being 'openly' gay. They hang so many negatives on that word, like it's something that someone would surely prefer to keep secret or is a bit shocking. Put the word 'openly' in front of the word 'racist' and you'll see what I mean. In tabloid-speak, only somebody blatantly behaving in a way they shouldn't does something 'openly'. Maybe the person who knocked on my mum and dad's door should apply it to themselves – 'I am openly a *Sun* journalist'.

Several months later, I found out that the paper had been sniffing around some of my neighbours as well. 'I just want you to know we had no part to play in any of it,' one of them told me. They didn't need to – I knew they wouldn't have spoken to a reporter in a million years. But I couldn't help thinking how awful it must have been for them to have been put in that position – 'If Alfie knows they called me, then he might think I've said something to them.' I imagine it was a deeply unsettling experience. I know the tactic they use: put the person under pressure. Make them feel as if they are being besieged. It had happened when I was still married to Jemma. On that occasion, a tabloid had gone round my neighbours asking if they'd seen any men going in and out of my house. They went to the pub across the road and asked the same question. Anything for a quote that would back up whatever sordid version of the truth they wanted to present. When that gets back to you, it's bound to cause an element of paranoia.

Even after I came out as gay, killing that particular story stone dead, the tabloids still hounded me relentlessly. At one point, after Jemma and I had split up, I moved into a caravan (I know, the glamour!). As I put the key in the door one day, I spotted several people hiding behind a grassy mound. Reporters. How do I know? My friend who owned the campsite had a conversation with a photographer while the guy was cleaning his camera in the toilets. He told him he'd been sent down by a tabloid newspaper because there was a rumour I was 'shacked up with the gay lover who I'd left my wife for'. They wanted to get a picture of this imagined couple together in the caravan so had set up their telescopic lenses.

At that time, my head was so rattled from the earthquake of being honest about my sexuality that I didn't care. I had bigger problems to worry about than a few idiots up from London with a fancy camera. Forget whatever fantasy existence they thought I was living, my real life was all over the place, so chaotic in fact that they could have printed whatever they liked and it would barely have registered. I was out of control with no idea what to do.

Looking back now, the *Sun*'s plan that morning outside my mum and dad's was possibly to provoke me. It was never likely that my dad was going to deliver an instant reaction at the wheel of his car at a quarter past five in the morning and yet the reporter had leaned straight past me and gone for him. Was that to wind me up? Had I got out of the car ranting and raving, chances are they'd have got exactly what they wanted. To them, any kind of response can be painted as an engagement, a dialogue, a reaction. If anything had come from my mouth concerning HIV, then they would have had their 'in'. Equally, I knew that if anything was ever to come from my mouth it could never ever be through them. Putting a delicate emotional situation into the hands of the *Sun* is like handing a bone china teacup to someone wearing oven gloves.

At that stage, the *Sun* was being kept at bay, but, as with my sexuality, the strain of maintaining the secrecy was relentless. Some days I would take the window seat in a café in Bridgend and mull over my thoughts. I'd find myself watching passers-by, just as I had when I was in turmoil over my sexuality, feeling so envious of their normal lives. Of course, I was wholly wrong in doing so. How did I know what mental baggage any of those people were carrying around? Can anyone's life ever be described as normal? We all carry something. For all I knew, that young woman, that middle-aged man, might also be trying to come to terms with being HIV positive, might also be facing unimaginable pressure in their private life.

No one was higher in my thoughts than my husband Stephen. The last thing I wanted was for this incredible man, who had brought me a level of happiness I never thought possible, to be consumed in the soap opera that my life seemed forever destined to be. The strength of our relationship was its utter normality. Me and Steve didn't do 'centre of attention'. We did sitting in front of the TV watching films and eating chocolate. But this was an episode that inevitably he would be dragged into.

Unlike my dad, who has done so for years, religiously making notes every evening, I've never been one for keeping a long-term diary. But around that time, sat in that window, I did occasionally jot down my thoughts, a recurring theme being the fact that while I was living, I was far from alive. One day I felt utterly consumed by what I perceived as the hopelessness of my situation.

Today, I wrote, *I feel like I want to die. As I watch the world go by, I wonder again what my purpose in life is. Is it to breathe toxic air? I only survive from seeing others achieve and the love of my amazing husband, my family, and my friends. Will I ever find my purpose? Or will I die never knowing?*

I've come a long way from that moment and yet, reading it back now, I still recognise those feelings. I can feel the sharp pinprick of those emotions at the back of my eyes, the fear, the loneliness. I felt hounded. The *Sun* had been shackled but I knew for sure they, and others, were sawing away at the links on the chain. My trust shattered by the experience of the blackmailer and the savagery of the newspapers, I felt unable to talk to anyone. Those who I had told, meanwhile, in my view I had only burdened. I was so alone.

The day of reckoning would one day come. The only question was who, how and when? It took me a while to reconcile the idea in my head but in the end I started to piece those elements together. Instead of not knowing the answer to any of them, I realised I actually had the power to dictate all three. I came to see that I was capable of telling the exact same story as both the blackmailer and the journalist but in a much better, more compelling, positive and inspiring way. We had the same subject matter, I concluded, it was just a matter of how it was presented.

It was such a big moment of understanding I couldn't work out why I hadn't thought of it before. Maybe I could tell my HIV story *my* way – one that didn't involve hurting others or gaining power over them. Perhaps, if I was honest, and told my story my way, just maybe it would be welcomed, understood and embraced. Finally, I saw what had always been in front of me – I could come out as HIV positive in a way that displayed not weakness but more strength than could ever be imagined.

All I needed now was to find it in me to make it happen.

CHAPTER 6

HUNTED

I am in full make-up as the Wicked Queen's evil henchman replete with vast black leather coat and gloves when I knock on Samantha Womack's dressing room door. She opens it in a towering headdress and wraparound shoulder horns. She is the Wicked Queen in question.

'Hi, Sam,' I say. 'I really need to have a chat with you.'

When it comes to the HIV 'story', the tabloid pressure, which has never wholly subsided, has a habit of being applied when I'm at my most vulnerable. Christmas is a case in point. Not only is this a time when the emotional importance of family is heightened but it is also a period when I'm away from them. Performing twice a day means a detachment from my normal existence. Elements of the media know that, cast adrift from my support network, that is the time to come for me. You see, it's not that people who run certain newspapers aren't intelligent. They are just intelligent in a very odd way, where they need other people's misfortune and discomfort to stimulate and nourish them. They must have been hyenas in former lives.

In my case, the predators – them – know the intensity of the festive period means their prey – me – has little or no time to mentally unwrap whatever tatty gift of unpleasantness they threaten to send my way. 'He can't do panto and look happy as Larry when he knows we're breathing down his neck.'

A teaspoonful of common human decency would make all this mental torture go away. But some would rather dish out buckets of thinly veiled prejudice and hate. They want to get me at my weakest, and then make me weaker. Forget the usual five minutes of 'He's behind you!' – the gutter press never exits the stage. I am in *Snow White and the Seven Dwarfs* in Cardiff with Sam when once again the tabloid heat is turned up, threatening to expose my HIV status. Sam is a beautiful person. She has an aura about her, so open and empathetic. She never judges. She herself is a strong woman who has been put in corners and come out fighting. The more I get to know her, the more I have an urge not only to confide in her about my HIV but that I am considering going public. When I knock on her door to tell her, I suppose the costumes just add to the drama of the occasion – it will look good in the film of my life, right? We'll have a laugh about it later.

Sam invites me in at a time when my newfound will to come out as HIV positive is wilting. On the one hand, I am terrified of the story finding its way into the press. The stalls in front of me day after day are packed with kids. Will their parents still bring them along once a newspaper has ripped the billboards down and presented its own picture of me? On the other, I don't want to return to a place of dread and fear, petrified of people discovering my secret.

I am hopelessly lost. Make no mistake, coming out is a massive step. Not for the first time, the temptation to throw in the towel and shut myself away from public life is massive. I know only too well how unjustified media attention can make your life a misery and the *Sun*'s antics in particular have delivered a thudding reminder of just what some elements of the British press are capable. Do I really want to voluntarily invite this into my life?

'What is the point?' I think to myself. 'I could stop the fight right here. I could just bail out. Why not just admit it's too much?' Rather than coming out, maybe I should be doing pretty much the opposite – make myself scarce, become invisible and I puncture the power of the popular press. If I'm not on TV or in magazines anymore, then for them what's the point? Their whole schtick surrounds fame. Who do you think created this age of celebrity? Newspapers fill the trough and then feed from it.

No doubt then that flicking the off switch on the spotlight is an option – but it's an option where I will press stop on my life. I will stand still, stop evolving, deny myself the strength I have always accrued from overcoming the challenges laid before me. My family too will be denied the satisfaction of seeing me overcome the hardest of times and know that I am happy. They will know I let the bullies win.

I am desperate, one way or another, for the bright light of mental freedom. The *Sun* has been sitting brooding on its tale for more than two years now, hoping one day it will hatch into the 'world exclusive' that will drive the clicks on its website. Two years. Imagine what that does to the person whose life they could potentially be wrecking. Not just mine – anybody's. There is an invisibility to media harassment which makes it difficult for those on the outside to comprehend how deep it worms its way not just into your own head but those of your loved ones. It's like a tick, jumping from person to person, burrowing, painful, irremovable, nagging.

While I struggle to cope with that hostile environment, thanks to David Sherborne, and my previous experience with the press slavering over my sexuality, at least I have the slight advantage of understanding how the maelstrom works, the route the tornado is likely to take and how the worst of it can be avoided. Others – my parents, for example – don't have that knowledge. Why should they? There aren't night-school lessons in what to do when the press comes knocking.

But will coming out make it any easier? In my mind, I can see a family photograph unfurling in front of me. I look at each person intently, asking myself, 'How will my coming out affect them?' I have a big family, including nieces and nephews. What will kids say to them in the street? In school? Coming out won't end with me. All these people on this photo will have to go through their own process of reconciliation. And no one will see that side of the equation because it will all happen quietly and emotionally behind closed doors.

Stephen again stands out. I think of the assumptions that will be made of him. 'Gareth Thomas has HIV? You're his husband. You must have it too. That's how it works, isn't it? It's transmitted from one person to another.' He will have the stigma without even having the illness.

For his own part, Stephen wonders whether, if I come out, we might be treated differently. On a night out will we be subjected to stares, like animals in a zoo? Or worse, rejection, abuse? I know exactly what he means. I have been blessed with so much support and goodwill from the public, both as a rugby player and after I decided to be honest about my sexuality. So many people have told me that it means a lot to them to have heard my story. I don't want to lose this and a fear of rejection haunts me. No one wants to be ignored, dismissed, pushed to one side. To be alone in a busy room. I don't want to live a life where people – vocally or silently – don't want to be in the same gym as me, the same bar, the same restaurant. To be fearful of putting their hands on the same weights, their lips on the same glass, their mouth on the same fork, even if it has been through the dishwasher a thousand times. Just because these fears and prejudices some people still hold about HIV are based on long-standing misinformation, it doesn't mean they don't exist. A pneumatic drill hammers one simple question into my skull – would those previously pleased to see me now turn their backs on me?

It is in this confused and contradictory state that Sam finds me and she gives me the coordinates back to sanity. Choosing her as a confidante is one of the best decisions of my life. I know straight away from her demeanour, her absolute honesty, that I have been right to entrust her with my innermost secret. Not only does she listen but she completely understands. Just minutes before, I'd found myself in the solitude of my dressing room staring at an image of myself made shockingly, terrifyingly bright by the lightbulbs round the mirror, wondering whether I really should write the next scene in my life or if it is a version of me that should never see the limelight. Now, after a ten-foot walk and a quick knock on her door, Sam's negotiating me through one of my darkest times. Not so much Wicked Queen as Fairy Godmother. Sam doesn't have kid gloves for her role but she might as well, so gently does she deconstruct and reassemble my mental quandaries, as if they are workings of a watch that needs delicate attention before it can once again start ticking.

Everything she says seems to make sense. 'You're not someone who should be trapped in a corner. Why should that ever be the case? There is no stigma to a virus. We're human beings. We all get them.'

More and more I start to think the situation through in a positive manner. If I take control and tell my own story in my own way then I can use my experience to educate people. I'm not naïve. I know it will be an intensely difficult journey, reawakening endless painful memories of my diagnosis and the anguish and soul-searching that followed. I gave a tiny spot of blood that day that has turned into gallon upon gallon of tears. But I feel somehow it will be worth it. In the most basic of ways, I know it is the right thing to do.

It's typically bizarre that one of the most deeply affecting conversations of my life should happen fifteen yards from a stage dressed to look like a fairytale forest but, whatever the circumstances, Sam has made my mind up. I will come out in public as an HIV-positive man.

CHAPTER 7

NO LIMITS

There was zero doubt in my mind that if I was to come out as HIV positive, I needed to do it in a way that made a statement. I wanted to banish forever the media-fed stereotype of a person with HIV being frail, liable to snap like a twig, on the verge of death. I wanted to smother the misconception that HIV is the result of a lack of mental fortitude, a failure to do what is right, to behave within the accepted norms of society. I wanted to stem the flow of verbal diarrhoea that says HIV affects gay men because they are naturally weak or effeminate. HIV has no more to do with weakness than it does strength. It sits hidden in everyday existence, transmitted through the interactions that the vast majority of us experience. HIV isn't weak, isn't strong; isn't right, isn't wrong. It's life.

A thought occurred to me. Wales Ironman was nine months down the line. Widely considered one of the toughest in the world and starting and finishing just down the coast in Tenby, it entails a 2.4-mile sea swim, 112-mile bike ride and full marathon.

To take part would mean taking my physicality to a level I had never experienced. Rugby's tough but, no matter how full-on a game, it's over after eighty minutes. In a best case scenario, the triathlon would take me around twelve hours to complete. Worst case scenario? Well, let's put it this way, I couldn't swim.

I come from the *Jaws* generation. When it comes to my fear of the sea, that film has a lot to answer for. They might not have great whites in Tenby but they do have massive jellyfish the size of a car tyre which have a nasty habit of popping up right in front of you, and for me, that's plenty enough to have the Welsh equivalent of Sheriff Brody screaming, 'Mynd allan o'r dŵr!' ('Get out the water!') from the nearest beach. Even without thinking about what lurks beneath, getting in a deep, swirling mass of surf has never seemed a particularly good idea to me. I've always been ultra-aware of dangerous situations and what can go wrong, and water seems to offer up more possibilities of an early demise than most. Seas, rivers, swimming baths, I've never liked any of them. More than anything, it's the fear of my head being underwater. I have always found it so horribly claustrophobic – the water enclosing me, my panic quickly rising as a sensation of utter helplessness grips me. I just could never reconcile it as being in any way normal. You can breathe out but you can't breathe in? I'm not wrong in thinking that could kill a person, am I? And, therefore, surely I'm perfectly justified in being afraid of it. We've learned to adapt to that environment but it can never be natural to us. It's the reason we're not fish.

While as a kid, I'd go in the swimming pool with my mates or, if I was on a rugby tour, mess about in the sea with the lads, I never wanted to be out of my depth, to have that horrible 'Oh shit!' feeling where you reach for the bottom with your toe only to find it's not there. I would never put myself in a position where I might go under. As I got older, I became more honest with myself about my fear and so simply avoided any situation that might entail me ending up in deep water or the sea.

If I was to turn a loose idea to take part in the triathlon into something more concrete then my phobia of deep water would have to be overcome – an overwhelming mental gulf I would need to cross before I'd even begun to take on the vast physical challenge of the event itself. In entering the Ironman, I wasn't so much avoiding deep water as laying out the welcome mat and inviting it in for tea.

The sea arrived in the rather less threatening and altogether more reassuring form of renowned swimming coach Dave Tonge. Dave has an 'endless pool', which is basically a big tub, shallow enough to stand in, in which a current is turned on for you to swim against, like a treadmill for swimming. Mentally, it made the process so much easier. I didn't have to deal with the vastness of a pool where the sides can seem a distant prospect if you are out of your depth.

Dave took me through a series of micro-steps. I would put my head under the water for ten seconds, then fifteen, then twenty. The next stage was to put my head under and breathe out. He was teaching me to trust the water. The downside in those early stages was I began to see him as my lifejacket. His presence was so hugely reassuring that I could only imagine sinking if he wasn't there. The point had to come where I put the onus on myself. In the triathlon, there wouldn't be a supporting hand to rely on or, if things went wrong, to blame. I had to take responsibility. Whether I was in an endless pool, swimming pool, or the vastness of the sea, only I could put my head under the water. Only I could control my thoughts. Dave could help me and guide me but he couldn't live my mindset. He knew that as well as anyone. All the time, as he took me from stage to stage, almost by stealth, he was slowly removing himself as a buoyancy aid. 'Click moments', I called them, where all of a sudden I felt I had progressed.

Dave was a deeply perceptive operator. At an early stage, when I still couldn't swim that well, he took me in some really rough seas, where massive waves crashed into and over me. Even now I can swim relatively strongly I wouldn't go in the water in those conditions. But he had figured out how I think and he was giving me a psychological comfort blanket – the knowledge I had faced extreme scenarios and overcome them. None of this was spoken. I had no idea at the time he was stretching me, strengthening me. And yet, there he was, with his bricks and cement, adding another layer to my sea defences. His actions meant that, if conditions were bad on the day of the Ironman, I would know I had already dealt with an angry sea when I wasn't particularly good at swimming, so dominating negative thoughts in the maelstrom of the triathlon would be so much easier.

Before the Ironman itself came the Long Course Weekend, a key moment of preparation where, across three days, competitors get to experience the set-up for each discipline. At that point, two months before the real thing, I hadn't swum anywhere near as far as the 2.4 miles that I would have to complete for the real Ironman and I was not short of nerves when I stepped into the waves at Tenby for the dress rehearsal. It was a daunting prospect; I knew I needed to overcome my very real phobia of water for not one minute, five, ten or twenty, but more like eighty or ninety.

I considered my nervousness understandable – I was putting myself way outside my comfort zone into an environment that had real, not imagined, perils. Equally, I knew I had prepared myself mentally for the challenge. I had considered the state of mind I needed to adopt, emphasised to myself that I was physically strong enough, that even if there was an issue there were plenty of safety marshals to help me, and Dave would be in the water too. And yet I got just a hundred metres into the swim when my pre-built wall of strength was breached and I was consumed by panic.

'The shore is disappearing behind me! I'm out of my depth. I could go under. Everything is out of my control.'

And then one final overwhelming thought – 'I could die here!' I was properly freaking out.

'I'm not doing it!' I shouted to Dave. 'Get me out of this water! I can't do it!'

He swam closer and tried to calm me down. There were three buoys dotted across the 1.2 miles of water, which constituted a lap.

'Let's just go to the first buoy,' he told me. 'We'll assess the situation there.'

I was crying now, gripped by fear, but Dave's words, his reassuring tone, proved enough to get me moving. I worked out a basic plan. I would count fifty strokes, stop, get my bearings, calm myself, and then set off on another fifty. Eventually, we reached the buoy.

'Right,' Dave told me. 'Everything is OK. We'll just do one lap and then we'll finish.'

By the time I staggered out and on to the sand I was in a state of physical and mental exhaustion.

'Thank God, it's over,' I thought. And then Dave got hold of me, dragging me back across the sand and into the water. I had no strength to stop him. The waves hit me in the face, my head went under, it was horrific. He grabbed the spluttering mess that was me and pulled me out again. The nightmare, surely, was finally done. I'd barely sucked some much-needed air into my lungs when I was being hauled back into the sea again. It was as if he'd gone mad. But Dave knew exactly what he was doing. He was helping me overcome the fear, not just by confronting it, but by taking me to an awful place and showing me I could survive.

Before that day, I would swim in the sea for a few minutes and then pretend my goggles were leaking, or there was some other issue, cramp, something wrong with my wetsuit. I was the master at creating a reason to stop and gather my thoughts. After Dave's kind trick, I could put my head in the water and swim constantly for hours. I knew I had gone to the absolute limit and been all right. I knew even if I had a panic attack in the Ironman itself, I'd be able to gather myself, draw on the mental strength Dave had given me and go again. That was important because swimming in the sea alone or in a small group is very different from doing so among 2,000 other people. That can be scary and unnerving.

I knew the triathlon swim would mean me constantly having to overcome, overcome, overcome. So to realise I had mentally cracked my fear of not being able to swim confidently or strongly enough to survive a length of time in the sea was massive. I know also that plenty of others share my issues with deep water. I would never wish anyone to go through what I did to banish that anxiety. If it wasn't for the Ironman, and what was riding on it, my desire to show the truth about HIV, then I really don't think I'd have stuck it out. It was too traumatic an experience to go through just to have the ability to stick my head in the sea and swim.

That's what I thought at the time anyway. Time, as it tends to, would change my perception of the sea considerably.

CHAPTER 8

SINK OR SWIM

While the *Sun*'s tide of negativity was on the wane, it was always itching to come back in again, and a month before the Ironman they printed a story about an unnamed gay sportsman about to come out as HIV. I knew exactly what they were doing. They were jabbing a finger in my chest. 'We're still on to you, pal.'

Their little plan backfired. When I saw the article, I couldn't believe my luck. They had published right slap-bang in the middle of me filming a major HIV documentary for the BBC. Due to be screened a few days after the event and, therefore, a project known only to a few trusted individuals, it would form an important part of my coming out, with one of its most important elements being the debunking of myths and inaccuracies surrounding the virus. Another major motivation for making *Gareth Thomas: HIV and Me* was to show the *Sun* I was no longer afraid. But when they printed the anonymous sportsman story, it turned out to be a gift.

It was Ian Durham, the documentary's director, who rang me with the news.

'You're on page three of the *Sun*.'

A gay man on page three? Well, at least that was a break-through. We decided that I would read out the piece to camera. Thanks to the *Sun*, we had the perfect illustration of pitiful games played by certain elements of the tabloid press and their abject ignorance.

The headline immediately set the tone: 'SPORTS STAR IN HIV SHOCK.' What does the word 'shock' deliver? Negativity. It's a shock, therefore it must be bad. 'A British sports star is set to publicly announce they are HIV positive,' it reads. 'The international intends to break the news on social media to fight the stigma of living with the virus, which can cause AIDS.'

'The sports star,' it continues lower down, 'will follow in the footsteps of US basketball legend Earvin "Magic" Johnson, 59, who announced he was HIV positive in 1991. He takes a daily cocktail of drugs to prevent his HIV progressing to AIDS.'

'British figure skater John Curry,' it adds, 'who won gold at the 1976 Winter Olympics, announced he was HIV positive in 1987. He died of an AIDS-related heart attack aged 44 in 1994.'

Why does the journalist keep mentioning AIDS? For one reason and one reason only – to sensationalise HIV, somehow dirty it in readers' minds. Why use John Curry, who died over twenty-five years ago, as a reference? Simply to reinforce stereo-typed and hackneyed ideas about HIV, homosexuality, AIDS and death. Instead of John Curry, the journalist could just as easily have mentioned the name of any of those living a healthy and thoroughly unblemished life with HIV.

A 'cocktail of drugs'? I take a single pill every day. Even without this kind of lazily misleading nonsense people have enough misconceptions about HIV treatment. So often they find it hard to accept there is only one small pill involved, as if HIV has turned me into the Incredible Hulk and one tablet could never be enough to switch me back into Alfie – 'Surely he must rattle like a sweet jar after all the pills he's taken to stop himself dying.' No wonder people find it hard to comprehend the reality when the country's second largest newspaper prints this kind of shit.

'The brave personality, worshipped by millions of fans,' it carries on, 'is timing the announcement just before a sports event next month in which they are competing.'

Brave? Why brave? Don't patronise me. I'm not brave. I'm just getting on with my life, the same as millions of others with HIV across the world do every day.

I don't know how the *Sun* knew I was taking part in the Ironman. Again, it's a question of 'who can you trust?' I know for a fact that no one in my family and none of the documentary's production team would ever break the circle. And yet somehow the *Sun* had got hold of the information and put it out there in a way that would have meant nothing to anyone – 'Someone, we can't tell you who, is taking part in a sporting event, though we can't say which, of all the sporting events in the world, it is.'

Why bother? Why the silly games? They couldn't be that dim that they didn't know what I was trying to achieve by taking part in the Ironman. They claim to know everything else about me after all. But all that matters to them is 'We told you first!' After the Ironman they could boast, 'We told you he was going to do this!' Who gives a fuck?

Garbage like 'SPORTS STAR IN HIV SHOCK' shows both how important it is to change people's attitudes and what it is that we are up against, when this is the attitude of a significant player in British mainstream media. For so many people, dealing with so many scenarios, the tabloids block the path to enlightenment and positivity. Damned if you do, damned if you don't. If you are even remotely in the public eye and something difficult or sad or painful happens to you, you can stay behind the curtain and live in fear of a newspaper revealing your situation in their own scandal-shaded terms, or go public and risk that same publication using your openness as excuse to rummage around in your private life and harass your family and friends. Pretty unpleasant all round.

The only way of getting rid of them that I have ever found is by controlling your own agenda. Though that takes a lot of courage and the support of good people around you, as well as a degree of mental strength that, in times of severe turmoil, may well be lacking. In my case, as I had not given into their bullying, their prodding and poking at me, my friends and family, the *Sun* had been forced to use another tactic. In doing so, they showed themselves for exactly what they are and scored a massive own goal.

'What you have written here,' I thought, 'is the exact reason why I'm doing what I'm doing – to stop mindless, terrible, archaic and grossly misrepresentative articles like this being written.'

I think most people who read that piece would have seen it for the absolute shallow sensationalist drivel that it was. Nobody can be bigger than the press but at that moment I knew my voice was way louder than some journalist sat in an office in London spouting shit. At one point, they wrote that the aim of me taking part in the Ironman was 'to show you can live a healthy lifestyle with HIV'. The hypocrisy was astounding.

'Don't you dare write something supportive about HIV in an article that represents the virus so badly, and when I know how much you want to expose me,' I thought. 'Don't you ever talk about the subject if you can't be bothered to find out the facts. Stay away from it.'

My agent, Emanuele Palladino, and I sat down and discussed how best to break the news. It was never a decision that could be taken lightly and if I was to come out on my own terms, in a way that did both myself and others justice, the entire process had to be carefully planned. A tabloid newspaper was an option but one I was uncomfortable with. After everything that had happened with the *Sun*, all I'd had to do to keep the beast at bay, how could I now voluntarily enter the lair in which it lurked? A newspaper can deliver a platform. It can also deliver a trapdoor and a noose. In the end, however, I understood that, when a story is presented correctly, the press has a really powerful part to play in delivering the truth. I wanted a mass medium that could get my story, and the message it contained, across accurately, directly and responsibly.

I wanted to work with a newspaper that would break the news in a way which was not sensationalised but informed. By going with the *Sunday Mirror*, I realised, bearing in mind my history with the *Sun*, I could have been branded a complete hypocrite but I did so because I made it clear to the *Sunday Mirror* that it must tell my story my way. I would be in control of the message. The story must also be published on the day of the Ironman for maximum impact, to smash an irreparable hole in the dominant narrative that HIV is a byword for weak. I also made it clear I wanted nothing out of the arrangement but a strengthening of understanding about HIV. I donated my fee to the Terrence Higgins Trust. The last thing I wanted was it to be presented as some nonsensical celebrity tittle-tattle, people picking their newspaper up off the doormat or turning on their phone that Sunday morning and choking on their scrambled eggs as they shouted across the kitchen table, 'Gareth Thomas has got HIV! He's going to die!' I wanted those readers to see the truth, the nuance, of the situation. 'Gareth Thomas has HIV – and this is what HIV means.' The trust's involvement allowed me to raise awareness and deliver a message. A good part of the *Sunday Mirror* coverage would be given over to the charity giving a detailed explanation of HIV. I wanted the 'exclusive' to do more than tell my HIV story – I wanted it to educate.

Gareth Thomas: HIV and Me was based on exactly the same ethos. Now I had finally taken the decision to go public about this, I knew I needed to make the loudest, most positive and empowering story out of something that could, in other hands, just as easily have been depicted as deeply negative. I wanted to remove the cloak of fear and shame that appeared to come with diagnosis – that I had felt myself when I was first diagnosed – and deliver a message of hope to the hidden multitudes in exactly the same position. However, I knew that I was not yet in a position to do so.

Aside from my own little world, my own daily routine, what did I really know about HIV? Not much more than you could write on the back of a beermat in the bar at Bridgend rugby club. If I was to get up and say those six words – 'I've got HIV and it's OK' – I would need to educate myself. One of the main reasons I had wanted to invite the TV cameras in was it was my way of saying to an audience, 'How about you come along with me and we'll see what we can find out about this?' This way, I could actually allow people to follow my own HIV education. I, like the audience, would be learning.

When I came out as gay, going into interviews without preparation had come back and nipped me on several occasions as I replied to questions without a deeper understanding of what I was talking about. It's no good regretting mistakes afterwards – those articles will be on the internet forever. I needed knowledge and realised that if I showed that I was learning, educating myself, I could get things wrong and it wouldn't be held against me. Viewers weren't seeing the finished article. How could they when even I didn't know what the finished article looked like?

More than anything, I wanted to illustrate how arbitrary the reach of HIV is, how widespread the ignorance and how desperately unfair and traumatic its repercussions. During filming, I heard endless stories of disgraceful prejudice being foisted on innocent individuals. I met one young woman who had been helping children to read at a school. When other parents discovered she had HIV they sought to have her removed. The head should have nipped that situation in the bud. He should have spoken to those parents, reassured them and given them the relevant information. Instead he forced the woman to leave. She left not just her job but her dignity and self-esteem at the school gates. Imagine being in as powerful a position as a headteacher and behaving like that? Consider the discrimination, on all levels, he green-lit in his school by acting in that manner.

I also met a cakemaker whose customer base disappeared when she revealed she had HIV. No one would buy her cakes because they thought she could transmit HIV through them. I still ponder that sometimes. Do people really think like that? And, sadly, the answer is always the same – yes, they really do. Variations on all those situations will be happening right now.

The truth is that people can live with having HIV – they just can't live with others' reactions to them having HIV. I have met youngsters who have lost all their friends. Those who have been treated as outcasts in their communities. Just when they needed the strength that comes from support, the scaffolding collapsed around them.

Fear of judgement, disapproval, being cast aside, is over-whelming – something I know from deep personal experience – and is what stops so many people from revealing their diagnosis. Desperation to hang on to at least a semblance of familiarity and normality reinforces secrecy, which is why, when it came to the programme, I wanted to tell someone my truth on camera. Make no mistake, it's not easy telling somebody you are living with HIV. How would you do it?

You can come straight out with it – 'I have HIV' – and then as quickly as possible run through the bullet points while they're picking their jaw up off the floor. Chances are, though, as it did with me, the white noise will take over. Nothing will go in. At the end of your sprint through the basics, if they are anywhere near as ignorant as I was, they will be struggling for breath and still be of the firm belief you are going to die.

So what if you deliver the information in reverse, to explain exactly what HIV is and then reveal the diagnosis? Yes, there will still be shock, but it comes with perspective. Early on, however, I found explaining in reverse wasn't an option. How do you suddenly turn a conversation to HIV? 'Did you see the match last night? Oh, and what do you think about HIV?' In the end I found a middle way, combining my diagnosis with a parallel reassurance that first and foremost I am not going to die. It doesn't always work out – there are bound to be occasions where the person is too badly affected, traumatised even, to listen. All you can do then is keep delivering the basic information until they do.

For the documentary, I chose Shane Williams, a good friend as well as Wales' leading try-scorer, and veteran of more than a few Ironman competitions. On a bench overlooking the Ogmore Valley, near Bridgend, I explained to him my motivation for breaking my own self-imposed 'not in a million years' ban on ever taking on the hell of the three-headed monster of swim, cycle and run. The camera rolled. I turned to him and told him, simply and straightforwardly, 'I'm HIV positive.'

His reaction, as seen on TV, is pretty much the same as every-body else I've told – 'So long as you're all right, mate, that's fine.' But there was something viewers didn't see in the run-up to that meeting. The set-up hinged on his reaction to me telling him I was HIV positive. Shane, I felt sure, would be totally cool with it. But part of me felt it was unfair just to land the information on him, on a Welsh hillside, on camera, so, a couple of days before we were due to meet, I rang him.

'Look, Shane,' I said, 'I need you to know why I'm doing the Ironman before we do the piece for the documentary.'

He was having none of it. 'Don't worry about it. I don't need to know.'

'No, Shane, you don't understand. I'm not doing it because I want to be fit or because I want to make a TV programme. It's much deeper than that.'

'No worries, mate. Tell me on the day. It's fine.'

But I couldn't shake the worry I was putting him in a difficult position. What if his reaction wasn't a shrug of the shoulders and a quick pat on the back? What if – as I have seen happen – it was one of shock, maybe even fear?

'Look,' I said, 'this isn't something you will hear every day so I would rather you were prepared. You're going to be on film and I don't want the reaction you give to be anything other than that of the person I know you are.'

I might as well have been running straight into the Pontypool front row. He wasn't shifting.

'Alf,' he told me, 'I do not want to know because whatever it is it won't make any difference.'

In the end, while I don't think anyone can ever really be prepared to hear out of the blue that a close friend has HIV, his reaction was just that of one of two pals who now live miles apart but grew up together playing rugby. Like all true friends, we have a bond that will remain regardless of whatever happens to either of us. Shane's reaction was probably the best I have had in that it was barely a reaction at all. After I told him, he treated me exactly the same way as before and that is all I care about, from him or anybody.

If I was to come out with honesty and integrity, I felt it was important also that I accepted an element of blame for my HIV. I know precisely the moment where I put myself at risk of contracting the virus and I didn't act responsibly. I neglected the need to do so and will live with that for the rest of my life. If I hadn't had unprotected sex I wouldn't have HIV. That is an unavoidable and absolute fact. I am only kidding myself if I think I was somehow absent in the process.

There is another factor at play here. If you blame someone else then the negativity of anger seeps in. Much better to be honest and face up to the truth. To do otherwise creates an insurmountable mental roadblock which is impossible to live with. If I thought the other person had acted maliciously then, yes, I would feel aggrieved.

But just as I won't get angry, nor will I go the other way and act as if it's just one of those things. It's not good enough for me to go through life saying, 'It happened, don't worry about it. It's OK, move on.' That is disrespectful to the situation, those around me and millions of others who share my circumstances. I can never contract HIV again, it's done, but that doesn't mean I ignore the lesson learned – that for every action there will be an outcome. I have HIV and the ability to analyse my role in that fact is massive because the virus cannot then tie me down or drag me backwards. That is why I choose to take my blame. If I make mistakes, I own those mistakes, just like I own my medals and trophies that I've received for doing well in life.

I'm not saying taking responsibility is easy. To admit you have done something wrong is hard. Easier to put up the shutters. But accepting accountability has allowed me to move on. The brain might put locks on negative experiences but it never throws away the key. The door can swing open at any time. Making sense of what is inside has to be faced up to some time and, for me, remembering my responsibility has been a huge part of making progress. I am improved by owning my mistakes. I owe my success to them because, like most people, I find confronting stormy seas forces reflection. A paddle in a millpond takes you nowhere.

Of course, all of that is easy to say now but it takes time to work through. Blame did complicate my mindset. The fact that, by my own admission, a finger could be pointed at me meant that, while there was a similarity with coming out as gay – the unburdening of secrecy, the fear of the unknown – coming out as HIV-positive felt different. I felt more open to attack in a way I did not when I opened up about my sexuality. At a time when I would be under a lot of mental pressure, I didn't welcome the thought of people telling me, 'This is completely your fault. This is something that you could have avoided but you didn't.' People had every right to say, 'You've reaped what you sowed.' But that didn't make the prospect of hearing it any easier. I knew it was my fault without other people reminding me.

Eventually, mulling it over in my head, I came to see an element of hypocrisy in the argument. Let's face it, I could walk past hundreds of adults in any city centre any day of the week in the full knowledge that a large number of them will have had unprotected sex at one point or another. The vast majority of them will have thought nothing of it because there were no consequences and yet some would undoubtedly point a finger at me. I hold nothing against them for that. Had I not contracted HIV and discovered so much about it, chances are my mindset

– 'It's your fault, deal with it' – would have been the same. Sometimes the person in the mirror doesn't make quite such an easy target.

It's an attitude that also, as ever, focuses only on sex. It comes back to that repressed Britishness which for generations has portrayed sex as something dirty, even though it's something perfectly natural that we all do – and are all meant to do. To reduce HIV to sex is just a lazy way of discussing a very, very complicated situation. My identity as a gay man is not just about having sex with other gay men, it's way, way more than that. People fought for gay men to get married, for us to be able to walk down the street hand in hand, for us not to have to carry stigma. It's so easy to say being gay is all based on sex – it puts a full stop on the discussion. There is no need or desire to take it to any more depth. I'm a human being with sexual urges and so, yes, I have had sex. But, the same as anyone else, it isn't the be all and end all of who I am.

As someone who played rugby for years, I've spent a lot of time around groups of straight men. The reality is gay men and straight men are no different. The same with gay and straight women. They're all exactly the same and yet if a heterosexual couple is married, no one starts banging on about them sleeping with other people as well. If a gay man is single, the narrative is that they pick up men every weekend. Does a single straight man have his whole existence sexualised in this way? It is stereotyping of the worst kind, keeping society from evolving. It feeds the cloud of misinformation that hangs, or rather is placed, over the LGBTQ community. And it feeds misinformation about HIV.

I came to adopt a more pragmatic view of others' outlooks. If coming out as HIV positive meant some people believing I was a bad person, that I had done something wrong, so what? Let them think it. I have done plenty of wrong things. If that's the way they wanted it, let it be another on the list. Coming out was not about good or bad, right or wrong, it was about doing what was best for me. I understood an honest approach to my HIV would be better for my soul, better for my self-esteem and better for my future. Whereas once I would have done anything to avoid travelling down that path – even taking one that went straight over a cliff – it now felt exactly the right direction to me.

When I'd reached the conclusion that I had to take control of the story, Mum and Dad were both very sceptical, not to mention scared (for me, not them) of the reaction. They aired their worries and their concerns but ultimately their position was clear – 'If that's what you want to do, then we will support you.' It was exactly what I knew it would be. I've watched my two brothers grow up and I've seen how, as a family, everybody has managed to come together and support one another through thick and thin. There is a single underlying truth that, as their children, we have always understood – we are their sons and they will always love us regardless. That is our safety net.

I knew that, ultimately, I was doing all my family and friends a disservice by keeping my diagnosis to myself. Initially, I felt it was easier for them that they didn't know. I knew I wasn't putting anyone at risk and it seemed so unfair to burden them, to once again reveal an almighty secret about myself that they would mentally have to adapt to. Past experience of coming out sat heavy. Even though revealing I am gay led to better times for me, I can't pretend the shitstorm I created for Jemma, Mum and Dad, and many others, never happened. Even though they all reassure me now – 'Alf, we don't care! Move on!' – I still care. It is still there within me. But I was never comfortable with holding back such a big part of my reality. I wasn't going around telling deliberate untruths but I was most definitely being the opposite to honest. All these many amazing people had supported me through thick and thin. Who was I to keep such a major part of my life back from them? Not one of them would have said I'd been doing them a favour.

Some people think I came out as both HIV positive and gay because of pressure from the press. I will say it once and for all – I have never ever made a decision based on the media. I have only ever made decisions that were right for me and my loved ones. Coming out about my HIV diagnosis was about openness, honesty and empowerment. It scared me a lot to do it but it allowed me to speak about how bad I had been feeling and the burden of secrecy. It also led me to a realisation that, as a man open about his HIV status, I could do so much more. In making the documentary and speaking to others, it really hit home how many people must be suffering from the stigma created by the lack of will to present HIV in its true terms. By coming out I was refusing to wear the stigma that had been foisted on me by others and myself. I could make a difference.

On 14 September 2019, the night before the Ironman, Stephen and I left our rented cottage in Tenby and met some friends at the nearby Fat Seagull café. At this late, late stage, just the same as happened with the article ten years previously revealing my sexuality, I had a sudden attack of nerves. I knew the newspaper was going to run the exclusive and I knew it had to happen, but that didn't mean I had to be 100 per cent OK with it. I felt unsettled and, after a few bites to eat, decided to walk back to the house. At the top of North Beach, I looked down at the sea, pitch black in the dark, only identifiable from the noise of the waves.

'Fucking hell,' I thought to myself, 'in a few hours I'm going to be in there.'

Every crash of every wave seemed to mark a point on my journey to this place – diagnosis, despair, blackmail, journalists, panic, realisation, understanding, openness, honesty, strength. And now what? Acceptance? Rejection? Abuse?

I looked again down into the darkness.

'In a few hours I will either sink or swim.'

CHAPTER 9

MAN OF IRON

Back at the cottage, I make a short video for social media. I sit down in front of the camera and begin.

> *Hello, I'm Gareth Thomas, and I want to share my secret with you.*
>
> *Why? Because it's mine to tell you. Not the evils that make my life hell, threatening to tell you before I do. And because I believe in you. And I trust you.*

I pause, close my eyes and take a deep breath. The next four words are the hardest I will ever say.

> *I'm living with HIV.*

I gather myself.

> *Now you have that information, that makes me extremely vulnerable but it does not make me weak. Now even though*

I've been forced to tell you this, I choose to fight, to educate and break the stigma around this subject. And that begins today, when I take on the toughest Ironman in the world in Tenby and I push myself physically to the limits.

I'm asking you to help me to show that everyone lives in fear of people's reactions and opinions to something about them but that doesn't mean we have to hide. But to do this, I really, really need your support.

I use the word 'evils' pointedly and I use the word 'forced' advisedly. I do not mean it in the sense of bad people have made me reveal my truth. I mean that so much of my motivation is a result of them thinking I would do nothing about it. That I would always be in their grip. That I wouldn't have the guts to act. I mean it in a sense of complete empowerment – this moment of revelation is mine not yours to decide.

I load the clip to my Twitter feed and hit send. I turn my phone off and go to bed.

I don't sleep a wink. Even without the HIV revelation, I wouldn't have done. So pumped am I for what is to come that trying to relax was always going to be a losing battle.

Tempting as it is to reach for my phone to pass the slumberless hours, I have promised myself I won't switch it on again until I've completed the triathlon. Whatever is happening on Twitter, I don't want to see it. I don't want to get dragged into any conversations, debates, abuse, anything. I need to stay focused. If there is something that can hurt me, I have to stay away from it. I know that in a few hours I have to get in that water and don't want any potential negativity to stop me. Overcoming my fear of the swim is in itself a huge mental barrier; I don't need to carry more weight. I don't need to drown before I've even got in. In fact, I vow not to read any messages on social media until a year to the day after the event.

All well and good, but I'm still stuck in my own head, the same few thoughts ricocheting around my skull. *What have I done? What the hell was I thinking? Why did I do it?* These veer into *You have to do it. You are taking control. It's a really positive step,* and back again. As preparations for a twelve-hour triathlon go, it is far from perfect.

Eventually, the tiniest hint of dawn indicates it is time to get up. I drag myself from under the duvet, whisper goodbye to Stephen, get my gear together, turn the handle of the front door and walk alone through the dark streets of Tenby. There are hardly multitudes around – it has barely turned 5.30 – but even so, I put on a baseball cap, pulling the peak right down over my eyes, so petrified am I of what people might say after my Twitter revelation of the night before. I have arranged to meet some friends at 6am in the transition area. I am ten minutes early and lean against a wall, making myself as unnoticeable as I possibly can, watching people walk past.

No matter my disguise, I am instantly recognisable to my friends. If you're six-foot-three with a big nose don't ever seek work as an undercover operative. None of them mention either the tweet or the *Sunday Mirror* article, which by now will be up on the newspaper's website as well as in shops across the land.

Their silence is out of respect for me and the mental space they know I need to occupy ahead of the challenge. Now isn't the time. Also, they need to focus on themselves.

By the time the clock ticks round to the start an hour later, the town is buzzing. Heading down to the beach, people are, as ever, great with me, offering best wishes and asking for selfies, unaware, it seems, that there has been a seismic shift in my public life. I so appreciate all that goodwill but at the same time every fibre of me just wants to go home, grab Stephen, sit down and watch crap telly – to pretend nothing has changed and everything is going to be OK. I can't help wondering if those same people asking for selfies might still want a photo at the same time tomorrow.

At the start, 2,400 competitors are awaiting the off. I am in a group of similar ability who, like myself, aren't ultra-competitive. We are cautious of what's to come and understanding of one another's reticence.

'Hi – are you feeling a little anxious?'

'Anxious? I'm bloody petrified!'

'OK, let's try to chill out.'

I wonder if here might be when someone mentions the story but no, although I do notice one or two people looking at me. I look back and they quickly turn away. Automatically, I think the worst. Not that they are having a quick glance at a 'celebrity' entrant – which is actually most likely – but that they are looking at me as an object of curiosity or, worse, disgust. Putting my head underwater has gone from something I absolutely dread to the one thing I really want to do.

The whistle blows and I shuffle with hundreds of others into the water. Whenever the swimming element of a triathlon is on TV, all those arms and legs thrashing about looks absolutely terrifying, like a giant washing machine loaded with people rather than dirty clothes. Now, when I stick my head up through the surface for the first time, I find it is even more horrific. Forget the pre-start camaraderie, everyone has gone into survival mode. It's dog eat dog, people tugging each other's goggles, kicking, lashing out. No way would any of these people punch or kick someone in real life – well, hopefully not – but for now the normal rules of engagement have clearly gone out the window. If this is halfway back, I can only imagine the melee of competitiveness up front.

'Forget everyone else,' I tell myself. 'All that matters is that I get out the other side.'

Even so, it's difficult to avoid contact. I feel someone touch my feet with their hands. I can't help but instinctively kick out. I hope I've not caught the face of the poor devil behind.

Because the course entails two loops of the bay, it's not long before the elite guys and girls start to lap the slower swimmers. All of a sudden, everybody is mixed up with everybody else and things get a little brutal. This isn't like encountering a slow walker on a canal path – 'Excuse me, would you mind awfully if I came past?' Fellow competitors will quite happily swim over you if you are in their way. I get off lightly, with nothing worse than a couple of tussles over the same few feet of water.

It's not lost on me that the swim delivers total anonymity. I am just one of a shoal, head down in the regulation dandelion-yellow swimming cap. The more I settle into the swim, the more I appreciate all that Dave Tonge has taught me, allowing me to relax in the water and enter a mental space far removed from the potentially overwhelming nature of an otherwise frantic day. I feel an inner peace and calmness. While millions, I assume, are opening up their Sunday newspaper, switching on their phones, reading about me and HIV, the subject of that story might as well be floating in outer space. I have gone from someone who felt abject fear about swimming in the sea to an entirely different person who doesn't want to leave it. As I pass the landmark Goscar Rock on Tenby North Beach for the second time, it occurs to me that for many long minutes I haven't thought of anything other than the water. Nobody else is there. Nobody else can see me. Only I can see me.

I desperately want to revel in every second of invisibility. 'I've got a few hundred strokes here,' I consider. 'I can either go for it and try to get out the water as quick as I can, or I can take them really easily and enjoy my last seven or eight minutes of being just another head bobbing in the sea. A last seven or eight minutes of not confronting what everybody else knows about me right now.'

The water becomes shallower and dry land beckons. Despite knowing I will have now lost my cloak of anonymity, as I drag myself from the surf, I feel a massive surge of relief. I know now I can physically get around the course. Cycling 112 miles and running another 26.2 holds no fears. Swimming 2.4 miles did. I take one last look at that amazing rock. My last moment as the me of before. I will have to face whatever consequences come my way.

And yet, while I am waiting for anonymity to fall from me like the last few droplets of Carmarthen Bay, actually, in wetsuit and goggles, I remain pretty much incognito, especially since the organisers have kindly allocated me a position in the changing area reserved for the professionals, who are long gone by the time my creaking body turns up. I'm relieved. I had worried about having to hustle and bustle through other competitors at this stage. Would they be OK with me, the 'new' me with HIV, brushing past? Reaching near them to get my bag?

I take my wetsuit off and begin running the mile to the transition area where my bike awaits. As if the twenty-six miles of the marathon isn't enough! The run takes me right through the middle of Tenby. But again I am able to avoid attention. My time of an hour and twenty minutes is common to a lot of other swimmers. Running in a bunch, we all look pretty similar, faces made puffy by goggles and time in the saltwater. It isn't like I'm wandering through town in a Wales rugby shirt. The sudden switch from lengthy swim to run also makes me feel disorientated. The mile is a blur of noise interrupted only by seeing Dave's wife on the other side of the barriers.

'I actually did it!' I shout to her. She cheers, and that's it, I zone back out.

I reach the bike and click on my helmet. Again, inconspicuous. One of many. And yet it is here I definitely begin to feel positivity from those around me. Some of it is spoken. 'Good luck, mate. Great thing you did this morning.' 'Oh mate, I love why you are doing this.' It is so lovely to hear and gives me a real boost. But it is the unspoken sense of togetherness that really moves me. I'm not a professional Ironman athlete, competing for a place on the podium, and neither are those around me. They are doing it for their reasons; I am doing it for mine. Some of them know my reason and they respect it. I don't know their reason but I respect them. It reminds me of how it was on the rugby field, professional or otherwise – not peer pressure, but peer respect, a silent acknowledgement that we are in this together; individuals, but part of a bigger, more intricate picture. It means that while obviously I want everybody to be OK with my motivation, it doesn't really matter. I don't need to know what everybody else thinks. In fact, it makes it more special to think that we are all complete strangers who together have sacrificed so much of ourselves to get to the start line of this race. I am desperately moved by that thought but equally I try not to let it dominate me, because the one thing I have to do is finish. I know I can't let emotion physically drain me.

For the next 112 miles, it's Soreen, Soreen and more Soreen. A great energy provider but I will never eat it ever again. As in the sea, I have absolutely no idea about any support – or otherwise – that might be forthcoming from the outside world. The only inkling comes when I cycle past Stephen.

'You're not going to believe it,' he shouts. 'Jeremy Corbyn has messaged you.'

What am I supposed to make of that? Is that good or bad? I conclude, from his tone, it is positive.

The taste of Soreen is still in my mouth when, gingerly, I dismount ahead of the small matter of a full marathon. As I remove my helmet, so I remove any last element of invisibility. I swap my cycling shoes for trainers and step out of the change-over tent.

I am hit by a tsunami of noise. I am in a daze anyway, my mind resetting to the sensation of running after 112 miles in the saddle, but this feels like a haymaker from Mike Tyson.

'Hang on,' I think, 'what's going on here? Is Alistair Brownlee out there or something?'

I turn the corner on to the long straight bordered by Tenby's ancient town wall. I know noise. I have run out as captain of Wales in front of 80,000 of my wildly fanatical countrymen and women. There are around 3,000 people on this street. Such is the volume, the cannon blast of support for me, that quite literally I am hit by a solid wave of sound, like a special effect you might see in a Hollywood action film that sweeps the hero off their feet. People talk about runners hitting the wall in a marathon – this wall hits me. It is one of solid cheering. It takes my breath away – I mean really takes my breath away. By the time I reach Stephen again halfway up the road I am panting, hyperventilating.

'This must be how a pop star feels when they walk out on to the stage,' I think. Except, if that is the case, I cannot compre-hend how they can possibly perform. I feel like I've been strapped to the top of a jumbo jet at 500mph. I am turning blue, trying to breathe out.

I cling on to Stephen. I want to hug him but I also need to hide from the sound so that I can get my breath back. My mum and dad are with him.

'You can't stay here and cry!' They are pushing me away.

'I can't breathe,' I splutter. 'I need to get my breath back.'

I know in that moment why I can't breathe. There is so much else, held captive within me for so long, that is now pouring out. The shame, the secrecy, the fear, the negativity. Breathe? How can I? There's no room for air. All that hurt is being forced from me as if I've been holding a hurricane behind a locked door. The Ironman, coming out, has finally provided the key. The emotional energy unleashed is terrific.

It's a bad idea to stop too long – the last thing I need is to seize up – and eventually I manage to jog off again. The tears which stream down my face are inevitable. Not just because of the reception, not just because I have seen Stephen and my parents, but because I have made it to this final stage of the Ironman, a day which is about so much more than sporting achievement.

If I am ever asked, 'What is the proudest moment in your life?' forget anything I did in rugby, any award I have ever won, it is this: the moment I set off on the 26.2-mile run at Ironman Wales 2019.

There is a simple ethos behind my urge to do the Ironman. I want to verbally try to educate people about HIV and, if they still don't understand, then I will physically show them too. And yet now I see that so many people have totally got it without me even doing the physical stuff. They aren't here to clap a man doing a sporting event. They are here to applaud the fact I am willing to put myself through these twelve hard hours to make the point. That is just incredible. Neither I nor anybody else had any idea what was going to happen today, whether I was going to be booed, cheered, or a mix of both. I'm sure every person in this crowd relates to what I am doing in a different way, but at the heart of it is a single unifying thought: 'This is a guy who has had a shit time and been made to feel really vulnerable, forced into a corner, who has decided to take control of his own life, his own narrative, and concluded the Ironman is the best reply he can give. I respect the strength and bollocks he has shown in doing that.'

Who knows how many of these people, for whatever reason, feel the same. They might not have HIV but they could well have their own issues to deal with. They may empathise with being misjudged or living with a secret. They may be over-coming personal battles. They may feel isolated or marginalised. They want to be part of my experience because they know what it feels like. They like the idea of someone getting up and telling the doubters, the naysayers, the prejudiced, 'You think I am not capable of doing something? Well, right here, right now, I'm doing it in front of your face.'

Maybe one day some of them will do something similar (not as extreme as an Ironman perhaps!), something that delivers a similar feeling of purpose and satisfaction. It doesn't matter what it is that we carry. The point is that none of us have to accept whatever others project on to us.

When the avalanche of applause buries me, I have a decision to make. Do I spend the next few hours walking round the course, taking the plaudits and making it all about me? Or do I do what I set out to do – my best – and finish before darkness descends on the Pembrokeshire coast? Actually, it is no decision at all. Do the latter and the message will be so much louder.

To achieve that goal, however, I know I have to blank out the crowd. As awful as it sounds, I have to make it a one-way relationship. That way I can still gain the strength from hearing the cheers, my name being shouted, but I won't be distracted from my objective. I can't take my eye off what I have set out to do.

I think back to being under a high catch in a game of rugby. If someone in the crowd shouted, 'Alfie, you are amazing!' and I glanced at them even for a nanosecond, I'd be guaranteed to drop the ball. I feel bad for the kids who hold out a hand for a high five, anyone who pleads for a hug. I want to, and I appreciate that love and support so much, but I can't afford to let this, the biggest and most vital catch of my life, slip through my hands. I have to finish what I've started. Oh, and I am extremely tired as well. When you've swum 2.4 miles, cycled 112, and are now running a marathon, it's hard enough to raise your feet, let alone a smile.

Oddly, I spend the majority of the run in the company of someone I have never met before.

'Do you mind if I run with you?' he asks. On a long run, you tend to find your pace matches that of a handful of other people.

'Mate,' I just about manage to reply, 'I'm more than happy for you to run with me but, whatever you do, don't talk to me. I'm knackered. I'm just digging in here.'

'No worries, mate,' he reassures me. 'I just want someone to push me along.'

As he runs with me, I realise I need the same. It's really cool, as together, unspoken, we help each other onwards.

By the time I get back to Tenby, Mum, Dad and Stephen have retired to the Fat Seagull. The route snakes past its front door and they are tracking me on their phones. I'm not sure they need the tech. I expect they can hear the cacophony, the crowds roaring, 500 metres before I arrive. I have been in the midst of this beautiful mayhem for four-and-a-half hours. I have never felt anything like it before – and I never want to feel it again. That might sound weird but if there is a definition of a once-in-a-lifetime experience then this is it. I can never relive it. And I will never have a greater purpose than I have today.

Just before the finish line, I have to part company with my fellow runner. I look him in the eye. 'Thank you so much,' I tell him. 'You have really helped me but I am making a TV documentary and I have got to cross the line on my own.'

He hasn't a clue who I am. He is in his own bubble, I am in mine.

'Mate,' he says, 'go for it. I'll go a bit slower now.'

I feel so bad. So much of me wants to cross the line with him. We have helped each other so much. I hope he knows how grateful I am.

The organisers have put out a red carpet at the finish line. I jog down it to the same big cheers and hear an announcement that Stephen is waiting with my medal. I weep for so many reasons as he places it over my head. Physically, I am absolutely drained. Emotionally, I am in pieces. But more than anything, I have conquered the Ironman. It has taken me 12 hours, 18 minutes and 29 seconds, and I have finished 413th out of 2,039 participants. But I know I have won because I have shown the world what someone with HIV can do.

And that is it, done. Six months of absolute hell training for this most crazy of events and within five minutes of crossing the line I am finished with it. Challenge over. Nothing to see here. I expect it's the same for footballers who win the World Cup. 'OK. What's next?'

Stephen and I put on our coats, fetch my bike from the changeover area and go home. I am so happy to do exactly that as it's something that all the other participants are experiencing. Yes, doing an Ironman is massive, but at the end of the day we all have to go back to normal life.

'What do we do now?' we wonder as we turn the key in the door. The answer, in my case, is to spend the night spewing my guts up. Energy gels will find a way out at one end or the other. After a fitful sleep, I wake in the morning barely able to move.

'I could die for a bowl of cereal and a cup of tea,' I tell Stephen.

He looks at me like I'm mad. 'You do know the Ironman was yesterday?' he asks. 'That's it now. No more training. You can have what you like.'

For one minute, I think he's going to refuse to present me with such a pitiful breakfast.

'You're not going to make me walk down the stairs to get it myself?' Thankfully, he relents.

Even when we go back to the Fat Seagull later that morning, where they have laid on a beautiful big breakfast, I'm still not hungry. Just walking through the town, though, is incredible. Many of those who suffered with me yesterday are down by the shop at the starting area contemplating just what they have done and quite rightly basking in their achievement. It is lovely to be in a place where, all of a sudden, I feel like everybody else, all of us there with a story in the background.

I look around. Maybe that woman has done it in memory of a family member who has died of cancer, or as part of a personal battle to address mental health issues. Maybe that man has done it to evolve as a person, to test his inner strength, to find out exactly what he is made of. Maybe they both just want to be the quickest triathlete in Whitby, Scunthorpe, Manchester, or wherever else they might come from. Whatever the motivation, everything suddenly feels pared down and normal. Not only has the razzmatazz of the event – the loudspeakers, the red carpet, the crowds – vanished, but for me so too has the burden of the previous six months. Those who threatened to reveal MY truth are firmly back under THEIR stone. There is nothing on which to gorge their abhorrent greed anymore. I have taken control of my own life, my own story. They can try to find another narrative if they want but there's nothing else to tell. Not only that, but they will now be swimming against a huge wave of public support, including the small matter of two princes.

'Gareth, you are an absolute legend,' tweets Prince Harry. 'In sharing your story of being HIV positive, you are saving lives and shattering stigma, by showing you can be strong and resilient while living with HIV. We should all be appalled by the way you were forced to speak your truth, it is yours and yours alone to share on your terms and I and millions stand with you.'

Prince William adds his own voice. 'Courageous as ever – legend on the pitch and legend off it. You have our support Gareth.'

No one down by the beach cares a hoot for any of that and nor should they. This is their moment too. Being part of that bigger picture makes me feel that not only can I be part of normality right now but this could be what the rest of my life looks like. I have taken control and discarded, like a pebble tossed into the surf before me, the fear of people judging me, of the press knocking on my parents' door. No more secrets. No more hiding. I am the same as anyone else, which is all I've ever wanted.

The thought feels a thousand times, a million times better than crossing the finishing line yesterday. I have confronted my

HIV and overcome the negativity, the stigma. I know I can be OK with it, know people aren't going to judge me. I need that. When I came out about my sexuality, I cared about what everybody else thought but at the same time I didn't really give a shit. Sexual preference, despite what some people bizarrely might think, is not a matter of choice and I had come to be happy with myself and who I was. But with HIV I have felt so judged. I needed the acceptance of others. Would they be OK with it or wouldn't they? I felt like the Ironman would be a good gauge of the rest of my life. To know that everybody is fine with something that could have been avoided is important to me. To know that I am able to walk down the street safe as someone with HIV, that I'm not going to be tackled or abused on every corner, is important to me.

I arrived in Tenby in handcuffs, I am leaving it free. No looking over my shoulder, no worrying, no baggage to carry. Nothing. In front of 40,000 people in Tenby, millions in a newspaper and millions more across the world, I have been me. I have real belief in who I am and what I am and I won't let anybody tell me different. No one.

CHAPTER 10

JUDGEMENT

On 15 September 2019, I truly realised my strength to overcome. I knew that whatever life could throw at me, I would get through. I had played rugby against New Zealand, taken the field in World Cups, European Cups, but never once had I been in a position where I felt I had challenged myself, mentally and physically, to my absolute maximum. Now I had – and I'd won. I knew that yes, something may hurt me, but I would always manage to deal with it somehow. I would always find a way through.

One year later, on 15 September 2020, just as I had promised myself, I finally took a look at the messages left on my coming-out Twitter post from a year previously. Famous faces from the world of TV, such as Gary Lineker and Gabby Logan, had left lovely messages, as had those from sport, including my old Wales teammate Shane Williams and rugby union referee Nigel Owens. But it was the welter of goodwill from those I neither knew nor had ever met that I found so moving and fulfilling.

'You are not a victim of HIV,' wrote one, 'you are a hero of humankind.' 'Legend. Whatever. Always,' said another. 'You have more support than you will ever know.' There were thousands and thousands of comments all dripping in the same sentiment. I was moved beyond belief as I scrolled through page after page.

I realised too how truly fortunate I am to have a pillar of public support denied to others. But if anyone keeping their HIV a secret is reading this, then I hope that you can see that those people are there in your world too. You just can't see them. And it's worth bearing in mind too that I am there in your world – and you can see me.

My sexuality and HIV diagnosis may have brought the axe of judgement to hang over me with what I imagined to be a razor-sharp edge. But fear of being judged affects us all one way or another – the way we look, the way we dress, where we live, how we speak, our background, actions and beliefs. There are times when we all feel the eyes of strangers, real or imagined, boring into our heads. We have become a society obsessed, from a very early age, with what other people think about us, many of whom we neither know nor will ever meet. I know because I've been there. It's so easy to become paranoid that we'll be judged in a negative way by people who have no relevance at all in our lives. It's not a bad thing to want to please people, to make others smile, but sometimes we attach more importance to that pursuit than we do to our own satisfaction. Why aren't we making sure that we are happy, that we are the ones who are smiling? We weaken ourselves and cause ourselves harm by not doing what's good for us for fear of offending, upsetting or not impressing others.

Like most people, I can trace my first experience of fear of rejection to when I was a kid. Back then, I wasn't the chiselled Adonis you see before you now. I had ginger hair, big ears and big teeth. (What's that you say? Only the hair has changed?) By the time my teenage years arrived, I had become a target. On one occasion after the class had been swimming, I got shoved in a corner of the changing room, surrounded by boys laughing at me and goading me as they whipped me with towels. Flick after flick, again and again. While they saw it as fun, I felt picked on, alone, and desperately wanted the 'game' to stop. At the same time, I knew that if I fought back it would only make things worse. It wouldn't be towels then, it would be fists, cracks round the head. In their eyes I'd have given them both the ammunition and the justification. Even if I'd wanted to, defending myself physically wasn't ever going to work. I knew I wasn't tough, that I didn't have it in me. I've never wanted either a fight or to be a fighter. In my rugby career I was always fearful of scrapping on the pitch.

There was another factor which made me so accepting of my fate in that changing room – the kids who were doing it were the rugby boys and I wanted to be in the sporty group. If I was the adult I am now then I would have had no qualms in telling them how they were making me feel but as a kid no way could that ever be an option. I really wanted them to be my friends, and friends don't go round complaining about how they are being treated.

Sport was all that mattered in the pecking order at Ogmore Comp. Swotty? Bottom of the ladder. Musical? Theatrical? On the lower rungs too. Brainy and sporty? Sorry, being brainy makes you a loser – you can't be rescued by athleticism. Sport and amateur dramatics? You're joking, right? Good at sport and don't care about anything else? You're in – welcome to the cool group. Except simply getting in the cool group wasn't enough. You then needed to stay in the cool group, which meant pressure to comply to its unwritten codes. Rebellion was part of the deal. You might have to do something daft, be disruptive, smash a fire alarm.

I look back now and massively regret some of my behaviour but that regret comes with the clear knowledge there was no way I could have challenged the system that encouraged it. No one in authority ever challenged our herd mentality. Nowadays, I, and I'm sure plenty of other people, believe in and actively promote the idea of young people exploring all avenues. Back then, however, few, if any, saw anything wrong with the situation. It was just the way it was. 'Inclusivity' wasn't in the school dictionary. And the sad truth is it wasted so much potential. What with peer pressure from fellow pupils and no interest from above, promise was allowed just to fade away.

It's often assumed that I trod a road to glory from an early age because I always had an ambition to play sport. But thinking about it, a lot of that ambition came from a simple fact – I wasn't any good, or deemed to be any good, at anything else. It's not like I could have said I wanted to be an architect or a lawyer. I was never able to engage enough in an academic environment to feel such intellectual occupations were on my radar. The only place I ever felt I could belong was in sport. Plenty of others, I suspect, felt they belonged nowhere.

Thing is, I actually liked some subjects but I could never enjoy those lessons because I felt a constant pressure to live up to the type of person I 'needed' to be to keep rejection at bay. I would never put my hand up in class to answer a question. Oh my God! Put your hand up in class and you might as well have pinned yourself to a target in a shooting range. The bullets would be flying for weeks. It was much easier to be someone who fitted in rather than use school for what it was actually meant to be for – the basis of an education and an opportunity to better myself.

But equally I was aware of a lack of interaction coming the other way, not even the slightest attempt to treat pupils as individuals. I had several abrupt and morale-shattering experiences of this attitude. My brother Richard, one year older than me, was academically gifted. Great – except whenever I went up a year, the teacher would automatically cry, 'Oh, you're Gareth! Richard's brother!' and assume I would be of similar level if not better. I sat down with just one thing on my mind – 'Here we go again! How am I ever going to live up to that?'

When my presumed academic brilliance failed to show, the teacher's positivity would turn crushingly into 'I see you're nothing like your brother!'

I was petrified of going into some classes. I might not have been the Brain of Britain of their imagination but I knew well enough that environment wasn't good for me, under pressure to perform like somebody else when all I wanted to be was me. The constant comparison with my brothers made me an easy target for classroom putdowns. And when those with power start singling you out, it gives the green light for everyone else, especially those with wet towels, to do the same. My solution? Retreat further into my group.

I hope that today's teachers know better than to make comparisons between children, be they related or not, because it delivers nothing but deeply harmful negativity that can last a lifetime. Even now, I can feel only too well that fear of placing myself in a vulnerable position by looking stupid. Invoices, bills, totting up a few digits – straight away I freeze. Even now I'm terrified I'll be the dunce in the room.

Though I did have someone in my corner at least. Not something all kids have, of course. My mother was having none of it. She would be in constant conflict with the school, called up there because I was considered lazy, supposedly wasting a talent for all things scholarly that existed in my DNA.

'He's not as good as his brother,' they would tell her.

'That's because he's not his brother,' she would reply, 'and you shouldn't treat him like he is.'

But even my mum's powers have limits. She was fighting a deep-seated lethargy. Nothing changed and so I became even more entrenched in the sporty group that at least offered a place in the pecking order – a shallow ranking which meant precisely nothing once I walked out the school gate for the last time.

Developing kids' ability to make their own decisions is vital and yet so often they are denied that chance to train their brain, instead steamrollered into following what other people want, never given the opportunity to expand their thinking or find their voice. For me, and I suspect many others, adult life hasn't always felt that different. But if you don't give people a voice, don't allow them to be heard, then they never have the chance to get it right, let alone wrong. They never learn to use, and trust, their brain. They go through life with one hand tied behind their back, their potential unused.

As a rugby player, all too often I found myself in situations where players were treated like children in a Victorian household – seen but not heard. I struggled in particular with coaches who just wanted to put themselves on a pedestal and teach – a lot of coaches are ex-teachers – telling players what to do and allowing no room for feedback or opinion. I was somebody who liked to contribute. I wanted to be part of the creative process, influencing the way we played, helping to making the plan to defeat the opposition, not just blindly going out on the pitch and doing what somebody else was telling me with zero involvement or explanation. How can that ever be conducive to a player or team performing to their maximum strength?

Thankfully, since I retired, rugby has gone in entirely the opposite direction. Many coaches now absolutely rely on their players' input, and rightly so. Players out there in the thick of it see so much that a coach on the touchline can't. A good coach will listen to that information, recognise it as something they are missing out on and act on it. They have no qualms about admitting that they are part of a process of shared decision-making. They will talk openly about how a senior group of players has helped them and give credit to all involved. A rugby union side consists of fifteen individuals, all with a different role, a different view of the game. Who in their right mind would not want to use that expertise?

Just like everyone, I am perfectly capable of getting things wrong and I am absolutely fine with somebody telling me that. Thing is, if you don't give people a voice, don't allow them to be heard, then they never have the chance to get it right, let alone wrong. They never learn to use, and trust, their brain. They go through life with one hand tied behind their back, their potential unused.

When coaches silenced me, they made me feel I was right back there in the classroom, a place where asking a question when not specifically invited to do so was made to feel like a crime. In circumstances like that, where you aren't even acknowledged, you shrink away internally until you feel you are nothing. I expect there are millions everywhere, in and out of sport, who have felt like that: muzzled by others and, rather than growing their leadership qualities, showing nothing but pig-headedness, disrespect and ignorance. A stronger person always welcomes the input of others but without confidence and self-respect it can be difficult to do this.

As the captain of any team I always took an encompassing approach. I felt like everybody had the right to a view. More than that, I positively encouraged it. I used to constantly push players to give their opinion, whatever it was. Even what might at first appear to be the most irrelevant of comments might actually be the piece that finishes the puzzle. Think about it, when you're doing a jigsaw with lots of blue sky, all those blue pieces don't appear important when you're busy trying to complete the main image. But the whole picture is never completed until that last piece of sky is in place. I wanted everyone in my team to have the opportunity to think for themselves, to contribute. Just as everyone should have that opportunity in the classroom. I hope schools have changed, I really do. Self-esteem is crushed, potentially for life, if people aren't given a voice. Those in charge deny youngsters that voice because they don't feel they have the life skills to give their opinions validity. They need to understand that giving an opinion *is* a life skill.

Feeling isolated, at any age, is more than hurtful, it rips your soul apart. Ultimately, we need to create an environment where anyone can be themselves without being consumed by dread. But it won't be easy. Forget Covid-19, peer pressure is a virus that is truly all-pervading. Every one of us lives with it every day. The minute we think 'What will other people think?' we are experiencing peer pressure. That question could apply to something major, such as getting divorced, or something minor, like what to wear for the school run. It's mad, and infuriating, how people, knowingly and unknowingly, put so much pressure on themselves and one another.

The end result is that down every street, there are millions hiding their true selves, building a wall of falsehood and bravado or putting a pretend version of themselves on social media. Just as with my old school, life has become one big popularity contest. People make statements on Twitter not because they believe in them but because it will bring them more followers – people who they don't know, never will know and so whose endorsement could not be more irrelevant. Crazy. No one would walk down the street, see a hundred people gathered in the park, and think, 'I must get those hundred people to walk behind me. I want them all to be my friend.' We wouldn't care in real life, so why do we care in a world that doesn't even exist? I met someone recently with 2.3 million Instagram followers. To them it defined success. To me, it was heaping a crushing weight of totally irrelevant judgement on themselves.

I do use Instagram – I acknowledge that pictures can be really powerful and uplifting – but I like my posts to have a purpose to them. When I moved home, I put up some photos of all my candles ready to be boxed up. This might have seemed like a superficial post, but it was my way of referencing that I was moving on again in life. I certainly never sit there at night and think, 'Shit, it's half past eight and I still haven't made a video.' I don't fit into a category of 'celebrity', I fit into a category of everyone else. When I go on a TV show, I don't do so as an act, I don't put my face on and go out there as someone I'm not. I'm just me.

People ask me how I have such a sense of my own identity, and I always tell them it's because I don't pretend to be perfect. Identity is the first casualty when you pretend to be someone you're not – I should know, as a gay man I spent years masquerading as someone other than myself. The second casualty is respect, both for yourself and others. I saw it once with a well-known former *X Factor* contestant. I was taking part in *Dancing on Ice* at the time and had been asked to present a prize during a radio awards ceremony at a posh London hotel. I was sat at a table in the bar with the singer in question and her entourage. The minute she started talking I had an immediate thought, 'I'm not trusting this is you at all.' I felt the same about the people who orbited her. I asked if I could buy a round of drinks. She and her group were straight in there. The bill came and it was absolutely crazy. Immediately they finished, they all got up and left. 'OK, fine!' I thought. It wasn't about the money, it was about behaving in a basic decent way, showing respect for other people, even if they are not in your bubble. Sitting at that table reminded me what it used to be like in a rugby changing room, another environment where people were so different and yet so often all trying to pretend they were exactly the same.

After they left, there remained a girl across from me. She'd kept herself to herself, separate from the showbiz posse all the way through. 'What would you like to drink?' she asked. She started talking and straight away I knew she was an absolute angel, so genuine, so completely different. I felt drawn to her, she was absolutely amazing. There was something else about her, a facial disfigurement from, I later found out, having acid thrown in her face. Thank you, Katie Piper. At that moment you restored my faith in humanity. The one person round that table who might justifiably have feared being judged and she couldn't have been more herself.

I feel for that singer and her 'friends'. I have learned the hard way that if we are to find inner peace, we need to believe that there is nothing wrong in being our true selves, warts and all. I know the best thing I can do from the off is front up that I have made a shitload of mistakes. I want people who know me to understand that I am not embarrassed about those stumbles. After all, none of us is infallible. Opportunities to balls things up present themselves to us every day. But think how many of those are deliberate. Most of us trip accidentally. We don't see a hole in the pavement, deliberately stick a foot in it and then go flying. We try a course of action and only by living that experience do we find it is wrong. What's worse, taking an unknown path and finding it overgrown with thorns, or not taking it and wondering forever what might have been down there? Regret will always gnaw away at you. A mistake, made for the right or compelling reasons, ultimately will not. We all mess up. Think of mistakes not as something you did wrong, something that will weaken you, but as turning points, opportunities to go another way. I have had some serious failures but I have learned to twist the natural urge to beat myself up into seeing those failures as foundations for success.

I take real pride in accepting that I am wrong and in accepting that I am going to make mistakes until the day I die. There have been times that I have tried to speak about something I believe in and it's not gone as I'd hoped. Ultimately it doesn't matter – you say sorry and move on. But I'm not going to live my life in fear of my actions being magnified. I won't be constrained by either public or media perception. If I want a release and go to a pub in Bridgend and get absolutely hammered, then somebody decides to take photos of me in that state, while I'd rather they didn't, I'm not going to be constricted by a feeling that I need to be a portrait of perfection. I'll never ever live my life like that. I like making mistakes. I enjoy screwing up. It makes me real – which is something I have occasionally seen lacking in the polished corridors of some of the buildings I've stepped into, false worlds where everybody smiles while plotting behind one another's backs. Worlds where, again, they are re-enacting days as children.

In any area of your life, by trying to be someone else, whatever the reason, you are undoubtedly limiting your ability. I spent much of my life as a sportsman trying to be the greatest rugby player. In my era, the best were the Kiwis, Jonah Lomu and Christian Cullen. I would watch those incredible players and try to be like them, train like them, figure out what they did in an attempt to be better on the pitch and, as I equated it (a common mistake), a better person too. Only later did I realise my greatest opponent was not Jonah Lomu, Christian Cullen or anyone else. It was me. Forget trying to be anyone else. First of all I had to learn to be myself. There will be millions of young people in all countries, all walks of life, looking at the very best in their field and wanting to be them. Why? Why the desperate need to judge our ability and strength in terms of others? Forget wanting to be whoever is your version of Jonah Lomu. Forget trying to be someone else. Why let a person you neither know nor have ever met set the height of your bar? Do it yourself, by being yourself.

When I started captaining Wales, journalists were forever asking, 'What role models will you be looking at?' At first, I would fall into the trap of trying to give answers. But when I stepped back, I knew exactly the position I wanted to take. I would be the captain I chose to be. I'd been asked to lead not because I offered what someone else had previously, but for my own skills and assets. My true answer to the question, 'Who is your role model?' was simple – 'Me!' I was the one who had worked my arse off to reach the top!

Of course, I never said that because I would have been considered self-centred, but actually I would have been speaking with total honesty. The conventions of society, particularly in Britain, mean that only the uber-successful get away with talking like that. The rest of us have restrictions on when we're allowed to be ourselves. Hopefully, that is changing as we all become aware of individuality, different patterns of thinking. I do think it's becoming more common to hear a sportsperson say, 'I want to be the best version of me,' rather than referencing a world powerhouse. And that is how it should be. None of us should ever feel the need to be a copy of someone else. Yes, have a hero, but seek to follow your own path rather than trying to be a clone.

I do occasionally wonder what I would have achieved if I could have been open about my sexuality from the start. But I do so with the knowledge that being completely myself was, at the time, as unachievable as being Tom Jones. So much, internally and externally, conspired against me, to the extent that standing up aged sixteen and shouting, 'Hey, everyone, I'm gay!' was about as likely as being selected for a space mission to Mars.

I hope those growing up now are better equipped to look inside themselves to find their potential, the solutions to their problems – be they real or perceived. The answers are always there if you look for them. When, finally, I searched within myself, I found them really quickly. For me, the realisation that I could be me was the biggest revelation of my life. It was a realisation that took a while to click, but when it did, I found, much to my surprise, I actually really liked the real me.

It's one of life's little tricks that it can take until you're older for you to like yourself – another reason why it's unfair to hang regrets around your neck or look back with hindsight. Whatever you did, it's always worth remembering you weren't to know. You were at the start of a journey measured not in weeks but in months, years and decades.

However, I don't want a teenager to read this and think, 'Hang on, I'm going to have to wait until I'm forty to find out who I really am?' That could be a bit of a blow! While it *can* take time for you to understand and like yourself, and you shouldn't blame yourself if it does, what I'm saying to teenagers is to have those conversations with yourself now. Explore what your mind, your instinct, is telling you to be rather than what other people assume you should be – and act on it. Life is about individuality and enjoying who you are, not trying to fit into other people's expectations.

I do know that there will be youngsters sick to the back teeth of hearing the likes of me deliver the 'just be yourself' mantra and then trotting back off into the sunset while they are left clawing for the light switch in the dark. That's because, while the message is true, too often it is presented in an over-simplistic way. None of us can read three words and, just like that, switch our mindsets. You need to take one step at a time. Question yourself, set realistic and goals personal to you and tune in to instinct. These are the three key steps on a stairway that will end in a free and unburdened life.

I have long known that it is not in a fancy house, a big car, massive TV stuck on the wall, where personal contentment lies. It is honesty and normality, and everyone should be allowed to experience it rather than be held back by fear of being judged. It is my sincere hope that we are working towards a time where no one feels compelled to suppress who they really are. Where no one looks with bemusement at those around them and thinks, as another small part of themselves dies inside, 'You have absolutely no idea who I am.' That is a horrible place to be. Life shouldn't be like that. But so often we find ourselves in surroundings which dictate to us who we should be.

Fear of judgement crushes hope. I should know. I justified not telling anybody about first my sexuality and then my HIV because all I could see was a world where I wouldn't be accepted. 'You are right not to tell anyone,' I told myself, 'because they are going to hate you.'

I find it tragic that we live under such a cloud. It is so damaging because it stops us moving towards so many positive life changes and exploring areas that will deliver truly incredible benefits. It's too easy not to try at all than to risk being mocked and belittled.

Exercise is a case in point. The message that fitness is something for people who are already fit is hammered home hourly in the media by endless images of toned, athletic individuals. As a result, the biggest step you can take when it comes to fitness is often the one that takes you outside your front door. The minute you turn the latch, that little bit of optimism, of self-assurance, determination, that was there when you did the unimaginable and actually bought your running gear takes a 400-foot plunge into the chasm of other people's supposed derision.

Such is the power of the myth of the 'perfect body' these days that those lacking in confidence can even start to assume that those who are already fit and slim only want to be around others the same, or have no time for those who are different. I have seen it myself. If someone who is overweight is with someone who isn't, they will often feel awkward or embarrassed, or will do their best to cover themselves up. It's a defence mechanism and it's unhealthy, particularly when it reaches a point where someone feels shame. Instead of seeing themselves in the mirror, they see what they believe everyone else sees – somebody who doesn't care, eats crap, and can't be bothered.

But if I see someone who doesn't fit the lean and mean stereotype out running, having a swim or whatever, the last thing I'm doing is judging. I get a thousand times more satisfaction seeing a normal person exercising than I do a person in great shape. It takes strength to do that, strength that comes from doing what is best for you and is then reinforced by the discovery that the real world is not actually anywhere near as judgemental as you thought. What actually awaits you, be it from friends, family, strangers or others down at the gym, is a huge amount of support. I deliberately go to the gym at unpopular times because I don't want to train alongside people who are ultra-fit. I'm just not interested. I find normality a better, more motivating, environment. It's where real people exist.

In 2016, I made a show called *Alfie's Angels* for BBC Wales. I was asked to undertake to train a hundred women to run a half-marathon. Hmm, I thought when the concept was first discussed, why would they listen to me? I'm a retired rugby player, not an athlete. The last thing I wanted was to stand there every week and tell them what to do. The reason I think it worked was they could identify with me. I might not be Mo Farah but I know what it's like to be riddled with self-doubt. The point was we would all do it together – 'I'll live your experience and you'll live mine. I will listen to your stories and I will tell you mine.' Once that was established, they believed in me. In one fell swoop I had gone from ex-rugby international to being just one of 101 people motivating each other to succeed. As with so many important new experiences, feeling a connection to others was at the heart of it.

At any point where your self-esteem is low and pulling away from peer pressure and fear of judgement may seem beyond your strength, one way to deal with the barriers this creates is to have someone you trust make the decision for you. Other people have a different perspective. They aren't blinded by the fear that may burn so fiercely in yourself. Sometimes, so hard are you concentrating on the worst-case scenario that the best-case scenario is lost in the mire.

Believe me, it works. When I decided to come out as gay, I was gripped by fear. With hours to go until the newspaper article would be published, I convinced myself it was the worst idea I'd ever had. No way did I want to go through with it. In that case I had entrusted someone with the decision – my manager, who, lacking my fear, had a better view of what was good for me than I did myself. When I then faltered, he could justifiably say, 'You entrusted me with this decision. It's right for you and you are going to go through with it.' Which, of course, I did.

Thing is, it's so easy to bail out, to say no. But when somebody won't accept your no, and you know you put the decision in their hands, and they are someone with your absolute best interests at heart, you can then use their instinct instead of your own.

We all like our comfort zone. I am sat in mine right now and it may well look like yours – a living room, TV in the corner, slice of cake, cup of tea and a dog chewing Steve's slippers. But it is outside that comfort zone that we find out more about ourselves. What we need sometimes is someone to give us the push into a different environment. Maybe they will even take that step into the unknown with us.

I can trace my realisation that others might have a better angle on a situation than me right back to that time in the school's changing room. When those kids finally tired of their 'game' and I trudged back to my peg to get changed, I considered my options. I swiftly concluded I didn't have any. 'Tell someone.' That's what we're all told, isn't it? 'Tell someone and they will make it go away.' But, like most kids, I didn't believe in that ethos. Grassing in school was an absolute no-no. If the lads knew I'd gone running to a teacher, I wouldn't have been laughed at and had towels flicked at me, I would have been ignored and that would have been a million times worse. Yes, the bullying would have stopped, but with it would have gone the interaction with the very people I desperately wanted to be friends with. I would have been ostracised, left on my own, when actually, more than anything, I loved being part of them, part of the boys.

The incident weighed on me all night. Next morning, I got ready as usual, had breakfast, put on my school uniform, stepped outside – and promptly burst into tears. It was a boiling-point moment where I was simply too afraid to go to school. My mum twigged straight away that I had been picked on and the story came tumbling out. She said she was going to ring the school – exactly what I didn't want. I pleaded with her not to but, looking at me crying on the doorstep, she had decided to intervene.

'I don't want the boys to know that I've grassed,' I sobbed as she picked up the receiver.

Mum was having none of it. She wasn't going to let a few daft kids sway her decision.

I don't know what she said – I couldn't bear to listen, so mortified was I by her actions. Neither was anything ever said to me by the school. My guess is that it was dealt with in a collective way, no names mentioned, with one of the teachers telling the sporty lads as a group to chill out. But whatever happened, it became the catalyst for a different dynamic. All of a sudden, attitudes towards me changed and my fear of being singled out disappeared. It meant that if I got things wrong I could trust in an environment where I wasn't going to be laughed at, spat at, mocked, or towel-whipped. Suddenly I had permission, on the sports pitch especially, to step out of my comfort zone. This had a big impact on my rugby as now, in search of my true ability, I would attempt new moves and new techniques, without the fear of screwing up or being blamed for letting everyone down. I felt the freedom to be able to express myself rather than playing safe all the time. Up until that point, as much as I loved rugby, I was never really any good at it, but my renewed confidence made me a different prospect.

I have looked back on that incident often. If it was up to me, I wouldn't have done anything. Thankfully, Mum was there to make the decision for me. She unlocked my mental trap and gave me freedom.

In fact, you could say it was my mum's call to the school that morning that gave me my big break.

CHAPTER 11

SEEING IS BELIEVING

If we are truly to encourage people to love themselves rather than wince every time they see a mirror then we need to give them visible role models. Instead of shelves of tatty magazines body-shaming celebrities with pictures of them coming out the supermarket in a big jumper and a pair of joggers – LIKE WE ALL DO – we need a narrative where normality is, well, normal. Where people of all shapes, races, genders and sexualities are represented with positivity and equality.

When I completed the Ironman, I felt I had cleansed myself of any last remnant of self-judgement and peer pressure, be it from the tumultuous times I had been through as an adult or maybe even left over from the childhood bullying in the showers. I felt like a different person. And, when I walked into WHSmith at Paddington Station and saw myself staring back from the magazine shelves, I realised I looked like one too.

When my agent Emanuele rang me to tell me *Men's Health* wanted me as their cover star, I genuinely thought I'd misheard what he'd said. When finally I took it in, I realised straight away it would be completely ground-breaking, one of the most progressive moments I had ever been part of. Look at what *Men's Health* represents: fitness, strength, wellbeing. Things that a good few would consider to be in direct opposition to living with HIV.

'Gareth Thomas? Really? He's got HIV. Why the hell is he on the front cover of *Men's Health* magazine?'

What I would say to that is, 'Why not?' And as soon as they thought about it, I expect most people would say the same. They would realise the only thing making them react like that was their own pre-programming.

But that's not to say I didn't feel some trepidation. The photoshoot came just ten days after the Ironman and, while I had put my story out there in the *Sunday Mirror* and finally felt free of self-judgement, there was a part of me still coming to terms with everybody knowing I had HIV. There were still mental hurdles to overcome. Anybody who has come out, in whatever way, will tell you there's an assumption that you have your big moment of revelation and then wake up the morning after with the weight of the world off your shoulders. 'Great! Life is amazing!' But it doesn't happen like that. There is undoubtedly a strength that comes from being open, but it requires a lot of mental repositioning to reap its full reward.

In this case, I found a photoshoot, something I had done dozens of times before, difficult to rationalise. To be honest, my starting point with any photoshoot is always, 'Why on earth would anyone want a photo of me?' Imagine. You walk into the studio and are presented with a wardrobe department, make-up room, camera, lights, screens, maybe a set of some kind, and the entire focus of all that stuff is … you. 'What?' I'll be thinking. 'Me? Really?' And I'm glad I'm like that, because otherwise that would make me a totally different person. It's all too easy to have your head turned and go into a situation like that saying, 'I want these clothes, this make-up, this hairstyle' (well, the last one doesn't apply, obviously!). All too easy to let the ego take over. But then, actually, when you think about it, a photoshoot isn't about me at all. It's about everyone in that room combining to make something work.

I was introduced to the wardrobe woman who promptly handed me a pair of tracksuit bottoms. I looked at the label. 'Four-hundred-and-fifty pounds!' I spluttered – I couldn't help myself. 'Who the hell pays that for a pair of tracksuit bottoms?' She laughed. Yes, *Men's Health* has everyday people on the front, but they also have those from a world where four-hundred-and-fifty quid is a drop in the ocean. I did the photos in the gear. Fine, no problem. I even gave it back! Then came a request that knocked me back a little. 'Hey, Alfie, could we do some stuff with your top off?'

I've never had a problem with being asked to show my body. I've always worked hard physically and have few qualms about revealing it to the public gaze. Do a photoshoot in a suit and you hide so much. Do a photoshoot unclothed and you are delivering the ultimate open gesture – this, quite literally, is me. Whatever your body shape, it shows a willingness to display more of who you are. Especially for me – when I take my top off, I unveil my tattoos, each of which comes with its own story – love, loss, hope, self-loathing, personal redemption – attached. This, however, felt like I was revealing myself in an entirely different way. I wasn't the Gareth of the last fifteen photoshoots, I was the Gareth who had just come out as HIV positive.

I respected the fact they had to get the photos they needed but pointed out I wasn't in the best head space to do the whole posing this way – that looking moodily into the middle distance kind of business. They listened and totally got it. Instead of doing staged photos, with all the breath-holding and tension they entail, they suggested everyone just relax, chat, mess around, and they would take pictures as we did so.

As I put my own (much cheaper) clothes back on, I reflected on how much I had enjoyed the session. I then left and thought no more about it for a couple of weeks – until I walked into WHSmith. As usual, I had a quick glance at the magazine shelves and, bloody hell, there I was. Wow! I didn't even know it was out!

I have been on the front cover of magazines before but this was completely different. Another publication would no doubt have approached the Ironman element of the story in a really one-dimensional way. Me staring into the camera, snarling, stern-faced – 'Don't discriminate against me – I'm hard!' But this cover was so simple – me, just smiling. Instantly I recalled how, as the shutter clicked, the editor had been asking me about the Ironman and I had explained how vulnerable it made me feel. Perhaps that's why they chose the images they did – because they showed not a strong man pumped full of self-belief and confidence but a strong man who at times feels as helpless as everyone else. It sent out such a normalised message and, as I looked at it, I recognised myself not as someone living in torment, but as someone moving the HIV dialogue towards a better place.

I was still coming to terms with stating publicly that I had the virus and now here I was on the cover of one of the biggest-selling fitness magazines, one that was totally iconic to me growing up. I hope that for some of those living with HIV it felt as big a deal as it did for me. I hope it said to them that to have HIV didn't mean being treated like something dirty, hidden away on life's top shelf, but that it was a reality that major organisations, such as *Men's Health*, wanted to embrace. Here was a major media outlet deciding to take an active role in breaking HIV's every taboo, wanting and willing to move the discussion forward massively.

Never for one minute did I think anyone would be on the front of *Men's Health* for talking about living with HIV, let alone that the person to make that gigantic step would be me, but I do know that such visibility is huge. As a young man, struggling to come to terms with being gay, I had no one to relate to. Any TV or radio show that featured a gay character did so solely to mock. They made such people ridiculously feminine or camp. How could I understand who I was, how I might fit into the jigsaw of life, when, as far as I could see, there was absolutely no one at all like me? No one whose presence could give me the green light to be somebody completely different. No one to look up to, be inspired by. That even made me think, 'Hang on, maybe I'm not gay. Maybe this is going to go away. Maybe this is just an urge that I will quash in time and then I will be like everybody else thinks I am, like everybody else wants me to be.'

Even now, it shocks me how few gay men in sport there are for people to relate to. Me and the diver Tom Daley are possibly the most high profile but where do you go after that? Every day I look at the sporting world and think, 'Where are you?' From across my whole forty-six years I can probably name ten gay sportspeople – men and women – who are household names.

Searching for my own inspiration in rugby led me to the book of hard-as-nails Australian rugby league star Ian Roberts. Welsh-born, the former front-row forward hadn't come out as gay but nor did he deny his sexuality. A brutal player in the ultra-alpha environment of mid-1980s Australian rugby league, Ian did not suffer fools. I remember looking at a photo in his book. In it he was grabbing an opponent who had just, with great originality, called him gay, by the jersey and giving him the mother of all pummellings. The bloke's face was like a mashed melon. I was a young man when I read Ian's book, *Finding Out*. His story was helpful and gave me a certain amount of strength but Ian was a man distant – in time, geography and personality. I liked looking at the picture of the bigot getting his just deserts but violence wasn't who I was. I would never have grabbed somebody and hit them like that.

So, sadly then, as a young gay rugby player, *Finding Out* didn't give me the ability to see the path ahead. Certainly his story didn't make me feel I wanted to come out as gay. I didn't want to spend the rest of my career – if I was even allowed to have one – being the target for every bigot around and being forced to prove myself by punching each one of them to make a point. That was more than twenty years ago and I'm not sure if I was that age now I would feel any different. Even in a much more diverse and inclusive world, there are very few relevant examples of those who can give a real understanding of the experience of coming out. It's twelve years since I made my move – is that a really good point of reference for a player who wants to come out now in the world of rugby union? Mark Foster is the only swimmer to come out. He didn't do so until he retired and he's now in his fifties. If we cannot see the strength of others in our position, how can we be expected to shake off our own feelings of weakness?

That younger version of me was scared constantly of being found out. Only in confronting fear is there strength. But I could see no one, literally no one, who suggested confrontation was a good idea. I was left instead trying to make sense of myself in secret. This led me to Soho's Old Compton Street, which back then I saw as a dark cave. I didn't want to face what was down there but I was driven by a compelling urge and intrigue to do so. There must be others like me. I felt afraid so I took each step tentatively; what I found there gave me comfort rather than strength. There *were* other people in the same position as me, who moved in the dark, sat hidden behind corners and curtains. Maybe there were places where I could be 'normal' – whatever normal was – and where I didn't have to repress myself for fear of judgement. I was so happy for those gay men and women enjoying their freedom. But I still hated myself. I despised my selfishness, that I was lying to people I loved on a regular basis.

'Good on you,' I would think as I watched them. 'You have managed to do something I never will. You have chosen your life. You are going to be honest. You are not going to hurt anybody else.' Eventually, of course, I would find the strength to choose my life and I thank those people for the help they unwittingly gave a young man, starved of any role models, to make that move. I thank them for empowering me.

After I came out, it took me a while to think that there may be those in the background who were now gathering strength from watching me, and perhaps that was something I should be thinking about. Until recently, for instance, I had never felt the need to go to the annual Pride events. I had always watched the reports on TV and seen Pride as little more than a party. But then I realised that actually it's much more than that – it's a beacon of hope for those, like I was, watching in the dark, maybe on the pavement, maybe on TV. Pride is a vision of what could be. Until coronavirus caused its cancellation, Stephen and I were set to go to Cardiff Pride as a married couple to show how far we have been able to travel.

Just talking about it made me think back to those pubs in Soho, each one itself a mini-Pride where someone not too sure of themselves could stand in the background and witness an amazing spectacle of celebration, a place perhaps where personal shame could begin to be rooted out and replaced with the seed of something better. Imagine one person, a rugby player like me perhaps, confused about his sexuality, who accidentally-on-purpose happens to be on the streets of Cardiff when Pride happens.

Even though every time I came back from London, I was massively shrouded in guilt and hated who I was and what I had done, there was a very small part of me – a part I was still figuring out – who took such a lot from it. Yes, there was guilt, but there was also want, there was also need. Over time, in tiny increments, I came to understand that need. Instead of always coming home and scrubbing myself in the shower, I slowly began to realise this actually was the real me, that maybe I didn't have to live a double life. More importantly, I could stop lying to Jemma and my family. It wasn't easy. There were some desperate moments along the way where death appealed more than honesty, but in the end strength did emerge from those sorties to Soho because I finally found it in me to sit down with those I love and tell them the truth. Soho had shown me that a gay man can be accepted, a gay couple can walk hand in hand.

We are a social species. We take so much from seeing, listening to and watching others. There will inevitably be those whose views and actions you respect. The key is to see those people not as template images of who you want to be but as guides, and select them carefully.

When I was playing rugby, I would always watch my captains intensely, which in time gave me the confidence to stand up and speak purposefully like they did. I played my first European Cup final under the captaincy of the hugely experienced Fabien Pelous at Toulouse. I soaked up every word of his pre-match talk because I knew he had been here before. If the captain had been someone who had never been in a European Cup final and yet was telling me what to do, how to play, I'd have been thinking, 'Hang on a minute, you don't actually know how this is going to pan out.' The greatest captains and coaches I ever had were those who spoke from a position of honesty and reality. It is vital to identify those people in life and take all you can from them. They don't have to be the captain of a globally renowned rugby side, they can be a teacher, coach, family friend, neighbour, someone you work alongside. Whoever they are, make the most of them and use their advice to either kickstart or fuel your own motivation.

Being guarded about ourselves is natural, particularly if we are wary of the judgement of others, but that doesn't mean the barriers always have to be up. At some point we have to allow ourselves to trust. I sometimes feel that I've encountered most of the really important people in my life, the ones who I trust above all others, by accident. When I think about it in more depth, however, I see a series of very deliberate accidents that wouldn't have happened if I'd been closed to trust. Don't get me wrong, there have been times where I've been unlucky in meeting people who I thought I could trust before realising, in quite dramatic fashion, that wasn't the case, but it's a part of me I really don't want to change. Sure, after some of my bad experiences it could have been tempting to build up some high walls. But occasions where my trust has been misplaced have never made me want to change my basic philosophy. It makes me appreciate those I do trust, those I do love, my positive friendships, ten times more. There is another factor in all this – when you trust in others, you are trusting in your own judgement. You are trusting yourself.

Maybe that, ultimately, is what I achieved with the front cover of *Men's Health*. What was that image saying if it wasn't, 'I'm Alfie – this is me!' I hope, even if it was for just one person, the sight of me on the shelves helped to dispel at least some of their fear and replace it with something resembling hope and strength.

Think about it: a gay, bald man with wrinkles, HIV, big ears and a massive nose on the front of *Men's Health*. If that doesn't tell you that it's OK to be yourself, then nothing will.

CHAPTER 12

REMOVING THE MASK

My first homosexual encounter in Bridgend was a necessity. I could no longer ignore this part of me that I had spent so many years trying to avoid. It wasn't a moment of weakness or strength, it just had to happen. Amid the shame I felt afterwards, I knew I had opened Pandora's box. As my old Bridgend teammate Glenn Webbe says to me even now, 'Once you shake the bottle and open it up, you can't put the lid back on.'

I had found something that, while utterly petrifying, and which so much of me said I shouldn't be doing, felt very natural to me – the real me. The problem was it also felt wholly unnatural to the person I had created for everybody else. There were times during that brief encounter when I just wanted to close my eyes, open them, and be back at Mum and Dad's sat in an armchair watching TV.

But when I banished those thoughts I knew in my heart this was who I was. This was easier than any other form of sexual encounter had been. I didn't have to think. I didn't have to force myself to do it. I didn't have to put myself into a different mental state – the macho rugby player, the person who everyone else (I thought) wanted me to be. In that moment, I didn't have to play a role anymore.

Afterwards, of course, the blur of real and imagined life returned. I'd had the realisation of who I was, had allowed myself to feel the most normal I had ever felt, but I also craved the person I had created. I liked that person. Being him meant I had played rugby for Wales and Bridgend. He had given me an amazing wife and a lovely home. If the real me showed up on the doorstep one day, he had the potential to take all that away. I was an actor who had become addicted to his character. Easier to keep taking the drug when no one was looking. Cold turkey, in the form of honesty, would be way too painful.

For me, then, that edition of *Men's Health*, as well as being another revolution of the wheel towards a new and accepted narrative about HIV, represented absolute total honesty about myself. As someone who has spent so much of my life switching between a real and fictional version of myself, that felt incredible. It also meant that *Men's Health* could have been either a justified full stop or a comma. I saw it as the latter. It was a moment unlike any other in my life, and yet I didn't even buy a copy. Well, for one thing, you'd need an ego the size of an elephant to pick up a magazine with yourself on the front cover, walk to the counter of WHSmith, and say, as if you hadn't noticed, 'I'll just have this, mate, thank you.' For another, I knew when it came to helping others find their true strength, the wheel hadn't stopped turning. The magazine wasn't a destination in itself and, unless I kept that wheel moving, I would never know ultimately how far it, and I, could progress.

For me, honesty about emotion is at the centre of strength. As a sportsman, I embraced my feelings, just as I do now. I never saw them as something I should be embarrassed about. They are what makes us identifiably us. It's why I never paid attention to media training, when clubs spend vast amounts of money bringing in specialists to suck the individuality out of their players. Media training is, at its core, telling you not to be yourself. It is basically taking a big roller and applying a thick coat of blandness to any semblance of character. 'I'm just pleased for the team that we got the three points and now we'll move on to the next game.' Sorry, mate, what was that? I'm afraid I've fallen asleep.

When anyone speaks on TV, sportsperson or not, more than anything I want to see their personality, their passion. But so rarely does that happen because everybody's programmed the same, not just in how they talk to the media but in everything else. They train at the same time, eat at the same time, sleep at the same time, lift the same weights, do the same drills. They started out as individuals and became the Stepford Wives.

Why do people love the Frank Brunos of this world, the Freddie Flintoffs? It's because they've been honest about themselves. When we see our heroes are like we all are, it only endears them to us. But whenever I had media training – how to speak to journalists and deal with cameras – it felt like they were teaching us to be presenters. Believe me, when someone shoves a camera in your face sixty seconds after losing one of the biggest games of your life you are not going to come across like Phillip Schofield. In the end, I trained myself as I went along, learning how best to project myself and say what I felt needed to be said. Post-match interviews can never be an exact science.

Professional sport might be an extreme environment but in its hang-ups about emotional honesty, it is actually no different to any other walk of life. From an early age, we learn that covering up our emotional reality is the easy way to acceptance, a situation exacerbated by the fact that most teenagers just want to be grown up, and if they can't be grown up they want to look grown up. That generally means doing what adults do, and I'm not talking about sitting in on a Sunday night watching the *Antiques Roadshow*.

Aged sixteen, for example, I got my first tattoo. The deed was done in the glamorous back streets of Swansea, with Rhydian Phillips, a mate I played rugby with at Pencoed. The flagon of White Lightning cider that accompanied us might have had some influence on me ending up in a low-end tattoo parlour having Yosemite Sam inked on my leg. Don't get me wrong, I didn't go into that tattoo parlour with the clear intention of having a three-inch Yosemite Sam. I went in there because I thought, 'I'm hammered! Let's do something wild!' Let's face it, if you were a bit of a lad, a tattoo was what you did. 'Why Yosemite Sam?'

I hear you ask. Because after a flagon of White Lightning he looked fucking amazing. It could have been worse – around that time the Weetabix Men were quite trendy.

I was at least just about sober enough that day in Swansea to realise it would be better to have Yosemite Sam's trademark Stetson and violently red facial hair at the top of my leg. That way, even if I was wearing shorts, nobody would be able to see him.

Public invisibility was a trick I maintained through numerous other tattoos. The first time either of my parents knew my skin was a pictorial collage was when I played for Wales against England at Twickenham eight years later. They were on their feet as I scored a try but as I went over the line I was tackled near the neck and my jersey was yanked down. There, for all to see, was the top of the cross that sits between my shoulder blades. It didn't take long after the game for my mum to mention it. 'Gareth, what have you had on your back?' Hands up. It was time to do a bit of explaining.

A psychologist might see that first tattoo as an attempt to separate myself a little from the crowd but in fact it was more of a punt at fitting in, hiding who I really was, trying to do something overtly male and macho and deflect any suspicion from other people that I wasn't what I knew myself to be. Back then, not many people had tattoos and those who did were generally tough alpha men. Just my luck that within a few years they were the height of fashion among gay men as well! 'Shit! I've gone through all that and now they're one of the biggest indicators of being gay I could possibly have!'

To be fair to the tattooist, who didn't seem overly concerned that two drunken teenagers had staggered through the door, Yosemite Sam is still looking pretty good today. He has become, for reasons I could never have anticipated, one of the most poignant of the many tattoos that cover my body. Rhydian, one of the nicest blokes you could ever meet, would go on to become a detective constable. Tragically, he died aged just thirty-four when he fell twenty-two floors from a New York hotel window while on a rugby tour with a South Wales Police XV to raise money for the New York Police and Fire Widows' and Children's Benefit Fund following the 9/11 terror attacks. I'm so grateful for the time I shared with him.

As the flagon of White Lightning might suggest, when it came to drinking there was only one goal – to get absolutely howling. Bridgend had a big macho drinking culture, the opposite to everything I am now, to the extent I look back and think, 'Oh my God!' but at the time I loved it. Me and my brothers used to work at the Spar shop on Saturdays. Together we would nick loads of booze, sit on the bench outside, and wait for oblivion. This is how much times have changed – aside from White Lightning, my drink back then was Malibu and pineapple, which would definitely not have gone down well in the amateur rugby changing rooms I was frequenting.

That particular environment was very much about all things alpha – that was what rugby encapsulated at the time. I adopted that persona like everyone else. I had to. The alternative was to be called a 'bender' or deemed as weak. Your actions on a rugby field were only a small part of your relevance to that world. The majority of it was how you behaved in the changing room, in the pub, or around girls. I felt it was incumbent on me to be like that. I had learned the code of conduct from everybody else. To be quiet in the changing room, not talk about women, or not have a beer was not going to go down well, to the extent that players who weren't macho were seen as not caring as much, lacking the heart and guts for the game. I look back and remember how we would laugh at some players behind their backs when they went home early from the pub or had a quiet night in with their partner – 'What? He's going home? What a bender!'

Put me in that changing room now and I would tap that bloke on the back – 'What a tough man you are.' And I am not alone in that. As time has passed, I have come to see more and more players, who had been so desperate to be seen on the outside as alpha males, reveal themselves to be anything but, although in many cases it has taken until retirement for them to do so. My great friend Compo, for instance, is a completely different person now he doesn't feel he is being judged week in, week out, by how hard he is. That goes for so many others. Out of the game they are totally authentic – the person they were in the eighties and nineties was a character, manufactured in the great sporting factory of male bravado. They, like me, adopted that character because they considered it was what was needed to look strong and survive in a changing room. Interestingly, when we have Bridgend club reunions, bearing in mind these are people who haven't played for a long time, the alpha ethos comes back in a flash. The difference now is that there is an element of self-awareness, a willingness to mock. Anybody who is blatantly trying to reawaken their inner alpha from all those years ago soon shuts up when they find themselves on the end of some pretty heavy-duty piss-taking.

Men are so messed up when it comes to emotional honesty because we carry generations of learned behaviour with us. We are still shaking off the attitudes learned in caves. I don't go into rugby club changing rooms enough now to know whether that sexist, homophobic attitude still exists, but if I were a betting man I would put my house on that being the case. We might be evolving but we still carry around that inherited history lesson on what makes us hard, strong, tough.

What is it with men? Why do we need rules, unwritten and written, before we feel like we know how to behave with one another? Look at golf with its history of all-male clubhouse bars, cricket the same. Why are men so scared of women? We, as men, are supposed to be intelligent people. And we're not. Absolutely not. We have got the tools but half the time we just don't choose to use them. What kind of species is it that has the ability to think in an incredibly deep way, unmatched by any other animal on the planet, and yet chooses to act like sheep? If we want to create this much-vaunted environment where men can speak openly about their feelings then the existence of macho culture, which teaches them to do exactly the opposite, can only be damaging. We should be helping men to remove the mask, not tie it on even more tightly. Why make life hard when it needn't be? Why ostracise those who are emotionally honest?

I find people's attitudes to crying so revelatory. When a sportsperson cries during a national anthem, or like Gazza did when he was booked in the 1990 World Cup semi-final and realised that if England won he would miss the final, they are deemed heroes. Equally, a group of alpha males watching a player cry after missing in a penalty shoot-out would be deeply admiring of his passion. His tears mean he is strong, he cares. And yet a person crying because they are struggling with their sexual identity is deemed weak as piss. Cry for a macho reason – i.e. sport – and it's manly. Cry for a legitimate emotional reason and you are a pussy. Sadly, I expect there are more than a few dads around who, if their son bursts into tears, tell them, 'Stop crying, you big girl.'

For someone who has shed many a public tear, people may be surprised to hear I never cried as a sportsperson, be that in victory, defeat or to the national anthem. Sport was important to me but I always understood exactly what it was – sport. I enjoyed it, was never less committed than anyone else, but always had perspective, possibly because I had so much turmoil going on elsewhere in my life. The only time I cried in a sporting setting was when I got injured – not because of the pain but because, on an emotional level, long-term recuperation means loss of friendship, identity and purpose.

I have a good angle on my emotional triggers and so I usually know if a subject or situation is going to make me cry. The start of my HIV documentary is a case in point. I knew that going back to the start of the story, the place where I was diagnosed, would, on a very basic level, make me sad. Whenever I talk about the major points in my life, I really invest in the emotions I felt at the time and so, in that moment, as I pondered how in a 'fairer' world I wouldn't be in an HIV clinic doing what I was doing, saying what I was saying, I had two options – a shaky voice or just cry.

On a practical level, letting the tears flow allows my emotions to come out, which means I can then continue what I'm doing. There are times I've made TV shows and tried not to cry only to stop two minutes later because it felt unnatural, that I was denying myself something I needed to do. If you find yourself welling up, there is no point keeping those tears inside. Your mind is telling you it needs a release.

There are now more men than ever who will openly cry and that's a good thing. But there will always be those who resolutely refuse to accept or understand the need to shed tears. I cry a lot, so I'm honest about it both with myself and others. I expect there are those who are sick of seeing me in tears, who think I cry for no reason, but that is far from the truth. I laugh because it's an emotion; I cry because it's an emotion. Those people who think I just like crying tend to be the same ones who find crying a difficult emotion to deal with. They find being in the presence of someone in tears awkward or uncomfortable. I wonder what drives that narrative. In effect, it's saying, 'You are creating a bad environment and I'm not sure I like it, so stop crying.'

Others think crying is something people do to get noticed. Break your arm and it's OK to cry; suffer emotionally and you are just after attention. Truth is, physical pain has hardly ever made me cry. It's part and parcel of rugby so you just learn to live with it and, rugby aside, I don't think I'm much different from the vast majority of other men on that point. Having long retired from rugby, physical pain is now largely absent, but the emotional side of life persists, and if that causes me to cry then I am more than OK with it. I see it as an expression of both honesty and strength.

I also won't let others tell me what I can and can't do. A lot of people won't cry because they're afraid of what other people will say. I don't like it if someone mocks me for crying but at the same time I'm not going to allow them to dictate my emotions, the same as I wouldn't let anyone tell me when I can and can't talk, or laugh and not laugh. It's not acceptable for other people to create an environment where they say what it is OK, emotionally, for you as an individual to do.

Whether depression has ever been part of the equation I'm not sure but I do know there have been numerous occasions in my life when I've cried my eyes out because I've been so sad. And others when I've cried my eyes out for no discernible reason at all. Looking back on it now, I don't feel that when I cried over something unidentifiable when I was at rock bottom it was me being depressed. It was just me being me, trying to get over whatever I was dealing with or going through at any particular point in time.

Crying is a massive stereotype of the vulnerable gay man. But anyone who sees this as being 'soft' could not be more wrong – about me or anyone else, of any sexuality, who shows their emotions. The fact I am not afraid of my emotions or of openly showing them even though that makes me really vulnerable is what makes me strong, really strong. It is the clearest message I can send out that I'm happy with my identity. It is what allows me to connect.

I will not change. If there's a camera in my face, it will make zero difference. I am not going to pretend to be anything different from what I am. If people think I am being false, fine. I know it's me and in the end that's all that matters. You don't have to pretend to be strong. You don't have to put on a front and wait until you have closed your front door to show your emotions. I will not be pressured into changing for anybody. I know who I am and I know what I represent. I have spent enough time in my life being something I'm not.

I know there are multitudes of people out there pretending to be someone else, trying to keep up an image, whether that's one that has been painted for them or that they have decided is the best or most lucrative way to present themselves to the world. Or in some cases, it's something they feel they have to keep up to protect themselves from the wolves lurking in the dark forest of their imagination. It must be so mentally debilitating for those people. I for one can attest to how hugely damaging it is to lie about who you are. It leads to a state of constant fear, not just of people finding out, but of the real you. Deception has the power to affect you in the most negative of ways. A mental position is reached where you believe the real you is actually a threat.

Confusion is the constant companion of those seeking an inner peace. We are bombarded with experts, gurus, telling us we will find it with this strategy, this exercise, this lifestyle realignment. But the true answer is always inside ourselves. Better to listen to our own voice, make the most of what comes naturally to us, than try to change who we are. I don't want to force theories on others any more than I want to have them forced on myself, and yet the newspapers are full of them – 'Your Guide to Finding Inner Peace'. How's that going to work then? That person doesn't know who I am, or what my idea of peace is. They can push its delights all they want but I'm not likely to find myself halfway up a Tibetan mountain having colonic irrigation. I'd much rather be up the Bwlch in the Rhondda. Stood up there, the landscape before me, my dad's village of Ogmore below, I feel more emotionally connected to myself than I ever could in some spiritual retreat which means precisely zero.

One road up, one road down, the Bwlch is beautiful, the physical representation of so much I wanted to represent through rugby and life in general. I am happy with my achievements, the life that my skill with a rugby ball has given me, the places it has taken me, the people who it has brought into my life, but I would take precisely zero enjoyment from any of those things if I didn't feel I had that basic and ever-present knowledge of myself as just being a kid from Bridgend. That, as much as the big dramas – the sport, the HIV, the sexuality – is my emotional identity. I don't need telling the top ten ways to find the inner me and I don't think many other people do either.

*

I also urge caution in the way we seek to help those around us who appear to be struggling with their identity. Empowering others, providing a platform for them to speak openly and honestly, find their voice and trust in it, is a matter of pride for me, but when it comes to sensitive and deeply personal areas we must be careful not to put anyone in a difficult position.

For me, the process of coming out as gay was a very slow one, during which I had to tread carefully, see where each step would lead me. So when, early on in my career, the aforementioned Glenn Webbe rang me and asked me out of the blue, 'Are you gay?' I was sent into a frenzy of panic that my secret was out. Glenn's curiosity stemmed from seeing me in a gay bar in Cardiff which the team as a whole had visited on a pub crawl the week before. It's easy to think I should have seized that moment to unburden myself – a problem shared is a problem halved and all that – but anyone who has wrestled with their identity knows it is in no way as simple as that. In order to be able to tell someone else, first of all I would have to fully confront the situation myself. When that point finally came, the first person I told was the first person who should have been told – my then wife, Jemma.

While Glenn is a great friend and someone who is really tuned in to other people – hence why he asked me the question – I would never take the approach he did that day. He did so with all the best intentions, to let me know it was no big deal to him, but I didn't know that at the time and such a blunt question gave me no indication that he was thinking that way. For me to have been honest with him, firstly he would have needed definite knowledge that I was gay, then he would have needed to make me feel at ease with having a conversation. As it was, asking the question out of nowhere put me in a position of added fear. My natural reaction was not to discuss my innermost secrets but to build more barriers around me. Far from settling me, Glenn's question made me think I must be doing something wrong. I must have let my guard down, started to relax a little. My secret trips to Soho must have loosened my shackles and allowed me to be a little bit too open with myself. I must have been giving out messages that made people think I was gay. I would now have to retreat into my shell and create a bigger, stronger, and more convincing straight character. The question didn't take me a single inch forward. Instead it pushed me back a hundred miles.

What I learned from that experience is never to push people for information. I would never just come out and say to somebody who I thought was struggling with their sexuality, 'Are you gay?' because it is far too black and white a question. Better to have a natural, perhaps random, conversation around the subject so the other person sees you have an understanding of the nuances of the situation. At that time, I had no real idea of Glenn's acceptance or non-acceptance, whether he was there for me or not. I know him well enough now to know absolutely that would have been the case but my mindset at that time meant self-protection was my only concern. I had images in my head of him gathering the rest of the players around him in the changing room, ready to burst forth with this juicy information that surely everybody would want to hear.

As the first black icon of Welsh rugby, Glenn's question also came from a place of experiencing prejudice himself. I have massive respect for Glenn; he's a wonderful man, and incredibly strong mentally – as someone who took a lot of racist abuse on the pitch, he had to be if it wasn't going to affect him. By comparison, firstly, I could hide my sexuality, and secondly, I wasn't strong enough to be open about it. Even when I did come out, I still had moments when I thought, 'Why have I done this?' whereas Glenn is somebody who would never want to change who he is. He always stood his ground and defeated hatred with strength and humour. I didn't share those characteristics. Glenn was also much older than me so had experience on his side. I was little more than a kid. I had nothing on which to form a strategy. I just wanted to play rugby. Keeping something to yourself ultimately is damaging. But that's not part of the conversation when the dominant force is control over your own life.

Eventually, however, I found that amid all the complexities of life, the dead ends, the mental networks of passages and caves that take us further and further from the light, there is one simple truth. Honesty and openness is the only way to achieve anything resembling lasting peace for yourself and those around you.

And there is one other factor to be considered – it allows you to challenge the ignorance and prejudice of others. It allows you not to be cowed, but to stand up for what is right.

CHAPTER 13

ATTACKED

'You fucking benders. You pair of faggots.'

I am always really aware of my surroundings. It has become something that's natural to me as a gay man and sadly it will be a state familiar to many others who are deemed to have committed the sin of being in a minority. Generally, it involves an internal dialogue. 'Am I safe here? Who is around me? What is likely to happen here? Do I need to do anything to make this environment safer?'

On this particular occasion, me and Stephen are walking through a busy Cardiff city centre one evening, not exactly a situation full of potential flashpoints. We aren't holding hands but are close enough that it's obvious we are together. It is then I see a group of six lads, aged around sixteen to eighteen, coming towards us. Straight away I see the potential for trouble, to the extent I move a little away from Stephen – not because I don't want us to be seen as a gay couple, I just want a simple night out devoid of any hassle.

As we draw level with the group, two of them start with the abuse.

I process the situation in my head. 'Right, just keep walking. No point making a fuss. They don't know what they're saying. They're just ill-educated idiots.'

I walk a half-dozen more steps and then I stop. 'Hang on,' I think, 'everything you tell people, everything you represent, everything you stand up for, has never been more relevant than now. You can't just ignore this and keep walking, Alfie. You have to do something. This kind of thing just can't go on.'

I turn round. 'Hey!' They turn to look at me. 'You can't say that to people. Why are you walking around thinking that you can?'

They stand and stare. I can see in their eyes what they're thinking – 'We either carry on walking or we finish it.'

They unleash a torrent of homophobic abuse. The usual stuff, nothing I haven't heard before. But this feels different. Whenever I've been a victim of homophobia before it has always been in a sporting environment. On a rugby field there will always be the odd person who believes such talk is justified. It is, in their minds, part and parcel of the game. They are wrong, but they exist. Here, though, for the first time ever, I feel like I am really being attacked, really homophobically attacked, in an environment open to anybody, just here in the street.

The tirade keeps coming. Stephen is concerned with the sinister way events are evolving.

'Come on,' he pulls my arm, 'let's just go.'

They start walking towards us. 'OK,' I think, 'we can either retaliate or turn and run.' I know the latter isn't actually an option. If we run they will chase us. They have started the confrontation and will want to end it.

Strangely, my mind turns to the cows in the fields I occasionally encounter when out walking my mad pointer Boyo. On those occasions, I make myself big, stand tall, stick out my chest, make my arms and legs taut, and walk towards them, at which point the cows back off. But a gang of youths in a city centre is different. They have the herd mentality but it is fed by bravado. I walk towards them but they keep up the constant yapping off.

'I'm going to call the police,' I tell them. 'This is a hate crime. You can't be going round saying things like this.'

It now most definitely has turned into a confrontation; a question of who is going to back down first. I make it clear it isn't going to be me by walking faster. They turn to run but as they do so one of them slips and falls to the ground. I grab him by the arm.

'Mate,' I tell him, 'I'm going to call the police and they will get you and your mates for what you've done.'

As the words leave my mouth, his mates turn, see him on the floor with me crouching over him and fly back at me. Before I know it, the fists are flying. I am getting smashed on the side of the head. Then I feel a kick in the ribs.

My rugby training comes in handy. I have often done an exercise where a player puts themselves on all fours while others try to move him. It is incredibly difficult. On all fours you can make yourself really strong and that is the position I adopt now, over this kid while the rest of them are just battering me.

I am shouting to Stephen. 'Don't do anything.' If either of us hits out I know we risk them painting us as the aggressors.

A homeless guy comes over and begins shouting at them. 'Get the fuck off him!' Even in the gale force of that moment I appreciate massively that someone so vulnerable has put themselves in that position for me. Sadly, however, his intervention is unlikely to change anything. The blue lights that now flicker between blows are a more likely source of help. Several officers wade in and split up this very one-sided melee.

'They abuse me every night,' I can hear the homeless guy telling one of the officers. 'They come round here shouting at people, intimidating them, threatening them. They abuse me, they kick me. I want to report them.'

A couple of bystanders agree that my attackers' behaviour is far from isolated. It is clear they have got away with behaving in a horribly anti-social way time and time again. The witnesses also reinforce that this is a hate crime. They have heard what has been said and seen them kicking and punching me.

'You have to do something,' they tell the police.

By now, I am stood a few metres away from the gang. An officer comes over and asks me what I want to do.

'Look, butt,' I tell him, 'I just want to get on with my life, but ultimately I can't pretend this never happened. I feel like I've been the victim of an attack and I really don't want to feel like a victim.'

The officer says I can give a statement and tell them who has hit me. I'm pretty sure it's all of them but because I've had my head down protecting myself I can only point out one with absolute certainty.

They walk me over to the entrance to TK Maxx. People are starting to congregate, and the doorway soon becomes a centre of attention. I am standing there with the police when some diners emerge from the Miller & Carter steakhouse opposite.

'Alfie? You wouldn't mind having a photo, would you?'

'Well,' I reply, 'I'm going to be a minute. I've got a black eye, blood all down the side of my face and I'm talking to a police officer.' To be fair, they have brought serviettes out with them to help mop me up.

As I fend off selfies and wipe blood off my face, the officer asks, 'Do you want to do restorative justice?'

I've never heard of it. The officer explains that it's a process where the victim of a crime is allowed to talk face-to-face with the perpetrator. It sounds appealing, better than the whole tiresome and time-consuming process of giving statements and potentially going through the courts. I agree on the guarantee that the police will give them a talking-to as well.

The policeman goes back to the gang. 'Look, boys,' he tells them, 'there is CCTV round here. Basically, we've got you on camera kicking the crap out of this man. He will testify against you and you will be dragged through the courts for committing a hate crime.'

I can see from the looks on their faces they are starting to get very afraid, realising that actually they are in a lot of trouble. They say they didn't even know there is such a thing as a hate crime. They thought I had just made it up. I watch this group of teenagers turn into real children. Absolutely petrified.

I look intensely into their faces, struck suddenly by the fact they are Black or Asian. They are in a minority themselves. I go to talk to them.

'Why are you,' I ask them, 'as people with protected characteristics, going round abusing other people in exactly the same position? If I walked past you and said something awful and racist, how would you feel? How can you not understand what you are saying and how your actions make other people feel?'

I don't want to simply assume their prejudice comes solely from themselves. Maybe they have grown up in homes with little understanding of LGBTQ people or made to think that all gay people are bad – that abusing them, beating them up, is the right thing to do. Maybe this is the one opportunity for someone to stand in front of them and dispel that inherited mythology. From this most negative of situations, I can actually do something good for them.

'Do you know how your actions made me and Stephen feel?' I ask.

They seek desperately to justify their actions. 'We've said things to other people and they haven't had a problem with it.'

'Those people might have looked like they didn't have a problem with it,' I explain, 'because they were too afraid to confront you or just tried to get away as quickly as possible – which is exactly what we considered doing.'

They seem to take this on board, listening as I explain how damaging prejudice is, how it ruins people's lives and how it has the propensity to ruin theirs too if they don't become aware of its destructive power.

By the end, rather bizarrely considering how this whole episode started, they are hugging me, shaking my hand and saying how appreciative they are that I have chosen to speak to them rather than go down the route of the courts. Equally importantly, I no longer feel like a victim. This isn't a situation for winners or losers but I can walk away definitely not having lost.

My hope is they never did anything like that again. I want to believe that the next time a situation like that arose, because they had spoken to me, heard how they had made me feel, they would walk past in silence, understanding that prejudice and abuse can never be the right way, that it is merely a commentary on a person's own deficiencies rather than anyone else's.

I hope also that my talking to those teenagers face to face helped the homeless man. He said he'd been trying to report them for weeks. Just because a person is homeless doesn't mean they should be denied a voice.

I won't pretend to be a saint. There was never a single moment where I didn't feel I could have smacked every single one of those youths across the face and felt justified for doing so. But I also felt that the law would not be on my side. I would be the one in the dock being accused of using unnecessary force or taking violent retaliation. I am glad I held back because restorative justice delivered something much more satisfying. I came away from that awful incident with so much knowledge of myself and other people. I learned that while previously I had talked to people about understanding the importance of representing themselves, standing up for themselves, I had never personally really understood the potential dangers and consequences of actually being in that position. It would have taken only one of those kids to have had a knife and it could have been a very different story – possibly one I would never have had the chance to tell. That's why, in a weird way, I feel grateful for that horrible experience. When I now talk about confronting prejudice, I better comprehend fear. I have a greater knowledge of what and who I represent.

Until that day, I thought being homophobically abused in a rugby ground was the worst scenario I could face, but actually getting the same treatment on the street from a group of kids, or even one kid, is ten times worse. It is much more invasive. When I was representing a club, I was part of something much bigger than me. There was a barrier between me and the crowd, an understanding that nothing was ever really going to happen. In Cardiff, it was just me and Stephen, in our own space, in our own time. No barriers, no nothing. Just us. You realise on the street that the potential for abuse, or something a lot worse, is actually there. For great swathes of people, fear of being attacked, punched, spat on, is not baseless but very real, and I couldn't help but wonder how my own experience, and the attention it subsequently gathered, might make other gay people nervous about going into Cardiff. Fear feeds fear. It marginalises the already marginalised.

An assault doesn't have to be physical to be damaging. When people say 'sticks and stones may break my bones but names will never hurt me', they are talking complete bollocks. Names are worse. I'd rather somebody punched me than abused me. If someone broke my nose in two places, a month later it would be fixed. Call me something vile and sickening and six months later it would still be echoing round my head. In fact, six months is a best-case scenario depending on the environment and the nature of the abuse. If you happen to be unbelievably strong and names mean nothing to you, then I am pleased for you, but most of us could walk along a line of a thousand people, have 999 of them shake our hand, tell us how amazing we are, and just one tell us we are worthless, a piece of nothing, and it is the negative one who we would drive home thinking about. It is impossible to ignore being abused. People might not show it outwardly, but inside those barbs are scarring big time.

Hate crime has to be taken seriously, which is why, while those exposed to it should never act in a manner that puts them at risk, they should always report incidents to the police. So many hate crimes – racist, homophobic, transphobic, whatever – go unregistered because people decide, understandably, 'You know what? I'm just going to walk away from this. I don't need the bother. I'll try to forget it ever happened.' But remember, just because you don't confront the perpetrator, doesn't mean you can't confront the system. Accurate numbers about hate crime add weight to the need to legislate and act against it.

With the situation dealt with, I wanted what happened over and gone. I knew that was fanciful. My bloodied face in the middle of a load of police officers had been caught on dozens of mobile phones, and so next morning I attempted to head off the inevitable interest by putting a video out on Twitter. Wales is like is a goldfish bowl. If I'd kept schtum, I'd have had my mates ringing non-stop asking, 'Hey, Alfie, what was going on in Cardiff last night? Why were you fighting?'

To me, the best way of nipping the story in the bud is to take control and do it my way. I didn't want to do a newspaper article, with any kind of 'poor Alfie' angle it might contain, so I decided to use Twitter for one of its more positive reasons – to explain briefly what had gone on and say thank you to the police and others for helping me.

I look battered and bruised on that video because that's exactly what I was. It was important to me to show the reality of what hate crime can do to someone. At the same time, I understood I was one of the lucky ones. Restorative justice at the scene had allowed me a degree of closure. I had a few physical scars but the mental ones, those that really matter, that can open up again so quickly, had already begun to heal. For sure, there would be those for whom such an experience would deliver a mental lockdown. They might never dare to venture out at night again. For their sake, it was important to end on a note of hope.

'There's a lot of people out there who want to hurt us,' I concluded. 'But, unfortunately for them, there's a lot more who want to help us heal.'

With the video out there, I felt I could move on. Not quite. Because I had been honest with the police and told them I could only identify with absolute certainty one person who had hit me, when the incident did come to be reported in the media it was done so as if it involved a lone assailant.

Sadly, and very predictably, machismo rose to the surface. A typical Twitter reply I received in the aftermath was along the lines of 'Hang on, you're six-foot-three and being given a mouthful of abuse by a sixteen-year-old kid? Why didn't you just knock him out? What a pussy.'

It's hard to reason with people like that, but I'll try. First up, even if it was one sixteen-year-old kid, that doesn't make knocking him out right. Secondly, if I had hit him, then that would have been it – I would have been in the wrong regardless. It would have put me in a difficult position with the police and I would have missed out on the great learning opportunity that was restorative justice.

I couldn't win. You can bet your life that if I had hit one of my attackers, those self-same people who were calling me out for not using my fists would be insulting me for clocking a mere kid. 'Big man Alfie, hitting a sixteen-year-old!'

It was a scenario I hadn't created, that I didn't want to be a part of, and yet here I was having to justify my role in it to people who had no idea of the delicate dynamics of the situation. As the police said to me that night, this was just one gang of kids – in the surrounding square mile there could be twenty others. I'm a big strong bloke, but it only takes a couple of minutes and there's thirty kids surrounding you. Then what happens to me and Stephen? There will be people reading this who know that only too well, because they have gone through the terrifying experience of street violence.

I can live with the usual nonsense on social media but when I had friends asking me similar questions, I almost wished I had taken the assault through the courts so everyone could see the CCTV footage of the group attacking me and feel OK about me being a proper victim, not a man who had cowed to a lone teenager.

Thankfully, I came to a more reasoned standpoint. I shouldn't have to justify why I didn't knock out a kid for calling me a 'bender'. What happened in Cardiff was not about being an alpha male, showing who's the toughest, it was about changing attitudes. My life, my way. Living by other people's rules of engagement is, as I well know, rarely a route to happiness.

Having said that, I did end up doing that selfie!

CHAPTER 14

DISCRIMINATED

I'm about to strip off in front of a bunch of other people. Not for the first time, obviously. I've spent half my life in rugby changing rooms, no place for the easily embarrassed. It's why the post-match showers are rarely dropped in upon by a passing nun. The difference this time is that I'll be stripping off in front of several women as well as men. I am filming a show based around *The Full Monty*. Across a number of weeks, we have put together a dance routine leading to the famous full-frontal finale. The film of *The Full Monty* features an all-male strip, but the TV show, rightly, includes women in the process. In previous years, male and female celebrities have disrobed separately. This time, however, the production company has decided we should all do it together. No problem as far as I'm concerned. If anything, it shows an enlightened attitude.

Beforehand, the men are gathered together. We are reminded that this is a professional environment and so we shouldn't look at the women's bodies. At first this doesn't strike me as odd. I understand completely what they are saying. It is inappropriate to look at them in a way anything other than as a colleague performing a role. And while I think most people would be more than aware of this, it's still worth saying. But then a thought occurs to me. This is classic sexual stereotyping. The language being used is based on everyone being straight. We are being subjected to unconscious bias.

After the meeting, I speak to a couple of the other blokes. They don't see the problem. Maybe it's because they're young, *Love Island* types and so haven't quite got the life experience. When I speak to a couple of the women, however, they can better see I have a point, perhaps because of the endless sexual bias they come up against every day. I am glad they have seen what's wrong but the lack of comprehension elsewhere worries me. I can't help thinking that this kind of lazy sexual bracketing too often flies over our heads. We never make the link. I expect there have been times when I've been as guilty as anybody.

I don't say anything to the production company. I'm not going to create chaos by screaming and stamping my feet. I can only try to change inequality from a place of calm. Strength comes from action built on reflection. I get my outfit on, get out there on stage and get on with the show.

It's not me I'm worried about. In the big scheme of things, this was just one small incident, no insensitivity meant. But it's important we build a place where people realise that what they're doing is wrong. There has to be more consciousness of bias in everyday life.

Make no mistake, bias and discrimination, conscious or otherwise, is all around us. Me and Stephen can walk down the street hand in hand in what we might think is one of the most enlightened places on the globe but there will still be the occasional person glancing back after we've passed. That's us as part of a well-established and largely accepted minority. Imagine what it's like for others. Routinely they will experience people staring, pointing or even laughing at them. There are those who appear to see minorities as a selection box – 'I'm OK with gay men and lesbians but everyone else? No thanks, I don't like those.'

There have been times when I've challenged that way of thinking. 'Hang on! You can't just be OK with gay people and not those who, say, are trans or gender fluid. They are still people. They still exist.'

Thankfully, increasingly we live in a world where confronting prejudice is accepted rather than mocked but it is still endemic in society, and many of those at its epicentre don't even think they have a problem. Basically, it's the large-scale version of that old chestnut, 'I'm not racist – one of my friends is black.' Believe me, it happens. I was in a text conversation with a contact when he insisted, 'I'm not homophobic, I've got a gay friend,' yet his previous messages had contained several deeply offensive terms. I pointed out to him that he was homophobic – his messages proved it. The fact he had a gay friend was neither here nor there.

It was nothing new to me. Before I came out, I would hear fellow rugby players make negative comments about gay people all the time – 'Hey, boys, we'll win today, no bother. I've heard the other team have got two benders in their side.'

Funny. Nobody ever said to me, 'Mate, don't kick the ball to him on that wing because he's gay and really good.' It was always, 'Kick to him because he is gay so he's really shit.'

'OK,' I would think, 'so am I not kicking it to him because he's gay? Because he's gay so he must be shit? Or just because he's shit?'

Those teammates didn't consider themselves to be homophobic. It would never have occurred to them. It was just part of the chat, the language of the changing room.

Back then, the route I took was not to confront prejudice but to strengthen the version of myself others expected me to be. I became a social junkie, someone who realised he had to be like everybody else and who also realised that such a skill was not going to come naturally. I would study intimately the actions, mannerisms and words of those around me. That way, I could detect if they were on to me or posed a threat to my hidden truth. I could also make sure my own behaviour mirrored that of the classic big-boozing, womanising, macho man. Everyone in my sphere became a subject, part of my education.

But after a while, I became so good at studying others that I knew I could see what they didn't – frailties in supposedly strong people; real strength in those considered fragile and weak. I so intently watched them, so intently listened to what they had to say, that I was effectively a walking lie detector. I came to really like some people and really not like others because I knew, unlike anybody else, who the true characters, the honest individuals, were. One week, someone would tell a story, then I'd hear them tell it again the next week but, depending on who they were talking to, there would be a difference.

I understood how to please people. It was an ability that allowed me a comfortable way of living, allowing me to exist through the personalities of those around me, giving me a quick trapdoor through which to disappear from my reality. But even though I could spot the lies and the people who were pretending, and I knew I myself was an actor in every scene, I still liked what I was creating. I actually wanted to be this person.

But even so, the way I heard men talk about women so often made me feel really uncomfortable. I found myself in situations where I would hear something and think, 'I don't agree with that. I don't like the fact you're talking about a woman in that way. It doesn't make me comfortable. You're so wrong if you think that's cool.' But of course I said nothing. Back then, if someone had spoken up and challenged that way of thinking they would have been on the end of a mouthful of abuse. The person spouting the usual crap about women could justify their opinion because it was the perceived consensus of the majority. There is an unspoken dynamic at play there – 'If you want to raise the minority view, we'll ask ourselves why. We'll make an assumption as to why you think differently. And that assumption will centre on your sexuality.'

In many ways, rugby is the best and worst thing that ever happened to me. I love my rugby mates. They have been so brilliant to me through everything in my life, and to a man they were hugely supportive when I came out. But rugby was an environment where individuality was never really considered. Everybody assumed everyone else was the same. Nobody gave any thought as to the effect their language might have on someone who was different. If it didn't offend them, how could it offend anyone else?

So naturally, as I came to understand myself, I became very afraid of what others in that environment would think of the real Alfie. This was, after all, my only environment, where all my mates were. Rugby was my life. Only when I finally bit the bullet and went to Soho did I see that actually the rugby changing room was far from the only social set-up out there. There were other ways to be.

While times have changed to some degree, still there are people out there who don't understand that just because attitudes and words exist in everyday life doesn't mean they're not discriminatory. If you say to me you refer to gay people as 'benders' but don't mean anything by it, don't expect me to shake your hand.

It needn't be so obvious. Some words carry less weight but, when you think about it, are equally insulting. 'Tolerant' is one that always gets me. 'We are tolerant of ethnic minorities in this country, tolerant of gay people, tolerant of immigrants.' To me, to tolerate something means to put up with it. It is a shorthand way of saying, 'I don't like it, but I know if I speak out I will face a backlash.' If you are tolerant of black people, then really you are racist. If you are tolerant of gay people, then really you are homophobic. If you are tolerant of trans people, then really you are transphobic. End of.

I find 'tolerant' people very obvious. Those of us who are in a minority tend to have a sixth sense for them. When I encounter them, I will quickly know who they are. There will be little in the way of warmth or conversation. Unlikely ever to be on the receiving end of prejudice, if they find themselves in a group of what they assume to be likeminded individuals, they will feel empowered to use discriminatory language. If I am there, then their approach will change. The last thing they want to do is *look* homophobic or racist but, within the safety of their own environment, they feel that they are OK to say what they want because nobody is affected, nobody has got a camera pointing at them. People talk about religion, race, sexuality, identity, everything, using words, terms and stereotypes that they would never use if someone who was from one of those groups was sat next to them. These people exist in all areas, at all levels. It is the ultimate hypocrisy and yet it happens on a daily basis.

When it comes to prejudice, the American civil rights activist Malcom X made the distinction between wolves and foxes. The wolf, he stated, doesn't try to hide its prejudice. Its constant snarl means its target is always aware of its venom. Foxes, meanwhile, show their teeth but pretend they are smiling. 'No matter what,' says Malcolm X, 'they'll both eat you.'

I'm not going to pretend to be holier than thou. Everybody has a form of discrimination within them. Humans are wired that way; we evolved making snap decisions about people – friend or foe, ally or threat. I might look at a stranger for a second longer than I normally would or make a judgement about someone based on the way they talk. But I know also that I'm always trying to strengthen my knowledge.

I was at an awards ceremony with my step-daughter Anna when Sam Smith, one of the most famous gender-neutral people, made a speech.

I turned to Anna. 'Isn't he great?'

'You can't say "he",' she told me.

'But I don't know what word I'm meant to use. I don't know what to say.'

She talked me through it. While I always thought I understood Sam Smith in terms of feeling different, I just didn't know the correct terminology I should be using. By listening, I educated myself. But I know I still have a long way to go.

Thankfully, much headway is being made to banish discrimination. You can tell it's working by the insults spewing from those who feel threatened by such progress. According to some of the infantile abuse thrown about by professional shit-stirrers in newspapers, I'm a 'snowflake' for wanting equality. For the crime of playing a small part, along with millions of others, in helping society evolve, the rent-a-gobs and their disciples want to shut me down with a silly bit of playground abuse. Not only does this reveal them as little more than the school bullies they probably were, in 'snowflake' they have found a term as contradictory as it is condescending. Snowflakes, as defined by those who spray the word around, are offended by people's opinions. And yet nobody could ever be more offended than those who so despise others for displaying a degree of enlightenment and empathy. I've got news for those people – if I'm a snowflake, you're a drift, ten metres high.

I also understand that free speech means everyone can have their say. In 2017, I was making a documentary called *Gareth Thomas v Homophobia: Hate in the Beautiful Game* and I attended a football match between Brighton and Hove Albion and Crystal Palace, a fixture loaded with historic rivalry. Brighton is known as a town with a large gay population and some Crystal Palace fans use homophobic chants as part of their 'armoury'. I knew it was unlikely to be pretty but, watching from the terraces, I was still shocked at the level of abuse targeted at the Brighton fans – the usual inane nonsense, grown men behaving like kids.

After the match, I challenged ten Crystal Palace fans who had left homophobic messages on social media to meet me in a pub in Croydon, near Crystal Palace's home at Selhurst Park, and talk face-to-face about their behaviour. Surprise, surprise, none of them turned up. I respect the fact we live in a country where everybody is allowed to have an opinion but freedom of speech also means that others are allowed to react to and challenge that opinion. In this case, it would have been an easy argument for me to win, which is perhaps why those supporters didn't turn up. If someone is being openly discriminatory, there are so many reasons why they shouldn't behave that way as opposed to why they should. Maybe some of those fans also didn't actually consider themselves homophobic. They were just going with the crowd. Or 'herd', as sheep are called.

One argument used by those who think 'free speech' means they can discriminate against who they like is that there can't be any comedy if comedians have to always be worried about offending people. But clever comedy doesn't spread discrimination, it highlights it. People often assume I would be offended by Matt Lucas's 'only gay in the village' character Dafydd Thomas on his and David Walliams' sketch show *Little Britain* and when it came out I did watch it thinking, 'This is wrong. This is making fun of gay people.' But when I looked at it in more depth, I changed my opinion. Rather than poking fun, it was highlighting the problem of being different in a small place and I was definitely someone who knew about that. I found it funny because it was a reality. By making fun of marginalisation, Matt, himself a gay man, was acknowledging its existence. It was a form of education in a very light-hearted way. There will be people who started out laughing at Matt's creation only to stop and think, 'Hang on, this is exactly how me and my mates talk about the gay bloke in our village.'

If we talk about a really serious subject and no one is allowed to laugh then I'm not sure we break down many barriers. It's important to me that I can laugh at myself or equally make a joke that isn't coming from a place of discrimination or hurtfulness, even if such comments can occasionally be misinterpreted, perhaps wilfully so. For example, an off-the-cuff remark I made about England prop Joe Marler after he had grabbed Wales captain Alun Wyn Jones by the testicles in a rugby international.

'It would've never happened in my day,' I joked in the studio, 'and I'm really upset about that – because if it had I would have never retired!'

As a pundit, I was merely trying to find humour in a situation. It wasn't, as was presented in some quarters, me condoning people going round touching each other in an inappropriate manner. For me, humour is a great way of engaging people. There's nothing more off-putting than an awkward environment. I like to create spaces where people can freely ask questions, talk and laugh about all sorts of subjects. But that has got to come from a good place, not one where somebody is being mocked.

Anything that helps normalise the conversation has to be welcomed. Do we want people to continue to associate the word 'gay' with otherness, a world occupied only by those who are perceived as 'different'? Or do we want them to see that the alien image in their heads is totally nonsensical? Think about it, if a town has a gay club often it is talked of as being somehow underground, separate. In Bridgend, there was a pub deemed to be a gay bar simply because it was run by a gay couple. Actually, it wasn't a gay bar at all, but for some that was all it took, and on that basis they didn't want to be seen in there. I have seen the same attitude applied to a gay couple in a 'normal' pub – 'Oi! What are you doing in here? You should be in the gay bar down the road.'

Still I hear people say, 'I have no problem with gay people but I wouldn't drink in a gay bar.' Well, you have got a problem with gay people then! That person will be perfectly friendly to a gay person and never think of themselves as discriminatory but of course they are. And that attitude can all too easily become that of an entire town. 'We've got a gay bar. Therefore, we are a place that is OK with gay people.' When I hear someone say something along those lines, I can't help thinking, 'Well, if that's the case, why don't you go there? Why don't you embrace it, go with your wife and help make it a place where people don't feel the need to walk in with a baseball cap pulled down over their face?' Until people question themselves, or their friends point out the contradiction, then they will never see they are doing wrong.

If someone asks me a question about my sexuality or HIV in a clumsy way but I know their intentions are good, I'm not going to jump on them because they are trying to educate themselves. I worked recently on a TV show with the actress Ruth Madeley, who has spina bifida. She told me that kids will go up to her and openly ask, 'Why are you in a wheelchair?' At which point she'll explain her condition and the kid learns something. If a parent drags that child away, on the other hand, they will stare at the next person they see in a wheelchair and the one after that. The parent will then tell them not to look. But they aren't looking in a discriminative way, they are looking because they are inquisitive. By telling a child not to talk to or look at someone in a wheelchair, all we are doing is creating a stigma which that child will carry with them through life. Similarly, if a kid asks me and Stephen why we are holding hands, I'll tell them, 'Because he is my husband.' Again, that child has found something out. Learning only comes from conversation, and that applies to all ages.

Sadly, some people don't ever want to open up their minds. When the Australian rugby player Israel Folau announced on social media that 'Hell awaits homosexuals', he defended himself by saying the words he was using were from the Bible. I take a different view – once you say something you own it. I could read a book justifying the Holocaust, put sentences from it on social media and then say I am merely repeating someone else's words. But to do so would be deceitful. If I go out and spout those words of hate against Jewish people, that means I own that opinion. Folau has come up with a great way to hide his prejudice but it doesn't wash with me. He owns those opinions and should accept the consequences.

What hurt me most about the Folau incident was that he used rugby, a game based on good values, as the platform from which to broadcast his prejudice. That platform wouldn't exist were it not for the hard work of others. Folau is a great player – in a team game. He could never be who he is on his own. His disrespect for the people who surrounded him in the Australian dressing room and at his club side, New South Wales Waratahs, offended me deeply. They didn't represent what he was saying but he didn't care about that. As far as he was concerned, their part in his success was nothing more than the battery for his loudhailer.

When I heard Folau's vile words, I could only think what hurt he must have caused. He had gone against what so many of his colleagues were about, including those who are very pro-equality, such as David Pocock, a great supporter of the campaign for gay marriage in Australia. That's without the potential fallout of Folau's comments in communities across the globe. As a kid, I emulated my rugby heroes in every way I could. When I was on that patch of grass outside my house, I'd be copying all the greats I so admired. Imagine kids who idolise Folau. What are they supposed to think? You cannot become a role model and express such nasty, horrible views that are going to affect so many.

Folau might argue that I should be tolerant of his views, that I should understand where he is coming from. I do understand. But I also understand that he is a man who thinks people like me have no right to be here, that we deserve to burn in hell. Yes, he has the right to state those beliefs, but he is wrong to do so for so many reasons, which is why, when Rugby Australia terminated his contract, he paid the price – the right price for the wrong view. He was capable of causing so much damage, making life so difficult for so many people.

Had I still been playing, I would never have done so in a team alongside Folau. If the club didn't make him walk then I would have gone instead. The only thing in Folau's favour is he is a wolf. At least he bares his teeth, which means I can see him and keep him at arm's length. It's the ones who sit next to me and smile while absolutely hating who I am I really need to be wary of.

I am sometimes asked to deliver a talk to a business about strength and achievement. I tell them that just because they have the window dressing – an equality committee, an advert for a Pride rally on the staff noticeboard – it doesn't automatically mean they have meaningful diversity in their workplace. That applies just as well on an individual level. People can feel comforted by their understanding of discrimination – racism, sexism, homophobia – without realising that by commenting on an overweight woman out running they are adding to exactly the same problem.

Sometimes, my frustration at the pace of change boils over into anger. What will be different, I wonder, in my lifetime compared to those of my dad and my grandad? As much as we have evolved as a society, it is still difficult to stop the thought processes already in place, passed down from generation to generation. Put ten strangers in front of a large element of the population and they would stick their mortgage on being able to identify if any of them were gay from the way they spoke, dressed, did their hair or walked.

Forget 'puff', 'bender' and all the rest, from a very young age just the simple term 'gay' is routinely used in a derogatory way. If a youngster misses a goal at football or wears a pair of trainers that aren't the latest go-to brand, chances are they'll be called 'gay'. I've heard children use it in the playground, teenagers use it on the streets, adults use it in the pub – all generations using it as a way of attempting to hurt people. While I try to stay out of difficult situations, if I hear the word being used in a negative or aggressive way I will be strong, stand up and say something, hence what happened in Cardiff. To me, the more who stand up against that cheap form of abuse, the more who will realise it is no longer something that is acceptable. We are all equipped to change others' attitudes.

I thought about my own role as a voice for change as I was out walking Boyo this morning. At first I was downbeat – 'Why should I bother? What's it going to change?' Two miles later, with the clarity that comes from half an hour trekking down country lanes, across streams, through fields, I felt different. I know that to say, 'What's the point? I'm not getting involved. I've got a comfortable life, none of this affects me,' is the ultimate cop-out. Actually, it's impossible for it not to affect any of us. It involves our workplace, our homelife, our community, our family.

'Why should I bother?' Because if I don't, how can I look those who are subjected to discrimination in the eye?

CHAPTER 15

HOPELESS

I never made the Olympics. I had a decent turn of speed but was no Colin Jackson. Nevertheless, here I am in Tokyo, designated city of the next Olympiad. I have been invited to speak at the city's Pride House, a space put aside for LGBTQ people either participating in or visiting the Games. My talk has sold out. Sounds great, until I find out a sell-out means twenty tickets. Once again, I am overwhelmed by the feeling of being in a cultural timewarp that has followed me round pretty much since I stepped off the plane.

I have travelled to Japan for the Rugby World Cup of 2019. When I visit any country, I always want to find its truth beyond the well-known cultural touchstones, the tourist traps. In Japan, as expected, I find the infrastructure and technology is way ahead of anything I have ever seen. But when it comes to diversity, it is a different story. I will spend more than two months here and in all that time I will never once see a same-sex couple hand in hand, never once see a rainbow flag in a bar or restaurant.

This is a year before Tokyo is supposed to be staging an Olympics. The Pride House has been a feature of every Olympic Games since the 2010 Winter Games in Vancouver. Well, I say 'every', but predictably the Russians put a stop to the idea at Sochi in 2014, claiming that 'propaganda of non-traditional sexual orientation can undermine the security of the Russian society and the state', an attitude that the International Olympic Committee clearly had no great qualms about. Ahead of Tokyo's big moment in the international spotlight, the city is trialling its own Pride House. I make sense as a speaker – not only am I a gay man but I was an ambassador for the Pride House at London 2012. On that occasion I felt honoured – but as I enter the Tokyo Pride House, my feelings are a little different. In fact, I am shocked and disgusted. Not only is this a poor imitation of what I saw at London – smaller, functional, lacking that all-important welcoming feeling – but it soon becomes apparent that those who have come along are taking a huge chance. Discrimination against gay people in Japan means that if they are seen going in or coming out of the Pride House, they risk being ostracised and losing their job. This most grotesque of ironies isn't lost on me and I am so grateful, while also extremely worried, that they have come despite this threat.

Speaking to them, I discover just how far behind Japan is in terms of gay rights and precisely why I haven't seen any diversity. The stories of discrimination they tell me are heart-breaking – relationships led in secret, lovers separated, people victimised, isolated and left without hope. I am staggered. I genuinely can't believe what I'm hearing. Japan hosts the Rugby World Cup, the Olympics, invites the world to its door and yet doesn't cater for the diversity which the world brings with it? How is that allowed to happen? It might not be illegal to be gay in Japan but there are more ways than laws to keep people down.

Over the coming weeks I investigate further. Japan, I discover, has yet to allow female succession to the throne of its Imperial household. While gay bars exist in Tokyo, they are underground and invisible. In a city of 37 million people, I meet just one man willing to say on camera that he plays for an inclusive rugby team. No one else will be filmed for fear of repercussions. What I see hurts me deeply. I want to be involved with the World Cup in Japan because I believe rugby is a great way of promoting diversity but when I see the extent of what is happening, it's hard not to feel like I'm here only to bang my head against a brick wall built on the foundations of deeply held and institutionalised prejudice. I can't let that pass. The truth of anybody who feels discrimination is my truth. It is important to me that I challenge the game at the highest level and ask exactly what kind of legacy it is leaving behind in a country so non-accepting of LGBTQ.

'You have an opportunity to drive change, so what are you going to do?' I ask various representatives from World Rugby, the game's governing body. They are all very on-message in what they say about equality and diversity but still I can't help but wonder how that will actually translate to real lives. What will happen when the Rugby World Cup finishes, and the Olympics – subsequently delayed because of coronavirus to 2021 – pack up?

What will happen when the spotlight is turned off? I can't help but feel that Japanese culture just isn't ready to open a debate on sexuality and equality. What I have found is a very gender-specific society where, more often than not, the man goes out to work and the wife stays at home. If it is that far behind on the separation of gender, conversations about sexuality are unlikely to be high on the agenda.

Reform, it feels to me, as I board the plane home, is a hundred years off.

I don't mean to single out Japan here. It cannot be blamed for seeking to host global sporting events – it just should never have been given them, the same as China should never have been awarded the 2008 Olympics and 2022 Winter Olympics, Russia the 2014 Winter Olympics and 2018 World Cup and Qatar the World Cup in 2022.

Just reflect on that. In the space of just fourteen years, the biggest sporting events on the planet have been handed on a plate to three countries where homosexuality is subject either to state-sanctioned prejudice or a death sentence. It's a bit of an understatement to say that doesn't exactly send a positive message to the minorities of the world. Instead of highlighting these countries as places of inequality, homes to deep prejudice sometimes enshrined in law, sport condones their attitudes by gift-wrapping them its showpiece tournaments. And then the International Olympic Committee (IOC) and FIFA claim they are welcoming of diversity. Try telling that to a non-straight person in Qatar fearing for their life. Those countries, and many others like them, should be highlighted, held up to ridicule and pressured to change their stances rather than fawned over and lauded.

I know full well that nowhere in the world is perfect. Wherever you hold an event there will be discrimination of some kind. In London, during the two weeks of the 2012 Olympics, there will have been black people unjustly targeted by police, women sacked because they were pregnant, a person with HIV asked not to come into school while dropping off their child. The key, though, is to be strong and challenge it.

Now that it has foolishly committed itself, when FIFA goes to Qatar for the 2022 World Cup it should promote the rights of LGBTQ people, as should the IOC when it goes to Beijing in 2022. When that same IOC heads to Los Angeles for the summer Games of 2028, it should do so with the Black Lives Matter movement lodged firmly in its brain. Go to the host country to stand up and make a difference. Don't just go there to hold a fancy tournament, make loads of money, go home and give yourself a slap on the back. How about, at the very least, recognising the brave efforts being made on the ground by activists and reformers? How about applying that notion of international solidarity that you hold so dear in sport to those who are working in the harshest and most terrifying of conditions to make their country a better place?

At present, these vast and powerful organisations prefer the easy option. They leave any diversity recognition to the host nation. So at the World Cup the Russians could chuck up a rainbow flag in a stadium and make themselves look respectful of the LGBTQ community, while knowing, and not caring in the least, that anyone who walked through the streets of Moscow waving a rainbow flag would quite possibly have seven shades beaten out of them by the police.

I have never been to Russia or Qatar. Not because I don't want to challenge those regimes but because I refuse to participate in a charade where they create a friendly environment which I know will be dismantled the minute everyone leaves. It's the sporting version of corporate PR – companies spending a fortune on making it look like they care about society's ills when really all they care about is themselves.

I understand that the entirety of a sporting occasion isn't about diversity and discrimination. You need brilliant infrastructure, amazing architecture, a fantastic atmosphere, but those elements come anyway. Legacy isn't a stadium – that's a facility. Legacy isn't Mo Farah winning a gold medal on Super Saturday – that's sporting inspiration. Legacy is the better moral, physical and human place that wasn't there when you arrived.

As it is, I'm struggling to think of any Olympics or football World Cup that has been life-changing, in a positive way, for a large amount of people. The true power of these huge sporting extravaganzas is just being thrown away. Countries who apply to host events should be challenged on their record of discrimination. If they push back, fine. Their chance is gone. Tell them straight – 'Our event celebrates inclusivity and diversity. If you don't want that in your country, then we won't bring it.' Don't allow a country to reap the kudos without doing the work, because as soon as the world has turned its collective TV off, they will just go back to what they were doing before, whether that's imprisoning religious minorities, encouraging gay-bashing, or shooting black people. Give someone else the chance to make a difference.

At present, sport is squandering its potential to inspire strength. Instead of its vast and powerful institutions throwing their immense influence behind positive movements, it is left to individual voices to do the hard work. If FIFA, the IOC or anyone else is going to make a difference, then make a difference! Turn the volume up to ten or don't have it on at all.

To effect real change, there has to be diversity within the governing bodies themselves. But where is that diversity going to spring from? Who inside those committee rooms is actually going to care? They are full of old men and (occasionally) women with no real understanding of discrimination, diversity and equality. They are often getting paid bags and bags of money for doing little, if anything.

We, the people, could change the status quo by boycotting events but I am realistic enough to know it would never happen. People care about diversity, but they don't care that much. Someone who is a massive England football fan is not going to miss out on a once-in-a-lifetime trip to Qatar to watch their team compete in the World Cup. I get it, I'm not immune. Despite the inequality that has been highlighted by Black Lives Matter, if in a few years' time, someone offered me a ticket for the 100-metre final at the LA Olympics, I would be straight on the next plane out of Heathrow. And there is the issue – people are being asked to make individual decisions when the responsibility lies elsewhere. Those paid to have that responsibility are letting everyone down. I might be calling out FIFA and the IOC in particular but so many sports – boxing, golf, swimming, cricket, athletics and so on and so on – are yet to properly confront the issue of inclusivity.

It actually hurts me that sport, especially in its most organised form, fails to recognise that its ultimate role – the strengthening of engagement, community and friendship – comes not through the riches it can earn but through the unity it delivers. Look at me. Yes, I kept my sexuality a secret for years and I often found the attitudes I saw expressed by certain players in the changing room and from elements in the stands difficult, but on the most fundamental level I always loved what rugby gave me – an excuse to get together with others who I loved and who loved having me around. I found people ready to show incredible commitment to me, willing to put their body on the line, to pick me up off the floor when I was down. And when I did come out, those exact same people were there for me all over again. On the rugby pitch when you are out of breath or your muscles are burning because you are so tired, there is always someone willing you on. Off the pitch, the same people have always got your back. Sport gives you something so often lacking in other walks of life. That's why teammates become a second family. Every time I took the field, whatever my flaws, they were committed to me. Priceless.

Being part of something delivers so much, as proved by the phenomenon of Parkrun. Every Saturday morning, hundreds of thousands of people of all shapes and sizes get out of bed to run five kilometres in their local park with total strangers. They could just as easily run round the streets on their own but they don't. Why? Because they get so much from doing it alongside other people. Who knows what their lives are like? They could just be cheerfully turning out for a fun and sociable event or they could be a victim of abuse, struggling with their identity, being bullied at work. I can only assume that they turn up on a Saturday because it gives them something to belong to. Team sport is the same. Whatever your problem, it offers an escape. Ability is secondary. It's about togetherness and everyone who comes along brings something with them.

I don't think that those who gather at luxury resorts to decide the location of sport's biggest occasions understand what sport does for the self-worth and aspirations of people. Perhaps they are so removed from the power sport has to champion diversity and what that can achieve that they never will. I'd like to suggest that they watch *Walk Like a Man*, a brilliant film which follows two gay rugby teams, San Francisco Fog and Sydney Convicts, as they battle it out for the biggest inclusivity prize in the sport, the Bingham Cup, named after Mark Bingham, who died in the 9/11 terror attacks. Mark, who had played for San Francisco Fog, was one of several passengers on board United

Airlines Flight 93 who fought with the hijackers, leading to the plane crashing in a field in Pennsylvania rather than reaching its intended target in Washington.

The film features a young man who was bullied as a kid. He plays just a few minutes of one game, not really knowing what he's doing, running around all over the place, but when he comes off the field he is literally bawling. It isn't that he's played that has prompted his tears, it's that he's become part of something, that he's representing his teammates, people like himself who have overcome so much adversity, so much discrimination and who now, through rugby, finally have an identity. It is so powerful to watch.

For his 'crime' of being gay, in Qatar that same young man could face up to seven years in prison. Maybe someone from FIFA would like to explain.

CHAPTER 16

WIN OR LOSE

'Hello, I'm James Cracknell.'

I look across the table. 'I know who you are, mate,' I think. 'You're a sporting legend. You've won two Olympic gold medals.'

I have been asked to be part of the process of selecting the nominees for the various categories of the Sports Personality of the Year awards (SPOTY). It is awesome. I am sat in a room with all these amazing stars, people who I have watched over the years with nothing short of awe. Next to James Cracknell there's Denise Lewis. Next to her is Judy Murray. I love these people and have so much respect for them, which makes it even more strange when, before the process starts, we all have to introduce ourselves – as if any of these incredible people before me have to introduce themselves! – and say a few words about what we would like to see come out of the process.

Everyone on the panel is saying how the awards needed to represent diversity. Gender, sexual orientation, colour, everything is mentioned. I am looking around thinking how refreshing it is that everyone should be so keen to include such factors in our decision-making. I am the last to speak. I know why I'm here, I'm not just here as an ex-rugby player, I myself represent an element of diversity. I tell the group how empowering it is to be in a conversation with diversity at its heart. But I also point out that neither should we dismiss a white, middle-class person because we feel compelled to vote for somebody who is from a black working-class community, or who is female, or who is LGBTQ. To do that will be discriminatory in itself when really this is a process intended to reflect sporting achievement. One or two of my fellow judges look at me – 'We didn't expect you to say that.' But it is the elephant in the room. No one is more pro-diversity than me but if we are deciding the best sporting performances then it has to be done, if you'll excuse the expression, on a level playing field. Equality is not about doing more for someone, or less for someone else, but the same for everybody. When we fight for equality, we fight for normality.

'Diversity,' I explain, 'is a pendulum. You want that clock to keep ticking, keep moving round. But push that pendulum too far one way and it will come back at you with force. At that point, both sides start pushing. One pushes too far one way, the other pushes back too far the other and somewhere in the middle of this war of words and ideologies, the whole point of the pro-diversity argument is lost.

'The trick,' I say, 'is to keep the pendulum swinging along at a point where both sides are happy and the hands progress.'

It turns out to be a productive meeting, one I am so proud to be part of, and yet one which, as I look through the lists of potential nominees, makes me wonder if sport really is doing all it can to build truly resilient structures that support diversity at all levels. Because without that foundation, discussions like this are meaningless. Choosing the winners for SPOTY is an end result, not a beginning. The unavoidable truth is that the names before a panel such as this can only ever reflect the efforts being made further down the chain.

It's a sad reality that the higher you go in sport, the less anyone cares about diversity. Governing bodies are an obvious example but individual clubs are no different. For them, sport is a business, graded in just two ways – win or lose. Sport is savage. Death or glory. Nothing in between. That driving force means those at the top are focused purely on winning. Nothing else is a consideration. Crazy, really. The very nature of team sport means it is built on diversity. People with very different attributes play in different positions. Put them together and they create a powerful entity. Take a step off the pitch, however, and it is a lesson that goes totally unlearned.

Football, bizarrely enough, given its global reach, has been among the last to see what diversity really means. While many of the world's biggest companies fully understand that having a diverse workforce is very much in their interests for a whole host of reasons, and so employ a huge range of people, you can bet there's not a football club on this planet looking at diversity as anything other than male and female, black and white; not a single one preparing for the future by trying to replicate the most forward-looking business organisations. Not one. Not a chance.

I find that truly astonishing – multimillion-pound sports businesses blind to the massive rewards they could reap by bringing in new minds, new mentalities, new voices. I expect there are some top executives who are positively resistant – 'We employ the best person for the job and that's that.' But no one can operate to their best in a non-diverse environment because it will lack original thinking. If several jobs have been advertised and all filled by fifty-year-old white men, chances are they will think the same thing, say the same thing and behave in the same way. That business is plodding along in lead boots and, in a rapidly moving world, will soon be way behind its competitors. The best talent will now actually investigate how diverse a company is before they apply for a job because they want to work in an open and embracing environment. They won't be fooled by empty gestures, employers who want the kudos of being diverse without making a meaningful effort.

Pride is a case in point. Many sports teams recognise the annual festival but so often their adherence to the cause seems forced, put on – an institutional lethargy that extends across the board. I can tell you right now how Pride is received in dressing rooms around the land – with a big sigh. When those rainbow laces are handed out, the LGBTQ community is the last thing on most players' minds. They'll be thinking just one thing: 'Really?

I've got to go through the hassle of taking out my normal laces and putting these coloured ones in now?'

I don't want to do a disservice to those players who are willing to be vocal and visible but they are never anything approaching the majority. And I'm not saying that it's pointless. Even if to most players and clubs, Pride is a PR stunt, a box-ticking exercise, it is one that does at least generate some questioning of the status quo. If a rugby team runs out to play a game in rainbow laces and that makes twenty people in a crowd of 10,000 step back a moment and think about what that actually means then that is an achievement. But to utilise its true strength, sport should be proactive from its deepest root to its highest branch.

Before that day on the SPOTY judging panel, I visited a Premier League academy to see how focused they were on creating an environment where young players could be themselves, where difference was celebrated. In reality, the likelihood was that just three or four of those kids would progress to the first team. And when they make it into the first-team changing room, the chance of them actively standing up and representing the ethos they have emerged from is slim. Much more likely they will want to fit in. They will mould themselves to fit into the existing environment others have already created, which may well put precisely zero emphasis on diversity.

Be it through their structures, coaching staff, backroom staff, supporters' club, players, or whoever, clubs need to represent their audience. A club which celebrates its gay fans, has a gay board member, a black physio, an Asian captain, is showing that they value diversity, that everyone is welcome. Much better to embrace diversity as a source of strength than pay lip service to it because it has been forced upon you or because you feel like you have to comply otherwise people will react in a negative way.

When Israel Folau was signed by Catalan Dragons after Rugby Australia had terminated his contract, a number of rugby league clubs used it as an opportunity to emphasise their own distaste for discrimination, lining up matchday events to show their support for the LGBTQ community and also emphasise that they would never ever allow somebody with such abhorrent views into their team. Take control, use the debate positively and it cannot fail to strengthen an organisation. At that point, it doesn't matter if a team wears rainbow laces, inclusivity is role-modelled at every level.

As a player, I would have loved to turn out for a club that really represented its community. Whenever I pulled a team jersey on, I always felt I represented the area too, and not just the fans who were watching that day. Making that wider connection always got the best out of me. But so many clubs and organisations are reticent about allowing sportspeople to play a part in highlighting discrimination. All they want them to talk about is soft areas such as the next game or ambitions for the season. They have no interest in them going off piste and talking about equality.

At least broadcasters are beginning to look beyond the tired old format of a bunch of middle-aged white men in a studio or commentary box. Inclusive sports coverage which has brought in new people has reaped particular rewards. On the ITV rugby team, we have Maggie Alphonsi, who is a legend of the sport, having represented England seventy-four times, scoring twenty-eight tries, winning a World Cup and seven consecutive Six Nations crowns. Not only does Maggie offer a different perspective to someone like me or Jonny Wilkinson, for example, but her knowledge of the game is simply immense. Yet I don't doubt there are plenty of men who see her on the coverage and say, 'Here we go, token woman.' But Maggie has won a World Cup, speaks with amazing authority and is always ultra-prepared. I love to think how much she is challenging received thinking. How, somewhere, leaning against a bar, a man is picking his jaw up off the floor at the sight of a black woman on a punditry panel who knows more than the men. A man who knows he can't truthfully do what every fibre of his body is telling him to – turn to his mate and say, 'She doesn't know what she's talking about.'

Same with Alex Scott. When I turn on the football and see Alex, I'm celebrating even before I've heard her talk. Again, her knowhow is second to none – she made 140 appearances for England and represented Great Britain at London 2012. But the real reason I'm celebrating is the fact that in front of me is a representation of society I live in. I'm not interested in television looking like some tired old-boys' club. I don't think I have ever seen a diverse panel that hasn't been either as interesting or more interesting than one that is predictably straight, stale and male. If you have a panel of four pundits who all have different experiences, different perspectives, how can that not be an improvement?

I am privileged too to have worked with and appeared alongside some incredible female presenters. Gabby Logan is simply amazing, a high-profile female in an overwhelmingly male environment. I hear people say 'she holds her own' as if that's a compliment. It isn't. Analyse those words and what they actually mean is that men are ultimately better and that Gabby does well to manage to stay with them. I'll tell you something about Gabby, she doesn't hold her own, she's head and shoulders above every single man I've ever worked with.

Then there's Jill Douglas. It doesn't matter what Jill's covering – rugby, snooker, cycling, whatever – she knows her stuff inside out.

The presence of these talented women on our screens is welcome but it is only a start. I still see only too clearly the influence of the male dominance that exists behind the scenes. For too long, sports channels have employed people to work in front of the camera who are clearly deemed as being 'easy on the eye' because they have made the assumption that everyone watching the sport they show is male and straight, and all of these men want to see a pretty female presenter and think, 'Oh, I'd give her one.' It's not just these women who are being discriminated against and diminished here, it's the viewers too.

Visibility is everything when it comes to diversity. What is it Michelle Obama says? 'If you can't see it, you can't be it.' TV, quite clearly, is vital in allowing people to make that mental leap. Whenever I'm on camera I'm 100 per cent aware that as well as representing my sport I am challenging those who think the status quo should stay as it is, that those white, middle-aged, straight men should still be there. I want to help to create a new normality, just like the one kids now experience when, as a matter of course, they see women's football on TV.

Tanni Grey-Thompson, the sixteen-times Olympic medal-winning wheelchair athlete and campaigner, and someone I admire deeply, provided visibility for those with disabilities. Tanni's a proud Welshwoman and declared the moment she led the Wales rugby team out in an international at Cardiff as the proudest moment of her life – quite something considering she has a list of achievements as long as her arm. Her influence on disability sport and the pathways she has fought hard to open up for thousands of others has been astonishing.

Maybe if there were more women execs in sport we would see a better acceptance of the importance of diversity, for they know only too well what it is, in all walks of life, to be pushed to the sidelines, to be ignored, to be made to feel secondary and insignificant. I also get the sense that because women within the sporting arena have generally had to fight a lot harder for recog-nition, they appreciate it a lot more. It follows that they carry with them the lessons they learned on the way, which makes them such effective modernisers. And yet, as it is, women in posts of authority in sport are minimal. There are many men who would like to keep it that way.

I dread to think how many male sports bores I have encountered in my time. Blokes who bang on about something they did fifteen years ago. It's like they won't open the door on the real them because they fear so much what people might think or say. I find it hard to contain myself sometimes, if I'm listening to someone talking about their past achievements. Usually, all I can think is, 'Well, you might have had a great career but it's ruined your life because you have no personality.'

These are often the same men who consider women's sport to be inferior, something I find offensive in the extreme. Just because men run the 100 metres faster than women doesn't mean they are superior, they are just different. All athletes have to work just as hard. And yet it is these men who so often end up in positions of influence in sport. Isn't that scary? What are they actually bringing to the table other than a tediously old-fashioned attitude and a complete lack of vision? When presented with such men, I have to stop myself asking, 'When will you grow up? When will you understand that you need to find out about people rather than lecturing them? Why the blinkers? Why the self-centredness?' The stereotype of the man driving round and round in circles because he refuses to ask for directions is not without foundation. Fine if he's the only one in the car, but when he's behind the wheel of a major sporting organisation, it is thousands of others whose journey he is affecting. Time to hand over the keys.

*

When I step into a football ground on a match day, though the law is on my side on the pavement outside the stadium, as soon as I go through the turnstile people can have free rein on my sexuality. The original Football Offences Act, which banned racist language and chanting, was added to the statute books in 1991. Four years ago, I first applied to get the Football Offences Act amended to include homophobia as well as racism. What does it say about attitudes to homophobia in football that another thirty years have passed and we're still having to campaign for change? How much homophobic abuse will have gone on in that time? I have been told that the delay to changing the legislation is down to Brexit and two general elections. Brexit and elections? Try telling that to the young footballer who had all the skill in the world but then decided not to play because he felt the environment wouldn't allow it.

Addressing homophobia in football grounds has to be enshrined in law. That gives strength not just to the police but to the vast majority of fans who don't want to spend ninety minutes having venom spat down their ears. At that point, homophobia is placed on an equal footing with racism – offenders can be arrested on the spot, banned, even have their passports taken off them so they can't go abroad to support the national team. The bigoted minority would then think twice before opening their mouths. Who knows? Maybe they might even start to question the attitudes that have landed them in that mess.

Point is, if an environment allows people to be discriminatory, then there will be some who will take advantage of that. Some make the excuse that football reflects society. Bollocks. Football reflects the worst of society. In ten years, I have experienced one incident on the street where I've been abused in a homophobic way. In football grounds, in ten games let alone ten years, I have heard homophobic abuse over and over again. The simple fact is you can use homophobic language in a ground and get away with it. Nothing has been done for so long that homophobia not being challenged is a given.

I have come across others in football's upper echelons who say, 'We don't need to do anything about homophobia because we don't have any gay footballers.' Are they so blind they can't see the connection between the two statements in that sentence? There are gay footballers. If, as government statistics state, 2 per cent of UK men identify as gay or bisexual and we have approximately 5,000 professional footballers in this country, how come none of those hundred players has publicly come out? The game's governors are oblivious to their existence because they have failed to provide an environment where they can thrive and be themselves. Do they really expect a player to come out as gay when homophobic abuse in football grounds is met, from the top down, with a blind eye and a deaf ear? When groups of fans chanting 'Does your boyfriend know you're here?' at their opposite numbers is deemed not only acceptable but normal? And legal.

While in so many other sectors, prejudices and preconceptions have been challenged, confronted and overcome, gender and sexuality remains one of sport's biggest hang-ups. Men's sport is still widely assumed to be a gay-free zone, while women's sport – as a chat with the tennis great Martina Navratilova made me realise – is seen as the exact opposite. A lot of girls don't want to play sport because they think they will be assumed to be lesbians. Wales' most-capped footballer, Jessica Fishlock, has spoken about how difficult it is to get girls to play the game for that exact reason. It's the complete flip of male sport and yet the underlying theme is the same – lazy stereotyping making great swathes of people feel uncomfortable about taking part.

Why do females back away from sport because they fear being deemed a lesbian? It can only be because of an established view that lesbians are some kind of oddity, a strange minority and, therefore, an easy target for abuse. Women are pushed down by the same stereotypes about femininity as men are about masculinity. I think that many women's first thought if they were asked to play rugby would be, 'I can't do that – everybody will accuse me of being gay.'

I ask again, what has anybody's sexual preference got to do with their ability to play sport? We need to drive home the message, at all ages, that sexuality, gender, has no relevance. We need to change the conversation so sexuality is no longer something putting off straight girls, gay men or anyone else from doing whatever they want to do.

That's why a prominent gay male footballer would be so positive and yet, globally, the very few who have come out have done so only with the security of retirement. The last UK footballer to play on after coming out was Justin Fashanu in 1990.

The prejudice he faced was relentless and he took his life eight years later. Some might say a lot has changed since then but in 2016, FA chairman Greg Clarke said he would be cautious about encouraging a player to come out because of the abuse they might receive. How does he expect a statement like that, dripping in inertia and negativity, to take the cause of LGBTQ forward?

I have had messages from gay footballers that have given me real insight into the bone-crushingly negative effect of the environment they are in. Such is the fear of being outed that often those who contact me are cagey, giving limited information about themselves. They are living a life I am only too familiar with, one in which every day they are forced to ask themselves, 'Who can I trust?' They are entirely justified in doing so. Rather than the unveiling of the first gay footballer being a positive moment in time, it will no doubt be massively sensationalised by the media. The football authorities, meanwhile, who have done precisely nothing to create a comfortable environment for that footballer, will waste no time in highlighting their hypocrisy by using him as the poster boy for their sport's openness.

They won't be alone in wanting their slice. Endless other organisations that represent LGBTQ concerns will also be hoping to work with and celebrate that player. Truth is that any athlete will balk at such an idea. Not only is it too much responsibility for one person to be the sole representative and role model of a gay person in their sport, a sportsperson wants to be judged on their ability not their sexuality. In football, as a gay man, there is no chance of that. Out of 5,000 pros, here, suddenly, is the one who is different.

As the first to do anything, you are always going to be a person of interest and there has to be some acceptance of that. But equally, others need to understand there is only so much one person can take. Yes, this is a big moment for society, but at the centre of it is an individual prone to the same mental stresses as the rest of us. To be put on a pedestal, described as a hero, a trailblazer, an icon, a role model, is a lot to handle at a time when you have got an incredible amount to contend with yourself.

A gay sportsman will be unpicked, analysed, discussed, written about again and again and again. Every move they make, whether they like it or not, will be seen through the prism of their sexuality. We have a knack of labelling people for life as well as celebrating them once. I have seen it myself, called on endlessly to comment on anything to do with homophobia in sport. Don't get me wrong, I want to talk about the issue, but I will only do so if I see the absolute relevance and can add something to the story.

I know, for instance, that were a rugby player to come out as gay next week, every news channel would want me to comment. Wouldn't it be more interesting to go to a teammate who isn't gay and ask his thoughts, rather than the guy who is obviously going to support him and be on his side? Which of those interviews is more powerful? That's why, on my HIV documentary, when I looked to tell someone on camera of my diagnosis, I chose Shane Williams, a typical hardman of rugby. I could have sat there with somebody who had HIV in the full knowledge I would receive all the sympathy, love and support in the world. But Shane – no holds barred, a bloke's bloke – represented a huge part of society. With his reaction, 'OK, no worries,' he said virtually nothing and in so doing said everything. It was exactly the same reaction I hoped for when I came out as gay. It's the normality that counts, not the difference.

Those in the media need to be a little more imaginative. The next time a sportsperson comes out as gay, put the captain of the team on the telly, the mayor of the town. When someone like that says, 'I am proud of this man and what he represents,' it makes a difference. The way the media operate now, they make gay people look like a club who exist to one side of the rest of society. 'Let's go and speak to them. Let's see what they think about it.' It's nuts. It winds me up. It's exactly the kind of thinking that maintains clichés and stereotypes, that places LGBTQ people outside the mainstream.

Is it any wonder then, that I sat around that table as part of the judging panel for Sports Personality of the Year, looking through the potential nominees, and wondered just when true diversity will be placed in front of those doing this job. I have to say that I don't see it happening any time soon. These are changes in approach and attitude that will take a very long time to filter through.

As things are, every time I watch those celebrated on SPOTY I can't help but think about others who never had a chance.

For them, no big fanfare, no fancy arena, no bright lights. They watch the show, switch off the lamp and go to bed. They, sadly, are a victim of a Catch-22 situation that affects plenty of others too – it takes more diversity to create more diversity.

I am not defeatist, however. Everyone who loves sports knows that, if you wait for long enough, victory always comes to the strongest, the best and most determined. I just feel so much for those who are lost, mentally and physically, along the way.

CHAPTER 17

ALL IN THE MIND

I am a white, middle-aged male, fortunate enough never to have been discriminated against for the 'crime' of what I look like on the outside. My battles were fought on the inside. I don't know exactly what a breakdown is but I reckon I've had loads of them. I've just never been clinically assessed. Whenever the possibility arose of being sat in front of a doctor to discuss my mental state, I avoided it like the plague.

If I had accessed counselling from the start of my confusion over my sexuality I think I might have built a useful relationship with it. I have seen it work so well, seen it be an absolute lifeline for others, opening up and exploring elements of themselves and their lives that would otherwise have forever weighed heavy on their minds, causing them intense mental and physical pain. But I can't now shake a perhaps irrational worry that the attention of a psychiatrist could unwrap the resilience I've built. That their digging might expose areas I feel I have moved on from and come to terms with, such as my identity and the situations I have faced.

I also now am lucky enough to have Stephen, who is to me the finest untrained counsellor in the business. No matter what my problem, he is always there to offer support. I have already talked about the immense strength I take from my mum and dad. In fact, because I have opened up publicly about such a lot of my problems, I feel I have any number of people I can turn to in an hour of need who will totally understand where I'm coming from.

Nothing pleases me more than to see the number of men in particular finally being open about their mental health. Each and every time a man talks about how he is feeling – really feeling – he lifts the stigma surrounding male mental health, the nonsensical code that 'men don't talk about that kind of thing'. It's not too big a step to say that each time a man talks about themselves in that way, they are going some way to saving another man's life. It's so important for someone in mental distress to see others around them willing to talk about their own issues. Openness feeds openness. It feeds life.

There was precisely zero mental health help around when I was a professional rugby player. Absolutely nothing. I started in the era when the amateur sport turned professional – or rather, an assumption of professionalism because in reality all that happened was we got paid to play and get pissed instead of just getting pissed as amateurs. At that point, in the mid-late nineties, nobody really knew what professional meant for our sport. Only when the paymasters woke up and smelt the coffee, or very possibly our breath, did they realise what was going on, at which point suddenly the game became uber-professional. 'We're not paying them to sit on their arses with pints in their hands. They'll do things our way from now on. We'll decide what they do with their time.'

It was an almost overnight transition, which meant there was no taking stock, no working out just what real professionalism should look like. In one fell swoop, the game went from free and easy to 'We own you now.' From that point on, all that mattered was working towards the game on Saturday and the game itself. Forget recovery, anything to do with me as a person. I was now a commodity, a machine, there to deliver the goods. Undoubtedly, I would have delivered those goods more effectively had I been in a better state mentally, but nobody ever considered that part of the equation.

In a way, I understand. If I own a cricket club and I want it to be successful, I need my players to be good at playing cricket. I might care about them a little bit but so long as they play cricket well that is all I'm really bothered about. In the same way, I want my best player to perform every week, to be the player I shelled out for, and if he comes from a different environment, so what? But to be so basic in my outlook ignores the link between the mental and the physical.

People seem to think that professional sportspeople rise from a coffin, Dracula-like, play the game, hear the final whistle and step straight back into hibernation until next week comes around. They don't go home, they don't have a family, they haven't got problems. But it is totally unrealistic to think like that. No one knows what a player is carrying on to the pitch. Sadly, I'm not sure many people even care beyond the point of maybe quite liking a player and loosely hoping they're OK.

Coaches are the same. I worked with some fantastic coaches who I loved and who I felt cared about me as a person, but ultimately the connection came down to my performance. Me doing what we were all paid to help me do. Stop doing the business and the player/coach relationship suffers. On the other hand, I care about my mate Compo, once a giant of the game and now a milkman. I will also still care about him when he stops being a milkman. That might be a strange analogy but the principle is the same. If somebody cared about me in my final game for Wales and then the day after didn't, it's obvious they only ever cared because they wanted me to play well for Wales. Sport, for the vast majority of people who run it, is all about what happens on the field and nothing to do with what happens off it.

This is why so many athletes emerge from professional sport into a barren emptiness. Sport can put so much demand on you, so much pressure, that by its very nature it traps you wholly in the present. Blindly you fulfil your obligations to it without ever understanding that when you get to the end of the ride there will be nothing unless you start to fill it now. I was no different to anyone else in my lack of understanding of this most basic of situations. No one ever came round and talked to us about that side of life, the fact that it had the capacity to destroy us mentally more than anything that could ever happen on the pitch or in the dressing room. They abandoned every player, no matter how long-serving, how diligent, to an unknown fate.

Professional sports clubs might claim they care about mental health, signal that it is something they deal with proactively, but the reality is they are shelling out for an employee to play, train and improve their skills. In their view, that, not sitting around talking about problems, is what will feed the business the results it wants. Even now, it is my belief that in the hierarchy of sport, few at the top are interested in creating a more open and mentally inclusive environment. Forget nuance. They'd rather their players completed a hundred passes in a game, two hundred bench presses in the gym. If something goes wrong, the answer will be found in the physio's room. All too often, it doesn't occur to them that players, and subsequently their performances, could benefit from support for the mental as well as the physical. I have seen it myself – at the elite level, everything is focused on what happens on the field. How we approach this penalty, this scrum, this line-out, this free kick. If a club puts aside an hour a month for you to mentally relax, let alone knock on a door and talk to a counsellor, then you are very lucky indeed. There is only one mindset professional sport is interested in – turn up at training at 9am on Monday and start working on the process of winning at the weekend. Mental wellbeing? Forget it.

This sends a message to a player: 'Mental health is a no-go area. Talking about it will single me out.' In sport, as in life, I learned quickly to be very good at hiding my emotions. Even given the opportunity, no way would I have gone and seen a psychologist. It would have felt too risky. If other players had found out – not difficult to imagine in the small environment of a rugby club – I might well have been considered weak. Also the psychologist would have been paid by the club and so I could have been forgiven for being suspicious about where their private information is going to end up. No wonder most players are reluctant to give too much away of themselves. I certainly was.

'If I reveal I'm struggling mentally,' I would think, 'and that gets back to the coach, there's every chance he's not going to pick me. Then what happens? I might never get back in. Then I will be really fucked. My head will be gone completely.' And so my issues would have been going totally unaddressed because I didn't want to give anyone the ammunition to knock me out of the team.

How often in interviews do coaches talk about the need for strength of character, a winning mindset? But what are they actually doing about it? Even with psychological help now more likely to be on hand, how many coaches really place any stock in its influence? In my case, by the time such help was introduced into the game in the mid-2000s, I had done all the hard work myself and, in my view at least, rationalised the person I am.

In this environment, when a coach came along who really did understand the role of the brain in sport, he stuck out like Shirley Bassey in a village talent show. During his spell in charge of Wales, Steve Hansen was a case in point. He understood that making connections with players mentally could yield just as positive results as anything that came from yet another training drill. Early on in his tenure, for instance, he showed the dressing room how facile it is for any player to go round boasting, 'There's nothing I can't do.'

It is totally forgivable for a professional to go into an elite sporting environment with the expectation they can do everything in their role. But no player is perfect. Trouble is, some players fear the perceived consequences of admitting they could ever have faults, which then stalls their development and their career. Forget sport, in any field it's difficult to tell your boss you can't do what they want. Rather than front up, chances are you will go away and give it your best shot. You might get away with it or you might end up looking a complete pillock. Either way, it's the wrong approach. Honesty would have been much better.

But if a player is to be open about their deficiencies then they need to be able to trust the coach to respect such an admission. It is important then to create an environment where people aren't going to be judged for not being the polished article. Where they know it's OK to fail, rather than holding in a dread of being exposed, which is very negative from a mental health point of view. Most people believe if they admit the absence of a skill, the next sound they will hear is that of the door slamming behind them. But look at it another way. Their boss might not even be expecting them to perform at such a level. They may also welcome an honest discussion. As in all areas of life, fear of judgement drives that lack of openness.

So one of the reasons why Steve Hansen was a gifted coach was that he never placed unrealistic expectations on anybody and I, and others, trusted that if there was something I couldn't do he wouldn't come down on me like a ton of bricks. Instead, he would suggest a coach to work with or deliver the knowledge himself. I wasn't going to be punished, I was going to be helped. That is precisely what I needed, it meant I could reach my potential and be the player we both wanted me to be – 'Trust in me and I will unlock it for you.'

Steve's tenure as Wales coach coincided with some of my most torturous times off the field as I wrestled with my identity. He never pried into my personal life but he knew there was something going on that was manifesting itself in a rebellious streak and the adoption of a guise that simply wasn't me.

Steve could be explosive when he needed to be, but only from the point of view of imposing himself as a leader. I respected this authoritative side of Steve. I had always struggled in classroom environments but I knew I needed an element of authority in my life. Steve would be firm when he needed to get a key point across but otherwise he would come at players from an angle of friend or mentor – someone who cared about more than the game, more than just winning or losing. He cared about people, in the full knowledge that natural instinct would create a better environment, a stronger team and, ultimately, better results.

At that point I had been playing for Wales for seven years. I felt I knew my game, knew my strengths and weaknesses. But he made me see that improvement, adaptation, never ends. He was a massive influence on my career as he made me go away, find my faults, put them right and come back as somebody with an improved mental attitude. He made me ten times the player I would otherwise have been. On the back of Steve's guidance, I became a British Lion.

The benefits of being personable to those in your charge are obvious but you'd be surprised how many people don't get it. The key to success in any area is good 'man' management and good time management. Simple as that. Don't waste time having people sitting around doing nothing for hours and hours, work with them and, as you do so, try to get to know them as deeply as possible.

As a captain, I felt tuned in to people's radio waves. I could tell whether the song playing in their head was happy or something a little more troubled. Indicators that were perhaps invisible to others were clear to me. A player might be a little subdued, or short-tempered. Their smile might suddenly seem a little bit forced. Age and experience don't nullify self-doubt. Some days I would look at even the most senior players and think, 'They don't look right today.' If that problem hadn't germinated from the dressing room environment, then it was something outside the sporting bubble. In both scenarios, if the individual, and the team, wasn't to suffer, the issue needed addressing.

Those who maintain the bluff and bluster attitude of 'just bloody well get on with it' don't have the first idea of the damage they cause. The tiniest crack can soon become a gaping crevasse into which first one player and then the entire team can fall.

If a player in my squad, no matter how peripheral, was feeling troubled, dispirited or marginalised, I would want to know. To me, everyone was relevant to the environment, whether they be the star player, the coach driver, the baggage man, whoever. I wanted everybody to realise that to me they were as important as each other and myself. Rather than a collective, we were a group of disparate characters lucky enough to be in this incredible environment. We owed one another everything for the fact we were here and, as such, we should look out for each other.

First on any captain or coach's list should be a willingness to accept emotion. Second on their list should be a willingness to immerse themselves in it. Sadly, all too often in my rugby career I was faced with captains and coaches who viewed emotion as weak, an inconvenience, a distraction.

Take the singing of the Welsh national anthem before a big international in Cardiff. I'm sure some will argue with me but I'm going to say it: for no other nation does the anthem resonate as much as it does for the Welsh. For me, the singing of 'Land of My Fathers', delivered at full volume by the most passionate supporters in world rugby, is sacrosanct, the best part of the day. Before my first game, I wondered what that outpouring, that torrent of emotion, would do to me. I soon realised the answer would never change. It didn't matter if it was my first cap, my fifty-second or my seventy-third, the anthem's power never wavered. For me, the national song was something I wrapped myself in. I sang it in the clear knowledge of what it represented. As the words flowed from my mouth, I would think how, around

Wales and across the globe, millions of people were singing those exact same words because, let's face it, wherever you go in the world, you will always find a group of Welsh people in a bar, who have somehow found a channel showing the game, belting out the national anthem before kick-off. It is a huge collective moment and to think of what you are part of is a beautifully overwhelming experience, even more so if you are captain. It is mind-blowing almost beyond comprehension, and so I quite deliberately chose not to comprehend it. I wanted it to exist on a pure emotional level. Singing the anthem as a player was an honour and privilege that may never come again. Accident, injury or non-selection could end my career at any time. I always sang the anthem as if it was my last time. Even now, that stadium choir, their voices rising and falling with the ebb and flow of that historic and deeply moving song, makes the hairs stand up on the back of my neck.

And yet, as a player sat in the dressing room at the Arms Park or Millennium Stadium, I had captains who would tell the team to pay as little attention as humanly possible to this unique moment in world sport. They saw it as a distraction from the pursuit of victory.

'Don't look at the crowd. Don't look for somebody you love. Don't let your mind drift away. Stay focused.'

What? Really? When I became captain, no way was I having that. I wanted them to see it is a positive experience.

'Forget what you have been told about ignoring the anthem,' I would tell my players. 'Forget what you have heard about letting it pass you by. This is the exact moment you should be taking everything in. You should be looking for your family, letting your mind drift away, thinking back to watching this exact same scene, the one you are now part of, as a kid, seeing the players stood in a line singing their hearts out and wishing you were one of them. Maybe you were stood in the crowd next to your dad or your mum as they proudly sang those words.

'This is not something getting in the way of the game. It is a moment to celebrate what you are about to achieve, the fact you are actually living your dream. In five, ten, twenty-five, fifty years, you will regret it if you look back and remember nothing.

'Enjoy it,' I would finish. 'It will affect you, so let it do so. Let it wash over you. Let it become part of you. Let it deliver its meaning.'

I meant every word. The memories I have of looking at my mother and father, my family, in the stadium during the anthem mean more than anything that ever happened on the pitch. I would see them, specks in the distance, and think, 'This is what it's all about. This is why I have spent weeks, months and years on the pitch and on the training field smashing my body to pieces. It was all for this moment.' I understand everybody's motivation is different but I didn't want anybody to feel like they couldn't appreciate that 'Wow, am I really here?' moment.

Then, once it was over, that moment should be cherished before being packed away and thought about later on. I realised that power early on and so separated the anthem and the game into two separate entities. The band finishes and you jog out of the line, ready to 100 per cent focus on the matter in hand.

I always wanted players to enjoy representing their country. I've been on the losing side with Wales and seen teammates absolutely crucified for wearing a smile at the end of the game, as if it was an indicator of some kind of lack of grit or will to win. OK, it's not the time to be grinning like a Cheshire cat but if a player has come off the bench for the last five minutes, realising their dream of playing for their country in the process, and has spotted his mother bursting with pride in the stands, his mum who has supported him every step of the way, then is he not entitled to share that moment in a human way that goes beyond the scoreline in the game? They both deserve that right.

So when I was given the captain's armband, I wanted to create a place where people would remember with absolute positivity doing the thing they had dedicated the best years of their lives to. You're a professional rugby player so you can't smile? You can't enjoy life? You can't enjoy playing for Wales? You can't enjoy running out at the Millennium Stadium? Why? Because if you smile, people will think you are happy and therefore not properly invested in the cause? Well, hang on a minute, what is sport's cause? To me, it is to entertain, to improve people's lives, offer an escape from the grind. If there is ever an arena where people should smile and be happy, it is sport.

I hate it when sport is described as a 'battle'. I understand why people reach for the analogy but it is not a good one. Nobody is going to die. Nobody is going to be shot at or have their lives threatened. Everyone on that pitch is going out to do something they love. As a player, I always tried to keep things in context. It was a game of rugby and my motivation was representing my club or country doing the one thing I absolutely loved and had always wanted to do. End of. That was enough. I didn't have to create a tribal atmosphere where sport is turned into a life or death enterprise because it absolutely isn't. Turn sport into something it isn't and all you do is pile even more pressure on people who are already experiencing a pressurised environment.

Through watching my captains and my coaches, the good and bad, I learned that you should never underestimate the influence your demeanour, your attitude, can have on those around you, not just in your own tight circle but on your environment as a whole. Positivity brings others with you. Let your spirits sink and chances are theirs will too. That could be in the workplace, it could be at home, it could be in the sporting arena, where I know only too well that positive energy has a key role to play.

Not many people will have the experience of this on such a grand scale, but an extreme example of this is in a stadium, where a crowd's character can swing in a manner that has a huge impact. There is an energy in most stadiums, especially modern ones. Designed with atmosphere and acoustics in mind, they have become cauldrons of sound. That energy can be helpful, which clearly is great – who wouldn't want the backing of row after row of deeply passionate supporters? – but rarely will it last across the full extent of a sporting encounter, simply because it's unlikely the game will always be going your way. That flipping of energy from plus to minus can be hard to deal with. While positive energy is loud, sometimes raucous, negative energy tends to be silent and damning, like you're being slagged off without anybody actually saying anything. Create it for the opposition and you're on to a winner – and in fact many teams, realising how difficult negative energy is for teams to counter, will actively put in place tactics to stifle the home side's creativity and change the environment.

In rugby, French crowds are infamously fickle. Start well against France and their supporters will quickly turn against them. Every captain I ever played under would talk openly about silencing the French crowd. You can bet, meanwhile, that in the changing room across the corridor, the French skipper would be pushing the need to keep the crowd on their side. Win this mental conflict and you could actually feel the negative energy swamping their players, just the same as it would swamp us in Cardiff when a game started to slip away. It is a very difficult thing to react against. After all, this influence is intangible. It doesn't physically exist. It's not like you can give it a swift right-hander when nobody's looking. Pulling the boys together, you end up giving a speech more reminiscent of the 1980s sitcom *Yes, Minister*: 'Look, boys, there are 75,000 people in here who really don't have any relevance to the way we play but we need them to have relevance because as irrelevant as they are they are always relevant.'

You try doing something with 75,000 people watching you – how can it not affect you? You can tell players 'don't let the crowd affect you' until you are blue in the face, but it's impossible.

'It is going to affect you,' I would tell players, 'so be prepared for it. There are going to be times when the crowd is against us. When we feel it, we must not allow it to oppress or embarrass us. We mustn't look around asking one another, "Shit, do you feel it as well?" We need to address the situation. We need somebody to do something to make sure we get this crowd back with us.'

I wanted my teams to be prepared for anything – physical, mental; tangible, intangible. A game plan can be as detailed as humanly possible but there will always be the unexpected. The key is freeing people up to act decisively and quickly, and again that comes from instilling a positive mentality where people embrace an atmosphere rather than be made to fear its consequences.

Some people still dismiss the suggestion that a crowd can affect what happens on the pitch. I can tell you, with absolutely 100 per cent clarity, that the crowd has an influence. Possibly my best-known moment on a rugby pitch, and my own personal favourite, is the interception try I scored against Australia at the Arms Park in 1996. I had to make it ninety yards, virtually from one try-line to the other, with, for the most part, the Aussie fullback Joe Roff on my heels. I wasn't consciously aware of it at the time – I was too busy concentrating on the job in hand – but how can the roar of 60,000 Welsh rugby fans not have given me something extra? The point where I became actively aware of the crowd was when I made it across what had effectively become the finishing line. I looked up for a split second and saw a group of about fifty people in the South Stand literally bouncing up and down. It was the oddest feeling, as if I was watching myself through them. It was lush to see how happy it made them and, as I slumped to the floor, totally wrecked, their joy actually became my celebration.

It was something that happened several times in games when I found myself with the space to run – seeing faces in the crowd and, taking in that ecstasy and understanding, realising I was living my enjoyment through others. So massively, spine-tinglingly, special. Think about it – it is never the physical that you take away from sport. I don't look back at that try and think about placing the ball on the ground to gain five points for my side. It is the mental. In those faces in the crowd I saw a representation of everyone who had helped me achieve that moment in time. My all-time favourite moment on a rugby pitch came just as much from the person who first put a rugby ball in my hands as it did from me; it came from my mum going up to the counter in Woolworths and paying £2.99 for my first pair of boots; it came from every single person who had helped me to that point. And that is why looking up into the South Stand and seeing those faces so full of joy will always resonate.

They were strangers, but I recognised each and every one of them. Connections run deeper than we think.

CHAPTER 18

DEDICATED

Whatever situation I have been involved in, however close I have felt to something, there has always been a part of me looking in from the outside. Not so much a heightened self-awareness, more a 360-degree vision of what's going on. It's a feeling that is totally ingrained and one I'm cool with. It makes me feel protected, as if being on the outside is a safer place to be. The only time I don't feel that way is when I'm with Stephen, my family or my closest mates. Then I know there's no need to be on the outside of anything. There is precisely zero to be worried about.

As ever, though, I am a walking contradiction. I cannot ignore the side of myself that also wants to belong. Eventually, after I retired, I moved to London. Aside from when I played for Toulouse, I had always lived in South Wales. I wanted to go to a big cosmopolitan place where my sexuality wasn't relevant, where I could be like lots of other people, where I didn't have to be 'the only gay in the village'. I wanted to experience London, not as a fleeting visitor or a fugitive, but as someone who lived, and possibly belonged, there.

It was an urge I'd had before, although in rather different circumstances. It was the early 2000s, when I was still yet to come out, and I'd picked up an voicemail message from Welsh Rugby Union head coach Graham Henry.

'The police have been in touch asking about your where-abouts.'

'Oh my God,' I thought, 'What's happened?' I rang him back and he asked where I'd been the night before. Henry's sudden transformation into Columbo was a little unnerving. He explained that my car had been seen in a part of Cardiff renowned as being a hang-out for sex workers. Even though I knew for sure it was a mistake, I was petrified. My first thought was that police officers would now be looking intimately into my life. Yes, they would see it was a mix-up, but what else would they find out? My truth as a gay man would be exposed. Detectives would be picking through a pile of scraps of information and somewhere at the bottom would be me.

I was in a state of absolute panic, so much so that I drove home, grabbed some money, filled a holdall with a few scant possessions, and decided there and then to head to London. I knew full well it was a place where a gay man could just disappear.

'I've got to find a way that means I don't have to live in fear anymore,' I told myself.

I was all set to go when I received another call. Again, it was Henry. He confirmed it had all been cleared up. The police had found it wasn't my car at all, just one of a similar model and registration number.

Even so, the incident stayed with me. I couldn't help thinking how many people there must be in small towns across the country who fear having a spotlight shone on them for their sexuality, who are denied the opportunity to live normally, who have to overcome stigma and fear to do everyday things like enter a shop or walk into a pub. Imagine what that feels like – it's something people who have never been on the end of prejudice can never truly understand.

My second flirtation with London soon after I retired from the game was planned but still impulsive. The first time I clapped eyes on the apartment I'd bought was when I moved in. Nor did I have a single friend in the capital. I didn't see either situation as an issue. I wanted to evolve and the challenge of living some-where I was effectively a stranger would, I believed, allow me to do exactly that.

From the off, I found London very exciting, very high energy compared to other places I had lived. I joined a gay gym down the road and quickly made friends. On the same Soho streets where previously I had lurked in the dark, I was now walking into cafés, bars and gay clubs like it was something I'd been doing for years. Every day I found the strength to do something that not long before would have terrified me.

After such a long time in the public eye, I embraced the anonymity London gave me. Whereas now I am widely known as a campaigner, at that point I was just a retired rugby player. As a gay man, I stood for something, but in a sport which I no longer played. If anything, during the period I was in London, I was defined by taking part in *Dancing on Ice* and *Big Brother*, both of which happened while I was there. But to the vast majority of people, I represented nothing more than 'Oh, there's that guy from the rugby.' It was great. I always felt like I fitted in, which was quite something considering not all that long previously, I had thought of myself as someone who would always live in the margins.

The downside was that I knew I was one of many thousands who felt a sense of peace and belonging in London that could never truly be found where they were from. For so many LGBTQ people, success is deemed as getting the hell out of the place where they were born. I found so many people in London who had gone there to escape their hometown or village. They had to be somewhere that allowed them to be themselves without fear of discrimination and the place where they were born was never going to be it. But then you end up forgetting those who have been left behind. Which is natural to a degree but still sad. When you think about it, you have changed nothing but your own circumstances. You have washed your hands of the bigger issue and left it for the next person.

Eventually, the pull of South Wales, the source of everything I truly love, would bring me home. I didn't miss London – I had spent enough time there to scratch the itch of discovery – but I did recognise how much I had learned there. More than anything, how easily lifestyles can be accepted in one part of the country compared to the freakishness with which they can be viewed elsewhere, where life for anyone deemed 'different' can feel like it is led under a magnifying glass.

I knew from the support I'd had after I came out that I'd be welcomed back in Bridgend. To the vast majority of people, I was just Alfie, home to stay. I realised how lucky I was, though. So many others must head home either still harbouring their secret or knowing that they will have to face the stares of those who deem them different. I, however, felt a remarkable sense of belonging as I unpacked my bags. Living in London was something I'd had to do but it was good to be home.

In my toughest times, when my entire identity was a source of huge personal turmoil and confusion, rugby had saved me, giving me a coat of security and, again, belonging. Rugby was the perfect game for someone like me – fitting in was seamless. So long as I underwent the initiation, I was in. Ah yes … the initiation.

Not many people arrive for their first day at the office to find their new colleagues waiting for them armed with a pig's brain, fifteen pints of lager and a bottle of tabasco sauce. And yet, back when I was in my twenties, craving to fit in, an initiation like this made absolute perfect sense to me. It felt like such an easy fix, like putting a coin in a vending machine, pushing a button and receiving instant acceptance, total togetherness. Basically, the unwritten rule of the initiation is this: 'If you are willing to do or eat something disgusting, perhaps painful or borderline dangerous, then that tells us you are willing to do anything to be a part of the group and, therefore, we open our arms to you and will look after you.'

Perhaps the worst rugby initiation I witnessed was when I was playing for Bridgend and we travelled to a match in France. On arrival, we went to an open-air food market where we happened across a local delicacy that can only be described as brains in trifle – the perfect welcome present for the new players in the group. Back at our hotel, meanwhile, we discovered the swimming pool was closed. It had been left to fester for so long that the water was now an off-putting shade of green. With dead rats floating in it. I'm assuming none of this was featured in the hotel brochure. The challenge for these poor guys was to dive into the pool, swim a length, get out, eat the brains in trifle, dive back in and make their way through the rats and the filth back to the other end. Over and over again. Health and safety would have banned it for the very obvious reason that someone could have died. Whatever was in this pool had killed rats. And yet there we were, whooping, laughing, cheering. Amazing, looking back.

An initiation is generally done after your first game – the match itself is a way of earning your right to the initiation – and I had one at every club I went to. Some were horrendous – a case in point being when tabasco sauce was applied to every (and I mean every) part of my body – and some I barely noticed. My Toulouse initiation, for instance, was nothing. A rarity in that it came before my debut; all I had to do was play that first game with my head shaved like a monk. Piece of piss. I just sat there as they went to work with the clippers. I was happy and didn't care. Doing this stupid thing was my pathway to belonging.

With the distance of time, I can see the similarities between the initiations I endured to standing in that corner of the swimming pool changing room as a schoolkid being towel-whipped by a load of other boys because I wanted to be part of the group. I shouldn't have had to go through that and I recognised at the time and for years after that it was wrong, and yet there I was as an adult doing exactly the same thing – letting other people do what they wanted to me just to be accepted.

Even now, while I know who I am, I will admit that accept-ance still matters to me. When faced with something I'm not altogether comfortable with there is still a voice inside that says, 'You know what? I might as well just do it. I've got them on side then.' It is a part of my personality I am not altogether comfort-able with.

Modern players increasingly refuse to be put through initia-tions. They see it as a relic of the past, like listening to the radio on the team coach when you've got an iPhone and earbuds. I genuinely don't know what would have happened if I'd done that, for the simple reason refusal had never been heard of. It was a given that you were going to be initiated.

Where initiations do still exist, they tend to be nowhere near as extreme as they used to be. Play your first game for Wales now and on the bus journey back to the hotel you will be required to stand at the front and sing a song – a lot milder than eating dogfood or downing horrific 'cocktails' of fish guts and pickle juice but the principle remains the same: are you willing to make yourself uncomfortable in front of the group?

To me, a better initiation would be to ask that new player to stand at the front of the bus and tell the group something personal or vulnerable about themselves. That way the situation is turned around so the onus is on the existing players to show how much they want to embrace the newcomer, rather than the newcomer having to prove how much they want to embrace them – surely a more powerfully uniting way of inviting a new player into a team. I'm not saying a player should stand there and reveal their innermost reflections on their sexuality or talk about the effect of a family bereavement. They could talk about anything, however big or small. The point is one of acceptance and understanding. Those who are listening make a joint vow not to use that information in any kind of negative way.

'You could tell us anything, bud. You could tell us your real name is Ethel and you're married to a dachshund. It wouldn't make the slightest bit of difference. As far as we're concerned, you're one of us.'

Some might ask, why not ban the initiation altogether? Why don't I, as someone who is so pro-individuality and anti-peer pressure, feel it should be consigned to history? But to do so would ignore its roots – the togetherness and, ultimately, strength, that it delivers. In team sports, commonality of purpose is huge. In professional sport especially, there is no time for messing about in achieving that. Initiation offers a quick answer. Some sort of pathway or initiation, however bizarre, however extreme or mild, happens in most sports one way or another. In real life even, you still hear of the new kid on the building site being sent to buy a tin of spotted paint. I wonder if in South Wales Police, newcomers are required to ring the Welsh Rugby Union and tell them one of their most high-profile employees has been spotted in Cardiff's red-light district. Just a thought!

Because of its unique nature – players from four nations thrown together briefly in a united cause, to challenge the best teams in the world – the British and Irish Lions was an environment where strength from togetherness was vital but much less easy to achieve, which led occasionally to mangled attempts to manufacture unity, thankfully at least not involving three onions and a tin of Pedigree Chum.

The Lions was infamous for its team-building sessions but I found them so alien as to be totally useless. A natural leader on a rugby field isn't necessarily a natural leader when building a raft. I can be committed to building a raft, I can have a laugh doing it, but I can't lead on it. Such a task takes no account of human nature. Ask a group of people to do something they have never done before and some will be good and some will be terrible. But an important thing to note is that, within that set-up, no one will want to be the one who is very obviously bad, which means caution is the overriding mindset, and so nobody really shows themselves. Far from being revelatory about character and personality, the task actually discourages honesty and individuality. That isn't great in an environment where it is hugely important that, from the first minute of the first team meeting, players feel OK about being themselves. The shift from your own dressing room, where everybody knows you and you feel totally at home in your own skin, to a Lions dressing room is difficult enough without adding a first day of school feel to proceedings, with individuals trying to fit the mould of who they imagine others want them to be.

Well before the Lions, team-building sessions had been a bugbear of mine. At club level, I had the misfortune of encountering them repeatedly pre-season. Every year I'd think the same thing – 'If they think one team-building course is enough to build the strength and resilience needed to handle pressure situations across the whole season then they are very much mistaken.' A team-building course is so surface. It reveals nothing of what is actually on people's minds. Also, as with the Lions, I didn't want to be in an environment where I could stand out as potentially being weak, my positives and negatives analysed in a very public manner.

There was always a focus on creating values, a ridiculously broad concept which I mention often whenever I am invited to speak to a group from the corporate world, which is similarly wedded to this kind of nonsense. So often businesses come up with three values to represent their core ethos. Fine, except in doing so they are surrounding employees with a self-made barrier. There may well be a good number of people in their organisation who, when they see the laminates go up on the wall, think, 'OK, but actually I don't live by any of those values.' A business thinks it is unifying its workforce when often what it is actually doing is driving a coach and horses straight through the middle. My way round that was to create my own slogan, just for me, containing the three values I lived by through my rugby days, and still live by now – dedication, sacrifice and enjoyment: 'I will be a dedicated person, willing to make sacrifices to make my life but also, more importantly, other people's lives around me enjoyable.'

It is perfect for me, accurately summing up my life aged twenty-three when I came up with it, and still accurately summing me up now at twice that age. Values must be individual otherwise you are just lumping everyone in together. You are asking people to be someone they aren't.

You might wonder why a team made up of the best players of the four home nations would need any psychological manipulation in the first place. But actually, in this case, the best players may not be the answer. Chances are the Lions, and by extension other manufactured teams, will fail if chosen on cold statistics. What's actually needed is to put the person before the player. After all, whoever is selected must be able to immediately commit not only to the cause but to several people who might well in previous games have once tried to tear their ear off. Make no mistake, in professional rugby, as in life, you come across people who you don't like, detest even. But instead of allowing negative feelings to gnaw away at you, draining vital energy, weakening the cause, it is far better to maintain an element of respect for their achievements. After all, you know how hard it is to reach that level – you have done it yourself. Mutual respect is massive in any team environment. Rivalries will, ultimately, weaken the unit and get in the way of the success.

Anyone given the Lions call must also commit to a brand with which they have never really had an identity. I, for instance, rarely describe myself as British. I tell people I'm Welsh, same as the Irish tell people they're Irish, and the Scots tell people they're Scots. The English are more likely to call themselves British but generally remain soldered to England underneath. Whatever your home nation, the Lions badge is unlikely to inspire the same passion.

But the fact that the Lions generally do manage not just to compete but sometimes achieve impressive victories over formidable southern-hemisphere teams is what makes the concept so intriguing and the team such a celebrated brand. Individual golfers coming together for the Ryder Cup and Solheim Cup offer similar fascination, as do tennis players in the Davis Cup, and sprinters in relay teams. Artificial teams, brought together on an occasional basis, should lack the strength that comes from long-term coaching and interaction. They will also have major divergence in culture. Welsh rugby union and English rugby union, for instance, is very different. In Wales it's a working-class sport, from which it derives much of its strength, whereas in England it's traditionally been based around the private-school system. Potentially, you might think, players' attitudes would differ – surely someone who has very little will have a greater desire than someone who has everything? – and yet the English way still works. Their normal is different to our normal but they still get it, they still understand that strength comes from unity of purpose, and so a combination of players from two very different cultures can work.

The concept of the Lions is just one example of how we are all wired to take our individuality and use it as a way of supporting something bigger. As people, we are always more powerful when we pull together in a common cause. My bond with the Lions could never be as strong as my bond to Wales but ultimately, no matter our background, when we have a unity of purpose, we find a strength which would otherwise have seemed unimaginable.

All through my life I have witnessed strength in unity. My family has always stuck together through thick and thin, and then when I stepped into the bigger world I saw how sport delivered a sense of closeness and community that went way beyond the dressing room. I know what can be achieved when people with a common purpose set out to achieve against the odds and it is a lesson I am never going to forget. The only question I ever ask about that principle is where I am going to apply it next. Sometimes you just need to define what it is you are fighting for.

CHAPTER 19

NEVER GIVING UP

'Let's pack up and go and live by the sea. We won't need to bother about anyone or anything.'

It would be easy after coming out as HIV positive, completing the Ironman and making the HIV documentary to say exactly that to Stephen. After going through the emotional wringer, I had every right in the world to do so. But that isn't me. I didn't do those things just so I could say, 'This is my life with HIV – accept me.' I did them because I had realised that I wanted to be a spokesperson for others whose lives have been turned upside down by the virus. HIV made me realise who I am and what I want to do; that my purpose in life shouldn't end with winning rugby matches and picking up trophies. It is about so much more than that. It is about spreading the message that HIV is not about death. It is about life.

I know that's not always going to be easy. The truth about HIV has been lost in the fug of a hangover that still persists from the 1980s, encapsulated in that doom-laden 'public information' film with its apocalyptic imagery, set in a fire and brimstone world, filmed with all the graphic intensity of a Hollywood disaster movie and narrated by the actor John Hurt with the intonation of a broadcast about what to do in the event of nuclear war. That tombstone still casts a shadow over the discussion about HIV and AIDS, even for those too young to remember it, as it had such a lasting impact on the way the disease was thought of. The government didn't want anybody who saw that image to forget it quickly. And four decades on, they haven't.

There have been attempts to change that narrative. Soaps especially have taken it upon themselves to educate viewers through HIV-related storylines, going right back to Mark Fowler in *EastEnders* in the 1990s, a character who contracted the virus from his girlfriend – an important retort to the widespread distortion of HIV as the 'gay plague'. More recent times have seen *Emmerdale* feature a storyline about an older female character diagnosed with the virus after a fling in Portugal, while *Coronation Street* introduced a young straight guy who lives with HIV. But all of these attempts to redress and re-educate have come from the realm of fiction, of TV drama. There has been nothing on a wide scale from the government and that, in my opinion, is a neglect of duty.

The reality of HIV – how it can be contracted and, just as importantly to allay stigma, how it can't – is a very basic health message any government should be getting out there. With coronavirus, there was a very deliberate and reasoned attempt to tell people how, why and where they could catch the illness. With HIV, those in charge appear happy for the majority view to be formed from a forty-second film first screened in 1986. A cloud of ignorance still sits over the country because the message has never been properly updated and, incredible as the HIV and sexual health charity Terrence Higgins Trust is, it simply doesn't have the resources to re-educate on that vast a scale. Where are the modern-day government campaigns, explaining the advances in treatment for HIV and the importance of being tested? Where is the new ad? Where is the counter to the old one? Why has it been left to charities and people like myself to get the message out there? When it comes to conditions such as diabetes or cancer, there have been intense efforts to inform. You'd probably have to walk into a sexual health clinic to pick up a leaflet about HIV. Go online and, aside from a handful of trusted sites, so much content is either plain wrong or outdated.

The lack of information and an unwillingness to address it is where so much misunderstanding and stigma comes from. People think they already know what HIV is and they don't. Why else, when I tell someone I'm HIV positive, do so many ask if I'm going to be OK? I'm not saying it's not nice of them to ask but it does show how little the subject has moved on. Even when I explain that I am well and my life is in no danger from the virus, they often don't believe it.

'No, that can't be right. That's impossible. You're just saying that. You're lucky to be alive.'

The only thing that makes me 'lucky' is that I live in an age where the science and medicine exists to create a treatment.

It is this level of misunderstanding, which in itself creates stigma and negative attitudes, that prompted me to launch Tackle HIV alongside the Terrence Higgins Trust and ViiV Healthcare, a pharmaceutical company focused on fighting HIV. Tackle HIV campaigns to change public perceptions, misunderstanding and stigma related to the virus. The statistics we presented at the launch truly did astonish people. More than 60 per cent of those surveyed said they would or might end their relationship if they found out their partner was HIV positive. Of those, 81 per cent said they would be worried about contracting HIV themselves and 17 per cent said they would be embarrassed if someone knew their partner had HIV. The survey also showed that just 19 per cent of people know that someone on effective treatment cannot pass HIV on to their partner. As a former sportsman, I found it sad that more than a third of those who said they played contact sports revealed they would not play against an opponent living with HIV and that 17 per cent would be worried about contracting HIV themselves. Twelve per cent said people with HIV shouldn't play contact sports, full stop.

Even journalists I really respected, who had covered some incredibly serious topics, had to admit there were gaping holes in their knowledge. That's people whose job it is to absorb and communicate information, so imagine how lacking other people's understanding of HIV can be. I wasn't annoyed (I would never be irritated at others' ignorance of HIV because so little has been done to educate society), in fact, I was glad as it increased the chances of their articles reflecting HIV as a bigger, deeper, more relevant subject than many people think. It proved the relevance of what I was doing.

In many ways, the misunderstanding and the stigma that still surround the virus is more dangerous than HIV itself, as it makes people less likely to seek testing and treatment, with serious, life-threatening consequences. Those who spread the classic HIV stereotype of sleaze and promiscuity rarely think of the frightened or ashamed mother not accessing the health services which could prevent parent-to-child transmission of the virus. Fear of judgement stops people getting help, which is essential if we are to stop the spread of HIV.

Think also how willing some are to use HIV as a hook on which to hang other prejudices. Knowing that gay and bisexual men, as well as black African communities, are disproportionately affected by the virus is all the ammunition some need to justify hate. This isn't some minor underground prejudice we're talking about. Lack of sympathy, antipathy and even downright hostility for those with HIV is widespread. In 2018, there were estimated to be 103,800 people living with HIV in the UK. We are talking significant numbers who quite easily can find themselves on the receiving end of other's prejudice. Worth bearing in mind also that 1 in 14 people living with HIV in the UK do not know they have the virus.

The aim of the Tackle HIV campaign is simple and ongoing. We want to reach as many people as possible who think they know about HIV but don't, or who believe they don't discriminate against those with HIV but do. That might be someone who previously had balked at the thought of playing contact sport against someone with HIV. Or one of the 79 per cent of people who, according to a YouGov poll, believe that someone living with HIV who is on effective treatment can still pass it on.

I couldn't help but feel that there was a certain irony at play when, just a few months after my 'coming out' newspaper article and HIV documentary, coronavirus appeared. Overnight, the mindset applied for so long to HIV sufferers now affected the entire population of the globe – 'I don't want to use your cup. I don't want to use your towel.' With Covid-19 there was good cause for that attitude, those precautions. But think about those with HIV who have, for absolutely no reason, lived with that stigma for years. It still shocks me that, before my own diagnosis, I had been someone who made those assumptions myself. I genuinely thought those were ways HIV could be transmitted. I had no other knowledge to tell me otherwise. Yes, I knew the virus could be passed on sexually or through shared needles but I thought for sure there was a multitude of other ways as well. I didn't even think straight people could have the virus, or that gay women could have it. I genuinely thought it was just gay men because that was all I had ever seen and heard. Nobody had told me all that stuff was bullshit and I had never sought the information out for myself.

That's what makes Tackle HIV so relevant – people think they know but actually they don't. Coronavirus proved the point. My mum and dad were really worried when the virus hit because they thought I would be in the 'at risk' category. Many others thought the same. And truth is I had to phone the doctor to check I wouldn't have to quarantine for months. I tell people constantly that I live a normal, happy, healthy life, just like anybody else, but then coronavirus popped up and my reaction took me aback – I still didn't know everything.

With the help of the Terrence Higgins Trust and the credibility their involvement brings, these were the kind of misconceptions I could remedy. I could shout from the rooftops that people in the UK who have HIV and are diagnosed early have the same life expectancy as everybody else. Forget those tired old rumours that somehow have survived from the eighties. You cannot pass on HIV by hugging, kissing, touching, sharing cutlery, crockery, etc. There is no need for anyone to feel like they need to say 'HIV' in hushed tones. It is not a dirty secret, a perversion, a matter of public disgrace. When I talk about HIV, I want to do so in my normal voice, which just happens to be quite loud! Who knows? Maybe loud enough to shatter that tombstone.

When I campaign I do so for everyone, but in my mind I do so particularly for that person with HIV sat in a house in a valley or a town where barely anyone understands what the virus is, how it affects people and how it is less threatening than a nettle sting.

Coronavirus delayed the launch of Tackle HIV a little but I was adamant that we shouldn't wait until the news agenda changed. HIV hadn't stopped just because a different virus had come on the scene. I didn't want to wait for a high-profile story in the news, or World Aids Day, when potentially there might be more momentum or interest. I didn't want Tackle HIV to be seen as reactionary. I wanted to be the kind of person I admire – those who are proactive. Be proactive in your message and then that spreads to those who take it on board. Comfortable short-term thinking is something we have all been guilty of. We see a headline, we react to it, and then we wait for the next thing to come along. When George Floyd died, I saw so many black squares posted on Instagram. That's fine but what does it actually achieve? Black Lives Matter didn't start overnight. It began years ago, but it took a flashpoint to gain mass interest. Why were there not more proactive, supportive voices from the start?

We're very good at reacting to situations but too busy getting on with our own lives to be proactive and prevent the long-term prejudice and discrimination that causes these issues to happen. We react in the right way but fail to be proactive in the right way. It's all too easy to react for a couple of days and we feel like we have solved the problem. In reality, it's like spraying an air freshener in a cow byre.

Look at what happened after the death of Caroline Flack. Coronavirus came along and everyone forgot about 'if you can be anything in this world, be kind'. And why weren't people saying that before a young woman felt compelled to take her own life? I want to live in a society where people confront or challenge discrimination consistently rather than wait for a terrible tragedy to prompt action, which may in itself have come from people feeling invisible, lost in a world that appears not to care.

I'm not saying people's feelings aren't genuine, but it is so easy to react, move on, and feel we have done our piece. Being proactive means thinking carefully about how to change views, environments, circumstances, so tragedy and discrimination is uprooted from society once and for all.

It shows how fickle a society we have become that body-shaming, once the hottest of topics, has slipped off the agenda. There was a time when designers were suddenly using real-size models, when airbrushing was deemed unacceptable. What happened to that? Where is the furore now? It has gone because, as ever, something else came along. Of course, there are still people working hard in that field but sadly, like so many other incredible campaigners, their voices are not being heard.

There are weeks dedicated to body confidence and weight stigma, same as there are for dozens of other issues, and I am sure they achieve an awful lot, but we cannot diarise discrimination when we know that the mental health and self-esteem of millions of people is battered every day by images of supposed 'perfection'.

Pride month is an excellent and life-changing concept, born from the moment in June 1969 when a police raid on the Stonewall Inn, a gay bar in New York, resulted in mass resistance and riots. The bravery of Stonewall patrons Marsha P. Johnson and Sylvia Rivera in resisting arrest and confronting police oppressors who had repeatedly harassed and persecuted members of the city's gay community provided the catalyst for the first Pride parades, a concept which soon spread across the globe. Understandably so – these days, Pride month is a time which creates so much joy and brings people together, as well as highlighting the love and support that can replace the fear and isolation and reassure those who feel anxiety about coming out. But equally it gives too many of us an opportunity to tick a box and say, 'Right, in Pride month I did this …'

When people ask me what they can do to be more supportive of gay people, I often say to them, 'Well, first up, bear in mind that being gay doesn't just happen in June. Neither does being beaten or killed for your sexuality.' Pride month is important, it reflects the liberation of gay people, but there are eleven other months in the year. By compartmentalising discrimination, we make it too easy for people to feel good about themselves. Liking a couple of Twitter posts for Mental Health Awareness Week is lovely, same as it is when a week comes round to highlight the plight of single parents, or refugees. But if I know one thing about discrimination, it's that it doesn't end at midnight on a Sunday. It's why I so firmly believe we need to talk about discrimination in general rather than splintering it into a thousand different shards. Focus on all prejudice all the time. If you are passionate about confronting one form of discrimination, then you should be passionate about challenging them all.

I also wanted Tackle HIV to exist away from the corridors of power I'd found so alien when I sought, alongside the MP

Damian Collins, then chair of the House of Commons Digital, Culture, Media and Sport select committee, to change the scope of the Football Offences Act to include homophobia. Being with MPs in the seat of power is amazing but the House of Commons isn't really me. I see it as an onion with a lot of layers that I know nothing about. I'm not stupid either. I know only too well that to some degree I am being played. Those in power find it difficult to address what are deemed 'taboo' subjects, more interested in votes than fairness and empowerment, and so rely on charities and people like myself to do that work for them.

That understanding should be instilled in schools. There is more to education than core subjects and league tables. Back in my day, sex education at school was: 'Man, woman – man does this, woman does this – baby' or 'Man, woman – man does this, woman does this – no baby.' No other areas were discussed. I would like to think things have changed but what I actually see is sexuality still discussed on a functional basis rather than as the deeply emotional element of human life that it really is. Kids need to know about the real world – and don't give me that crap about 'if you tell them, they'll just want to try it'. We're talking about the dangers of unprotected sex, not delivering a master-class in it.

At her school in Maesteg, my niece campaigned for HIV to be talked about in the classroom so young people could learn the truth about the virus and the stigma those who contract it so unfairly suffer under. Maesteg is a perfect example of a small place where knowledge can be powerful. I was so proud of my niece because it is actions like hers that empower people with long-term knowledge. Silence never gets you anywhere. The more kids know at an early age, the better. HIV will be a fact of their generation just like it is mine. They need to understand the normality of the way those with HIV are treated and the fact it isn't a taboo subject. Misunderstanding stands dead centre in discrimination. By being open and giving young people credit for their intelligence, we allow them to see that a person with HIV is just the same as them. The more we educate, the more we arm young people with the relevant information, the more we can prevent people contracting the virus.

We have to positively create change. I don't want the world to stay like this. I don't see why anybody would turn on the telly, listen to the radio, and think, 'Life works for me – therefore, everything is OK.' It's a really selfish outlook. My life, to a large extent, works for me right now, but I know full well that prejudice is present. It is impossible to deny. It is an unwinnable argument to say otherwise.

I do, however, understand the frustration, defeatism even, that some people feel at the snail's pace of progress. According to the Equal Opportunities Commission, at the current rate, it will take 200 years, or forty elections, for the House of Commons to become male/female equal. The Office for National Statistics, meanwhile, reports that in 2019 the gender pay gap in the UK was 17.3 per cent – on average women earned approximately 83p for every pound their male colleagues were paid. Women from ethnic minorities face the double whammy of both a gender and ethnicity pay gap. Official government figures show that black women are more than twice as likely to be arrested as white women. Closer to home for me, Welsh police forces reported hate crimes in the Principality doubled in the five years to 2018. I could go on.

The problem is that people have the attitude of 'it is what it is'. They don't ask why it is what it is. They don't consider doing something for the betterment of society. Only if something directly affects them are they interested. 'Coronavirus? We need a vaccine.' Prejudice? They have less desire to find the cure. They resist change, drag their feet or are deliberately contrary. For example, perhaps they don't know any gay people, have never heard homophobic language or spoken to someone who has been the target of it and therefore they insist that everything is fine. Step outside your own bubble and take a look at other people's lives and you begin to understand the reasoning behind change.

Those who have the power to make far-reaching social changes, to enact shifts in policy that redress deep imbalances, are not easy to reach, protected as they are by layers and layers of gatekeepers. Even if they do deign to answer your phone call, your knock on the door, often all you get is a political answer. And that is why, at times, addressing discrimination is so difficult, because so often you feel like you aren't getting anywhere.

Those times when you feel like you are walking through treacle you need to remember what history tells us – exposing prejudice will eventually force change. Whether that change will come in ten, twenty or a hundred years' time, I don't know. What I do know is that unless people shout it will never happen. I also know that I will carry on trying. My personal legacy, I hope, will be to have infiltrated enough organisations, ruffled enough feathers, scared enough complacent people, pointed out enough truths, uncovered enough lies, to have forced change. I am quite happy to be that person who makes a bigwig in an ivory tower splutter when they look out of the window, 'Oh fucking hell! He's knocking on the door again! When's he ever going to go away?' Never, mate, never. I know what I'm doing comes from a really good place. I have been fortunate and I want to help others who are struggling now. That is so important to me and it is what gives me the strength to carry on, whatever the knockbacks.

I know that campaigning works. The day after I announced my diagnosis, the Terrence Higgins Trust recorded high numbers of visits to its website. Many of those were specifically to the page dealing with treatment. The number of orders of self-test kits (which is similar to a pregnancy test) were three times higher than the average day. I have since joined the new HIV Commission, an independent organisation supported by the Terrence Higgins Trust, National AIDS Trust and Elton John AIDS Foundation, to find ambitious and achievable ways to end new HIV transmissions and HIV-attributed deaths in England by 2030. That is the kind of life-changing positivity I want to be involved in.

I hope we are in a world now that is more willing to heal the wounds of discrimination, but what I see is still capable of angering me, making me a bit more 'activist', a bit more 'fuck you'. I try to maintain positivity by not allowing space in my life for those with a negative presence, who have made a living by offering a constant negative voice. It is as if they traffic hate – and I don't want that traffic careering through my head. Carry hate in your pocket and you can't get rid of it.

One way in which I've tried to do this is in taking a step away from Twitter. Many good things happen on there which is why I do have a presence but I recognise what Twitter is, a business. It is a global money-making enterprise, not a social conscience. And unfortunately it is a really easy platform to fuel venom. Social media can preserve you in a moment in time. If you are in a poor state of mind, or just simply angered by something, you can vent your spleen in a tweet but then it sits there forever – even if you remove it, it may have already been reposted elsewhere. Truth is, anyone who engages with social media should be aware it can lead them down a maze of dark corridors. Some of them have a light at the end of them, some of them don't. When in your pocket is a phone full of images of everyone else's supposed success, it's easy to feel a failure. Look in the mirror and see a failure and you assume everyone else sees the same thing. When suicide takes the lives of so many people, it's vital that we recognise the possible thought processes going on. Young men are particularly prone to take their own lives. There are many complex reasons for that but the alienation that social media can bring at a time of life when so much of life is about fitting in surely has to be a consideration.

After I came out as HIV positive, I felt I was too fragile to expose myself to Twitter and the like, though there are also times when I find Twitter interesting and motivating. One reason is that it gives me an insight into how people are subconsciously bigoted or homophobic. It's important for me not just to acknowledge the people who stand by me and what I represent but also to understand what I am fighting against. That way, I am prepared. I might learn something that will help me to change someone's mind.

There must be times when all campaigners feel as if they are banging their heads against a brick wall but I know, as do they, that it is the little victories that keep you going. Sport has taught me there will always be barriers to overcome, situations to confront, and if you work hard there are positive outcomes. If millions of people watch a documentary I make and 500 of those are affected in a positive way, then that to me is worthwhile. That is what keeps me going. I have decided what I want to do in life, what I want to represent, and nobody is going to push me off that path.

I know that I am not alone in this. There are plenty of others seeking to question established situations and attitudes. Look at my mate Ian Watkins, better known as H from the pop group Steps. As a contestant on *Dancing on Ice*, he became part of the first same-sex couple to dance on British TV. No way was I going to miss out on being part of the audience that night and so there I was with Stephen and my stepdaughter Anna. I hadn't for a moment thought that it would affect me in the way that it did. When they came on to dance, the atmosphere in the audience was electric. Everyone was tuned in emotionally to this beautiful, poignant, powerful and mesmerising vision of two men dancing together. It would have been a privilege to be there whoever had been dancing that night, let alone someone who I could call a mate.

Afterwards, we went for a few drinks and one of the skating instructors, a lovely bloke, turned to me. 'Was it just me,' he asked, slightly confused, 'or was there something about that performance that was bigger than I thought it was going to be?'

I was a little incredulous but knew his question came from a good place. 'Don't you understand the significance?' I replied.

'No,' he said, 'I don't.'

'It was a massive moment in history,' I pointed out. 'A same-sex couple dancing together on prime-time TV, where traditionally the dynamic has always been the man and the woman – him bringing the strength, her bringing the vulnerability and the beauty. All of a sudden that barrier has been broken, beamed straight into millions of people's living rooms.'

It was only then that the significance of the moment really sank in for him. In some ways, I couldn't have been happier that he thought like that because ultimately the place we want to reach is one where two men dancing together on TV is no big deal. *Strictly Come Dancing* has since repeated the trick with the first same-sex female couple. What should now happen is that a same-sex couple appearing on a TV show is never a headline again. It should be treated as entirely normal, not even worthy of comment. Sadly, I am far from confident that will happen.

I'm not a big drinker but I have to admit that that night I got absolutely wasted! I didn't want that moment, that day, to end. I kept making toasts and so me, Stephen, H and Anna had drink after drink. Back in 2013, when I had done the show, there had never been any discussion about my having a male partner. Seven years later, H made a point of saying he would only appear if he could dance with a male partner. Not only was it never mentioned when I was there but it was never even on my radar. That shows how attitudes, expectations, can change in a very short timeframe. Inevitably, ITV had to fend off some viewer complaints but I'm sure the vast majority of those who tuned in that day were as filled with positivity, as emotionally invested in that performance, as we were. H had been proactive. He had made a difference.

I'll readily admit there are times when I'll agree to a request to be on a TV show just because it sounds fun, but most of the time I'll do something because it will show the issues I'm passionate about in a positive light – it will allow me to further my message. I know from experience that it's someone getting up and doing something that makes people sit up and take notice, whether that's seeing an issue for the first time or thinking about it in a different way. That can come from TV, or simply me speaking privately to an audience of business leaders, schoolkids or a rugby team, for example. Or it can come from me doing an Ironman, busting a stereotype, in the glare of publicity. When I came out as HIV positive that was a headline for a couple of days; the real impact comes from the positivity of what I do afterwards. When I came out as gay it was the same.

The fact I have a public profile makes me no more important than anyone else campaigning for equality, it just gives me a soapbox, which is exactly what I need. While those representing the LGBTQ community are thankfully much more numerous than a decade ago, well-known people who are known to be HIV positive remain thin on the ground. I will say this to anyone campaigning for change – use every tool you've got and use them well. Showing people that existing preconceptions are wrong is often the sharpest, most effective, tool in the box.

Thankfully, there are plenty who aren't HIV positive who are willing to ally themselves to the cause. When it comes to HIV and AIDS, Prince Harry is carrying on the work of his mother. In 1987, on a visit to a hospital in London, Princess Diana made a point of shaking hands with an AIDS patient without gloves. This was at the height of the frenzy of myths and misconceptions about the virus, the main one being that it can be passed on through touch. Diana's and Harry's campaigning has been hugely important, not only in increasing awareness and fighting stigma but in supporting those who work unseen in these environments every day. For someone from the royal family, respected and listened to the world over, to be talking about HIV, meeting those with the virus, banishing shame and embarrassment, and even, in Harry's case, being tested, is massive in terms of picking up HIV from the margins and placing it firmly in the mainstream. Prince Harry's global renown delivers such a powerful message. Remember, the stigma attached to HIV in the UK is nothing compared to places where diagnosis can lead to assault or even murder.

Harry's a friend and, like any friend, I would never automatically expect that he would do something for me, but when he sent me the text of his statement of support for Tackle HIV he made me cry:

> *It has been amazing to see how much progress has been made in the fight against HIV. Since I started campaigning on this issue, I have been honoured to spend time with people who are leading this charge.*
>
> *Thanks to them, we have moved from a time of social panic and hatred, to a time when the public came out into the streets to cheer for Gareth, a man living openly with HIV, as he cycled the length of Britain. But this progress hides how far we still have to go.*
>
> *Stigma, misunderstanding and discrimination remain the greatest barriers to defeating this virus. I hope everyone is inspired by 'Alfie', and will support him and the Tackle HIV campaign to improve understanding of it.*

Wow.

I know Harry through rugby, a game I loved which, thanks to the hard graft of those around me, gave me an amazing platform to speak from after I retired. But when I was awarded a CBE in 2020, I was delighted that it was for my work in health rather than sport. It said to me that I have been more successful in my life after rugby than I was when I was in the game. That makes me very happy because to my mind it is more important to succeed as a campaigner than it is as a sportsman. It has a bigger impact on people's lives and environments. I felt the same when I was given the St David's Special Award, chosen annually by Wales' First Minister, for my work in breaking down the stigma surrounding sexuality and HIV and being a role model for young people. I was particularly pleased to see that second part. The young, after all, are the ones left to sort out so much of the mess left by previous generations.

In my experience, you get the best out of yourself when you look to a bigger picture. Ask what you represent and you will often find an answer that leads you in a new and exciting direction, that challenges you, but is ultimately rewarding because it takes you out of a mindset where you are marooned on an island with yourself. My inspiration has always come from the bigger picture. As a sportsman I was lucky enough to play for teams I loved which gave me a massive dose of passion. I don't think I would have ever done an Ironman just to prove I could do it, to try to record an impressive time. But representing something bigger than me spurred me on through all those gruelling hours. It is unhealthy to occupy a mental headspace with only you in it. It's all too easy to enter a downward spiral, become inward-looking, put up an ever-thickening blackout curtain on the world outside. Ask that crucial question – 'What do I represent?' – and you will see there are spaces big and small you can occupy, be that campaigning, helping support groups, going on a march, or a million and one other ways. It is one of life's oddities that the more you immerse yourself in the lives of others, the more you learn about yourself, but that doesn't make it any less true.

When I climbed the stairs to that sexual health clinic at the hospital in Cardiff I wanted to vanish and never be seen again. And yet a vast painting of me sits on that very staircase for all to see. That to me feels like an incredible symbol of my personal journey from shame and fear to knowledge, hope and a determination to help make things better for others.

It's not just any picture either. When Welsh artist Nathan Wyburn was commissioned for the project, he came up with the idea of using red paint and fingerprints, symbolising the pinprick test from which comes the initial HIV diagnosis. I thought that sounded so original but had no idea until I turned up for the unveiling quite how powerful the image would be. Nathan, a massive supporter of LGBTQ rights, had already done two other pictures of me – one in mud reflecting my rugby career and one in glitter which hangs in a well-known gay bar in Cardiff – but this was something else. It really did portray how I felt. Somehow he had captured vulnerability as well as strength, epitomising that first visit to the clinic perfectly.

I know from experience how daunting that moment can be, leaden feet treading slowly up the stairs to be faced with that door. You have no idea what lies on the other side. So, so scary. The hope is that a recognisable face on the wall will empower first-time patients to take that final step, because I have no doubt at all that there are those who make it halfway up that staircase before turning on their heels and disappearing back into a mental void of apprehension and confusion. So many people don't get tested because of the fear of finding out they are positive. Even people who can feel themselves deteriorating will shy away from it, so manacled is the virus to stigma and others' negative perceptions. Choose not to have the test and in their mind they remain free of the virus. That is the psychological minefield that HIV can take a person into, even though the consequences of delaying a test are so, so serious, affecting the rest of their life.

What actually lies on the other side of that door is not the ogre of their imagination but friendly, skilled and deeply committed professionals who want only to help. I hope that perhaps some people climbing those stairs will relate to that picture – maybe there will even be a few who are only on that staircase in the first place because they have seen me talk about my story, my experience, and it has helped them make that first step towards dealing with their own issues, to come and be tested. If that has happened with just one person then every second of my campaigning has been worth it. To think that people might get tested early enough for them to lead an entirely normal and totally fulfilled life because of my campaigning feels unimaginably good.

Remembering my emotional journey made the unveiling of the artwork feel like an out-of-body experience. To see myself hanging on the wall was trippy. How the hell had I travelled from a hopeless person, hunched, weeping, believing I was going to die, to the content, confident, campaigning person I am now? Despite the momentous events along the way, it seemed like I had evolved without ever really realising it.

I was told that a survey by the Terrence Higgins Trust had found that 74 per cent of British adults are aware who I am and that I have HIV. How crazy is that? That's more people than will ever know I played rugby. Three-quarters of the people of this country now know the one thing I once never wanted anyone to know about me. But then again, that's what I'm about now – and proud to be about.

During the launch of Tackle HIV, I did many TV appearances, one of which was on Jeremy Vine's Channel 5 show. The programme's resident doctor, Sarah Jarvis, made a point of thanking me for being a vision of strength while also showing it's OK not to feel all right, to be vulnerable, to cry, and talk about areas of my life that most people would keep to themselves. I couldn't believe she'd even heard of me. But then when I thought about it, care, both physical and mental, is the exact field where the dominant force in my life now lies. While the thought of walking through a city and the people I pass knowing me as 'the guy with HIV' was at first abhorrent, then scary and then felt strange, now I have not only accepted it but I'm proud because it shows I'm active in fighting stigma; as Prince Harry put it, I am doing everything I can to turn 'a negative into a positive' and find a new purpose in life. I am incredibly proud of each and every trophy and medal from my career but equally I know that every day their significance wanes. I never realised it when those things came my way but their greater importance was in giving me a launchpad from which to campaign, something that, hopefully, I will be doing long, long into the future.

CHAPTER 20

FACING
FEARS

'Would you,' the person on the other end of the phone wants to know, 'be available to ride a bike from Cardiff to Aberdeen?'

It is BBC Sport. They want me to do a challenge for Sport Relief ahead of Sports Personality of the Year, this year coming live from the granite city.

'Er, well, maybe,' I say. I hate cycling. I mean, really hate it. Although my rather downbeat response is lost on the caller from the Beeb.

'In three weeks' time?' they continue.

'What?'

'Five-hundred-and-twenty miles.'

'Eh?'

'In seven days.'

Someone get me a whisky.

'Towing the SPOTY trophy?'

Actually, leave the bottle.

I tell them I'll have a think and get back to them. But I already know my answer. It's Sport Relief. It's highlighting discrimination and inequality. And it's not like I'm not a fit bloke. A few days on a bike won't kill me. Hopefully.

While three weeks isn't the longest time in the world to prepare for something of that magnitude, I know I'm built for cycling. I've got good power, good range in my legs, and know from the Ironman that I'm good at it. It's just that I find it one of the most boring things I could ever do. I know people who love it and routinely go out for eight-hour rides. The mere thought of that amount of time on a bike makes me feel queasy. Imagine still doing in the last minute exactly what you were doing in the first? Aside from the occasional gear change or braking it is just solidly the same. I'm not knocking people who cycle. For me, though, all I can think about on a bike is when I can get off it. I spent endless hours in the saddle preparing for Ironman but it was only because I had to. Riding 520 miles across seven twelve-hour days will be something entirely different. Especially considering I will be pulling the SPOTY trophy, which, I am told, weighs more than 20kg, in a trailer. Although surely it won't actually be in there? They'll just pretend it is, slip it in for a few miles at the start and end of each stage. I think that part of it will, at least, be fine.

It isn't fine. I turn up to set off on my torturous weave across three countries and there, in the trailer, is the trophy, all set and ready to go.

'It's not the real thing,' someone tells me. Presumably, they don't want it dented if I have a crash. (The real Gareth Thomas getting dented in a crash is all right.)

'It's a replica,' continues the person from the BBC. 'Actually, it's a bit heavier than the real thing!'

I'm beginning to wonder if I'm the victim of a hidden camera show – when the modern-day version of Jeremy Beadle is going to jump out.

The ride will be split between a solo bike and a four-person Quattrocycle – a four-wheeled bike with two rows of two seats facing forwards – the other three spots filled alternately by friends, celebrities and those who have benefitted from money raised by Sport Relief. Before I try it, I am quite looking forward to the Quattrocycle. Four times the people means a quarter the work, right? But when I get on it, I find it is heavy. It also requires sitting in a recumbent position, which makes it very tough on the legs over a long period. The solo bike will be the option for most of the time.

I don't eat that much before I set off. Despite the clear challenge ahead, there is still a part of me that remains a little blasé about how hard it will be. In fact, I've decided I will use the entire venture as a way of slimming down after sticking on a few pounds to get me through the Ironman. It's a mistake, a big mistake – by the time I get off the bike at the first feed point two hours later I am physically shaking. My blood sugar is through the floor. I eat healthily, about six packets of Jaffa Cakes swilled down with mugs of tea, and start to feel a bit better. But I have

STRONGER

had my warning – this is something to be taken seriously. If I don't, I won't even make it out of South Wales, let alone reach Aberdeen. This is December, after all, conditions aren't exactly going to be easy.

The aim of my journey is to help change attitudes to people either living in isolation or burdened by social stigma. I know from my own experience how many people lead a life detached, through no fault of their own, from the everyday life enjoyed by others. If I can, I want to do something so their voices can be heard. All along the way, I am doing interviews, radio shows, to keep the journey as high in the public consciousness as possible. That way we will raise more money. I also want to make sure that every day we sit down with an organisation that will benefit from Sport Relief. This is how, one lunchtime in Shropshire, I come to meet two homeless women. I am moved deeply to hear how they have ended up, quite literally, like something abandoned in the gutter. I find it as heart-breaking as I do unbelievable that people should be living like that in the modern age.

It is a freezing day and by the time I am back on my bike and have cycled a couple of miles the cold has got into my bones. One thing I'm not short of on my bike is thinking time and, with the two women still so vivid in my mind, it occurs to me how so often we try to raise ourselves or one another by saying we should think of people worse off than us. 'Look,' we say, 'it could be so much worse.' According to that mentality, I should now be making myself feel better by thinking about those two women sleeping, hungry, homeless, in the bitter winter cold.

How odd is that? How upside down is it that we should cheer ourselves by thinking of others' misfortune? I find it perverse that we should look at a homeless woman sleeping under a slide and think, 'Well, that makes me feel better. Maybe I haven't got it so bad after all.'

It's obvious that the actual way to feel happier about our lives is to do something to make that other person's life better, something we can do in a myriad of ways, be it donating, campaigning, volunteering, working in that field, or simply offering kindness and compassion. None of what that person is suffering is about us. But I know also that I am as guilty as anyone when it comes to reaching for others' pain to put my own into perspective.

The conversation in my head reconciles another uneasiness – I hate asking people for money, I find it really awkward. And yet here I am, constantly asking for donations. Now, though, I realise I can switch that around. I'm not actually asking people for cash, I am asking them to help other people. And in doing so I am offering them a chance to feel better about themselves, the same as how I now feel better about myself because I know I am doing something positive to help those two women whose lives are in a mess.

One day, I stop at the top of a particularly brutal hill to do an interview with Zoe Ball on Radio 2. Behind me, as ever, is a line of traffic a mile long – don't get stuck behind an ex-rugby player towing a trailer on a bike if you want to get anywhere quick. A woman pulls over and comes across to talk to me. Her young kids, she tells me, have been asking her what the hold-up is.

'There's a man up the front cycling with the Sports Personality trophy,' she has told them. 'He's been on the telly. He's gay and has been talking about living with HIV.'

'Mum,' one of the kids had asked, 'what's gay?'

I love that. Unbeknown to me, while I am toiling up that hill, cursing every turn of the pedals, I have prompted a really important conversation in that family. It makes me think how, every time I pass through a little town or village, as a man who is gay, and has HIV, I am leaving something behind. Little chats between people on the street. Parents explaining something to their children. Maybe I have passed the 'only gay in the village' that I once considered myself to be. Maybe I have passed someone recently diagnosed with HIV. Or maybe others who have had a sudden thought – 'I wonder if anyone who lives here has got HIV?' Equally, my grinding through the town crossroads on a bike, as someone known as an equality campaigner, might spark a conversation about sexism or ageism, or one of a dozen other topics. These thoughts make me see the quest in a new light. It isn't all about raising money, reaching Aberdeen, it is about what, in the bleakness of these dark dank days on the road, might be sparked along the way, what little barriers might be knocked down, what connections might be made.

As I pedal on, I become really conscious and proud not only of taking this iconic trophy that I have watched being handed out to legends year after year on TV through the wind and the rain from Cardiff to Aberdeen, but of actually carrying way more with me – a representation of stigma and discrimination and how to overcome it. That's how I come to think of myself over the course of these seven days, which is so much more powerful and meaningful than being an ex-rugby player making an unlikely bicycle journey from one country to another.

It is an odd feeling as I ride into Aberdeen's state-of-the-art P&J Live Arena, where the Sports Personality programme is being staged before an audience of thousands. My motivation to do the ride was to raise money and meet some of the incredible people who have benefitted from Sport Relief. As I snaked my way across the country, the ride took on an extra dimension, acting as a catalyst for conversation. I have collected hundreds of memories over the course of the past seven days and now, as everyone stands to applaud, this seems the least significant of them all. I am being clapped for getting the trophy to its destination when in my mind this part of the exercise has become almost irrelevant. No one knows any of that, of course, except me. I am appreciative of the reception, and respectful, but it isn't part of the equation for me. I would prefer the ride to end with its true poignancy, be that sitting down with some of those helped by Sport Relief, or in the middle of a tiny community in the middle of nowhere, or even on my own in quiet contemplation of what I and many other people have got out of this crazy journey.

Physical challenges – whatever that means to you – are a good way of expressing how much you care about something. I could quite easily have driven to meet those being helped by Sport Relief, but match it with a physical fund-raising effort and it becomes so much stronger and captures people's imagination.

I'm lucky enough to be friends with Davina McCall, who completed her own Sport Relief challenge in 2014, cycling, running and swimming 500 miles from Edinburgh to London in seven days. I was in tears as I watched her being pulled virtually lifeless from Lake Windermere. She chose to be in that position. She chose to get in that water and chose to swim until she passed out. Why? Because when you see someone willing to go to the limits you engage with their vision. People understand that if someone is willing to put themselves in that position then they must believe massively into the project – which, in Davina's case, was helping vulnerable women.

The training I did for the Ironman may not have left me with a love of cycling but my journey to conquer my fear of swimming in the sea did have a big and lasting impact. Once I had an understanding of its power and what I needed to do to survive in it, I returned to it again and again. I actually now find it an incredibly life-affirming environment, a place where I could die and yet never feel more alive, delivering mental release. Before I tried open water swimming, the closest thing I had to escapism, taking my mind to a different place, was rugby. But even then there would be long periods when I wasn't involved in the game. On average, my part in the action never extended beyond 15 minutes of an 80-minute game. Those other 65 minutes could be hard, the mental more wearying than the physical. But with swimming, because I remain relatively new to the discipline, effectively starting from scratch, all I can think about is completing my current stroke, then the next one and the one after that. Swimming removes the future, removes the past and puts me in the now. I have often thought how lovely it would be to live my entire life like that. But I have tried and I'm not wired that way. It's too much of an effort. The one time it isn't an effort is when I'm there, just Alfie, in the sea. The fear of the water remains. I'm still respectful of it and from that point of view will never be a natural swimmer but it will always be my way of finding real peace when, in good times or bad, I just want to be me.

Personal development is vital. Even now I still want to evolve. Just because I'm no longer a child doesn't mean I shouldn't want to better myself, to learn. That's the same for anyone. Whenever Usain Bolt raced, he wanted to go faster than he did the time before, because ultimately he wanted to challenge himself. Bolt is an extreme example, but the principle remains the same. By challenging ourselves – be it to improve our diet, to exercise more, or get out and do something rather than scrolling through social media – we create a stronger version of ourselves. I didn't really want to swim on my own without Dave but I knew I had to, otherwise I was just, metaphorically speaking, treading water. I was forty-five before I could swim properly. Deep into middle-age, I found more than a new skill, I acquired an everlasting reference point: 'You know what, Alfie? If you can overcome that, you can overcome anything.' Whatever the size of the challenge, no matter how minor or major, I now know what I have to do is not just confront it but take it as far as I can.

And all that came from showing vulnerability. Being open about fear is strength.

Accepting challenges, persevering in unfamiliar environments, overcoming fear, allows us to learn so much about ourselves and the world around us. It shows us just how much resilience, determination and drive we have inside, in direct opposition perhaps to how little we thought we had. That is why we should never be afraid of embracing new, perhaps daunting, situations. They should never be seen as a threat, rather they should be viewed as places of personal empowerment, a doorway to a better us. Step through that doorway and so often you find the person you thought you were is actually someone else completely. Where you might have believed you lacked strength, purpose, drive, ability, you will discover that you are actually someone who has all those things in abundance. It is just that circumstance, the relentlessness of routine, or the negativity of others has applied a blindfold.

Low self-esteem and low confidence will always seek to be our bedmates. By deliberately challenging ourselves, we also challenge them, while at the same time finding ourselves on the receiving end of a massive dose of perspective. When I set off from Cardiff on the Tour de Trophy, I didn't really understand what that bike ride would do to me. It was all so last minute. But as I carried on, I became more and more aware that, while I consider myself someone who takes notice of the world at large, I had actually been blinkered to so much that was going on right in front of me, to the point where the challenge itself, the endless revolutions of that bike chain, seemed utterly insignificant. I might have got off that bike in Aberdeen stronger physically, but that was nothing compared to how I had developed in my head. In every town, every village, I had encountered people dealing with situations of all kinds. Unlike the Ironman where I had been focused on the message my achievement would send out about HIV, here I was plunged headfirst into a myriad of issues affecting others. I saw that behind so many doors is someone with a deep personal story of one kind or another. It was as if a veil had been lifted – I had the power to see the truth of myself, as someone battling inequality and prejudice across the board, and others so much more clearly. The problem is, if we do not keep ourselves challenged, stimulated, that veil can all too easily fall again. We all need to continually keep asking how we can evolve – it doesn't even matter if we don't always 100 per cent succeed at everything we try.

Previously for Sport Relief, I had been hurled out of an aeroplane at 12,000 feet in a tandem skydive, for which I had to overcome my fear of heights. Even thinking about that would make my hair, when I had any, stand on end. Prior to going up in the plane, I did a course to try to overcome the phobia. The best method, I was told, was to think of a flashpoint with heights in the past – a childhood trip to a castle perhaps, or getting stuck in a tree – break it down, and make it a comfortable memory, reimagining myself as someone not afraid anymore.

It worked, to a certain extent, in that I didn't actually feel too afraid as the plane rose into the sky, something, heights aside, I have never liked, generally crossing my fingers from the moment of take-off until the 'ding!' signals I can take my seatbelt off. In fact, I was remarkably OK with the ascent, feeling relaxed even. But then a crew member got up and opened the door, at which point I nearly shat myself. I don't care what anyone says, when you're sat in an aeroplane at 12,000 feet it's just not normal for someone to get up and open the door.

Shuffling over and perching on the edge of the glaring hole where there used to be a comforting three inches of metal didn't feel hugely natural either. I peered down – not the best idea I've ever had – and couldn't even see the ground. I looked back into the plane, hoping it was nothing more than a bad dream. What I actually saw was the same man giving me the thumbs up. 'Mate,' I thought, 'there is nothing thumbs up about this. Nothing at all.'

And that was it, I was falling. At which point I did what any sane person would do – I closed my eyes. I was last out of the plane and so all my co-jumpers were already on the ground when finally, and with no shortage of relief, I landed. They were all thrilled, comparing notes and saying how exhilarating, how beautiful they had found the experience. How they would like nothing more than to get back in the plane and do it all over again. My view was somewhat different.

'Never again. Not. A. Chance.'

It wasn't easy being the only one who appeared to have left the ground a human being and come back down a jelly, especially since all my fellow parachutists were old age pensioners, the Silver Skydivers, who, as the name might suggest, like nothing more than spending their retirement at eye level with a buzzard. Actually, that's only part of the story. What they really get out of it is purpose and companionship. Because as much as my Sport Relief journey was about overcoming my fear of heights, more significantly it was about ageism, elderly people being made to feel irrelevant. It was an eye-opener for me, a form of discrimination I had never really considered, possibly because it is invisible to most people until they are right there on the end of it.

We're not just talking about discrimination from employers here. Ageism's tentacles extend, incredibly hurtfully, into family. While I would always want my mum and dad to live their life on their terms, I could just as easily be the sort of son who says, 'You're in your seventies. I'm going to bring the toilet downstairs and you can sit in a chair doing crosswords and never go out again.' That might appear a way of caring for them but actually I would be discriminating against them because all they want to do, regardless of their age, is live their life to the maximum. So often, best intentions are in fact ageism. That is its hidden face.

I was pleased that by confronting my fear of heights I had learned about and could highlight the unfairness of society towards a group of people who have so much to offer. However, I remained a little unhappy with myself. Truth is, jumping strapped to someone else meant that while I had challenged my fear, I didn't feel as if I had really confronted it to the maximum. Hence, unlike putting my head underwater, I still have the phobia of heights, and will do so until I go that step further. But before anyone offers to help me climb the Burj Khalifa, can I just say that the fear of heights is one I'm ready to live with. I don't feel like I need to challenge it to the max. Learning to swim has given me a life skill, one that not only do I enjoy but could save my life or indeed somebody else's. Yes, it would be nice not to be afraid of going on a rollercoaster but it wouldn't make me a better, more developed, person.

I inherited the fear of heights from my mum. She can't stand them either. I think possibly she was a little over-protective when I was a kid – anything more than two feet off the ground prompted a shout of 'Gareth! Stay away from the edge!' I hid my fear of heights as a youngster but didn't feel the need when I got older. There have been plenty of times when I've found myself high up and have absolutely panicked. I gathered the courage to go up Blackpool Tower once, only to get to the top and discover it's got a glass floor, people like ants on the pavement directly below. I couldn't get back in the lift fast enough. But it doesn't have to be anything extreme to get me going. If I was fifteen feet up a ladder, I wouldn't be happy. In fact, if someone else is fifteen feet up a ladder I don't like it. If Stephen goes up a ladder at home, I'm terrified.

When I was a kid, I also had a fear of the dark. I hated waking up to find my room pitch black. It made me feel as if I was lost in a tunnel and so I slept with the lights on. Even now, we have no curtains in our bedroom. I like, if possible, to go to bed when it's light because it has a calming influence on me. I'm not afraid of the bogeyman, it's just there's so much uncertainty in the dark. I like to know my environment, know where I am – the door is here, the window is there. I travelled so much in my rugby career that often I would wake up half asleep, not knowing what part of the world I was in, let alone where the light switch was. I found it very unsettling at times and it remains something I am wary of when I travel now.

Mastering a fear is not about just understanding it. What matters ultimately is facing it fully and honestly. You could flick the lights off for ten seconds, turn them back on, and see that nothing bad happens. Except that wouldn't be overcoming the fear. That would be the fear overcoming you. Stand in that same dark room for twenty-five minutes and reach the point where you couldn't care less if the light was on or off and then you are truly getting somewhere. By accepting that challenge you have improved as a person.

Claustrophobia too has been a burden, especially with rugby. I hated it when I found myself at the bottom of a ruck, unable to move my arms and legs, and then somebody would come crashing down, covering my face as well. When that happened, I would always close my eyes and count to ten – a system I know many people use to overcome panic – by which time the pile-up would usually have dispersed.

Lifts are the same. I will never get in a lift that looks full, partly because of the enclosed space and partly because I can't help feeling that a full lift has a lot more chance of falling. If there are already six or seven people inside, I'd rather wait and get the next one. People might think that's daft but I don't care. I particularly hate the clear-sided lifts that have become really popular in recent years. Worse are the idiots who, if they know someone is nervous, think it's really macho to jump up and down or lean heavily into the windows. You know what, mate? If somebody is afraid of something maybe don't put them in an even more anxious position. That's just being a dick.

By seeking to overcome, we gain an incredible sense of drive and, ultimately, achievement, but the majority of the challenges we face in life are not organised events we decide to take part in. They don't involve an entry number, something I was reminded of when coronavirus came round. Initially, like many, I found the situation overwhelming, consumed by the thought of what the virus might bring, the havoc it might wreak. Its power felt oppressive, as if the world had changed overnight, to the extent that on one occasion I found myself in tears.

There were times where I felt caged in. I wanted 2020 to be a year where I continued the HIV conversation I started in 2019 and it felt so frustrating that I couldn't get out there and, as an HIV-positive man, be seen doing really normal things to hopefully make people look twice at their preconceptions of the virus. I wanted the year to be a configuration of my story and normality. I wanted to keep planting seeds which would blossom into new conversations. Of course, it was not to be and, like so many people, I had to accept that something I cared about had, to an extent, been placed on hold.

Other times, when lockdown kicked in, I was overcome with guilt at not putting this sudden rush of free time to good use. 'I should be doing something,' I'd say to Stephen. 'It feels wrong not doing anything.' We helped out dropping off food deliveries to our neighbours from our nearest shop but still there was plenty of other time to fill. The answer to that restlessness was to listen to myself. Instead of feeling guilty, I thought about my situation with a little more clarity.

'Doing nothing isn't a crime,' I told myself. 'If you don't want to do anything, then don't. You don't need to feel bad about it.'

There were days when I just sat on the settee and watched films, some good, a lot absolute rubbish. Instead of feeling stressed, I felt happy. My mind used that time to do a much-needed stocktake. It kept what was precious and chucked the rest in a skip – a big skip – and I came out the other end feeling so much lighter. Without the clutter, I actually had a clear view of myself and where my life was taking me.

I could just as easily have filled every minute of every day with activities. I could have attempted to master the pogo stick or taught myself Spanish. While I like Spain and jumping up and down on a pogo stick probably has its merits, I learned something much more useful – that sometimes in life it is OK to do nothing. That is not a place that, these days especially, many us allow ourselves to reach. It's more common to feel we are wasting our lives, missing out on a welter of amazing experiences, which is partly a result of the daily distortion of social media, presenting the best bits of others' lives – the holidays, the restaurants, the parties, the shopping trips – as everyday, when really we are seeing a very heavily edited highlights package.

As someone who loves to be around people, and who is very close to my family, I was saddened at the start of lockdown not to be able to see friends. But then, as time wore on, I thought about it differently. I realised that, for these months in my life, I was going to be with the one person I've always wanted to be with – Stephen. Maybe not having other people in my life for a while will be something to treasure. And that's exactly what it was. We found ourselves having time to do things together that we never normally would, like walking the dog or having a date night in the house.

Putting life on hold gave me time to absorb everything that has happened in the past few years, to step off the rollercoaster and take a more rounded view. An element of distance allowed me to understand it more, and maybe it gave those around me time to understand it too. Perhaps if I'd carried on campaigning hard all year, I would have found myself really fatigued.

Having gone into the coronavirus lockdown full of restlessness and fear, I found myself adamant that I wouldn't be made to feel a lesser person or guilty for doing nothing. I love challenges, I love overcoming my fears, but I don't have to do it every day of my life. It was important to be reminded of this.

Remember, as much as others can help, as much as they can influence, only you can live your life. You know yourself better than anyone, so it is important to listen to what your mind and body is telling you. If they want you to step back a bit, slow down a while, then try as hard as you can to indulge them. After all, it is your mind and your body that will get you through the rest of your life. Just don't let them get complacent. When they have had a good rest, give them a gentle nudge to get you back trying new and different things. Freefall skydiving or a book club – it's up to you.

CHAPTER 21

ANCHORED

I am devastated as I drive past my mum and dad's house. A big telephone pole has appeared on the green, the small patch of grass where we used to play when we were kids.

'I can't believe it,' I tell her, 'they've ruined Wimbledon!'

'Well,' she points out, 'kids don't play out on the street like they used to.'

I can't bear to drive past every day and see this monstrosity in the middle of our makeshift tennis court.

'How could they do that?' I ask.

'Oh, get over it, Alf,' she tells me. 'Move on!'

I feel sometimes that although I grew up in the seventies and eighties, my childhood was like one of those black and white photos you see of kids playing in the street in the thirties. In my street there were a lot of children around my age. We grew up together, went through amazing things together, many of them based on that very green. Our shared experiences created amazing friends, amazing bonds. In fact, I am still very good friends with them all. Catching up with them in Bridgend has given me some of the best nights I've ever had, as we looked back on our street Olympics or grass-patch Wimbledon, seemingly throwaway moments that actually I, and they, hold really dear.

That's no lie. I played rugby for Wales a hundred times. Somewhat blurrily, I can remember my first cap, my fiftieth and a couple of others. Winning street Wimbledon, on the other hand, I can remember in high definition, the reason being it was momentous. For my development as a person, enjoyment of life, it was so relevant. Between us all, kids and adults alike, we created this safe place where one day I could go out and be Boris Becker, the next Steve Cram, and so on and so on. This little patch of grass was a place of freedom where children could live out their dreams. Deny children open space and you are denying them an essential building block of life. When I look back now, although I didn't know it at the time, plunging head-first into that dreamworld was giving me the first hint of what I could be.

Dreams are important. When I realised I had no academic skills, sport still offered me hope. I was half decent at it precisely because I had been running, kicking a ball, playing tennis, doing something, every single day of my life. Some might say I am over-simplifying, being sentimental. Lots of kids play out but never play a hundred times for their country. Those people don't understand. When I played those games – tennis, rugby, athletics, whatever – I actually believed I was Boris Becker or Jonathan Davies. On a tattered bit of grass in South Wales, I could imagine

I was as good as these sporting giants. This ability was a real character strength, one that I carried with me for the rest of my life. Now when I drive past the green and see my eight-year-old self running around, wishing I was playing for Wales, and I know that I did it, there's no question that it all started on that patch of grass in the street. In the heads of youngsters, we made it anything we wanted it to be, and for me my wish came true.

Whatever I've done in life, good or bad, I don't want to forget. Memories keep you anchored, give you perspective. I know also that my mum doesn't really want me to forget. Only the other week she talked about how lovely she'd found it to walk up the street and see some of those kids I used to play with, now adults in their forties, still living there. She walked past one house and ended up reminiscing for an hour and a half about the road and how it used to be. That's because it's part of our lives, part of our makeup, the scaffolding that supported us as we grew. People often ask me 'What is your greatest achievement?' and I always reply that it is being born Welsh, but more than that, I was lucky enough to be born in Bridgend and within that I was lucky enough to be born in that street. I had such a happy childhood, such a happy upbringing. Yes, we struggled. Yes, we had little money. But neither did anyone else. Instead, we created challenges, games, adventures and a really joyful, happy life that, while we didn't know it at the time, would give us memories for a lifetime.

My mum and dad were the foundation blocks on which all those memories were built; they are two very strong people but in contrasting ways. My dad Barry is a quiet man but when he speaks people listen. If there are five people having a conversation and my father decides to chip in, everybody goes quiet. They know that whatever it is he's going to contribute he will have thought about it. He will be logical, methodical and to the point. 'Wise' is an old-fashioned word but that's definitely how I see him. I, though, am more like my mother. 'Vonny', as everyone calls my mum, Yvonne, is passionate, hot-headed and can fly off the handle. My dad has that in him but will have to be pushed to the brink to be angry or excited in that way. It will have taken a lot of quiet absorption for him to reach that stage.

I do try to be like my dad and put the brakes on the passion but I was so close to my mother growing up, because, as a postman, Dad always seemed to be working, that her traits are instilled in me. Not that Dad's presence wasn't felt. He existed in the form of a threat. If Mum told me and my brothers she was going to tell Dad what we'd been up to, we knew we were in for it when he got home. Dad knew that if we'd done something that warranted her telling him then it must be serious. Mum knew she couldn't use Dad as an idle threat, though. If she said she was going to tell him, she always did. She knew if we didn't think she was serious we would continue playing holy shit. Dad would come home and bollock us, again in his quiet, controlled way, and we would listen. He didn't need to tell us more than once, same as he didn't need to tell us twice to go to bed. Mum could tell us 500 times and we'd still be sat there on the settee.

Dad may not be outwardly passionate but he is strong in character and strong in presence. And he can also have an incredibly calming influence. Take a problem to Mum and Dad, as I still do – probably a little bit more often than they'd like! – and my dad will come up with a definitive way of dealing with it. He has a habit of making solutions look really easy. He talks in layman's terms and doesn't complicate issues – 'OK, we'll do it this way and it will be fine.' Simple.

He was exactly the same when it came to dealing with one of the biggest challenges that can affect anyone – cancer. Dad was diagnosed with prostate cancer more than two years ago. It came as a shock to us all but thankfully the doctors caught it early and the condition is under control. We had a conversation about it and I couldn't help but be struck by the synergy of our lives, not just in the kind of language he was using – 'I've got cancer, cancer hasn't got me' – but in terms of his cancer and my HIV experience. He went for a test, was diagnosed early enough and now lives a healthy life, taking the appropriate medication to keep the condition at bay and having blood tests at regular intervals.

I listened to my mum and dad and it was as if I was listening to myself. Treatment, medicine, the wonders of medical advancement, were all discussed in a really open and positive way. Because I had never seen my parents close-up in a time of worry such as this, because I'd never seen them challenged in a way that I've felt challenged, I'd always wondered where I get my strength to fight, to campaign, from. My parents had never obviously displayed that side of themselves. Like most parents, I suppose, they had dealt with any serious crises out of sight of their children. But now, as I looked at them, I was struck by how much of a carbon copy of them I am. It was uncanny. I don't think I've ever looked at myself and seen a replication of my father. Like most men, I suppose, I always thought 'my dad is just my dad'. Now I was sat there thinking, 'Jesus Christ, it's exactly the same as listening to me talking about living with HIV. He's saying exactly the same words, using exactly the same terminology.'

It was empowering to hear him talk about it. Cancer, like HIV, is so often spoken of in the media in terms of loss and death and yet here was my dad being upbeat about living with the condition. From his point of view, it's not something that continually needs to be referenced. He's found the mindset that works for him – 'OK, we'll do it this way and it will be fine' – and now he's getting on with his life, the same as before, and I couldn't respect and admire him more for that.

I wish I was more like my dad. I really do wish I could look at obstacles in his rainbow fashion, combining every shade and colour and coming up with the definitive answer. I think he's become hardwired that way after being married to my mother for such a long time. Mum's way of dealing with problems is to come up with a million different suggestions. Dad will calmly sit there, pick one of those million options and decree it to be the simplest way of addressing the issue. He's the laidback lion to mum's Tasmanian devil. Together, somehow, the combination works.

Dad has never been a huggy man. When a close relative died and, due to coronavirus, there were restrictions on the number of people who could attend the funeral, a friend consoled my brother, 'It's a shame you can't be there to hug your father when he cries.'

'It's OK,' he told him, 'my father hasn't hugged me or cried in forty years. I don't think he's going to start now.'

Again, so different from myself. If I watched *ET* every day, I'd still cry. Dad? I had a really awkward shoulder-to-shoulder hug with him once and that was it. It doesn't concern me one bit, though. I know without a shadow of a doubt that he loves his sons as much as we love him. The fact he doesn't show it by hugging or that I've never seen him cry doesn't mean he's any more or less passionate about his family than the rest of us. Maybe for him it's a generational thing. Maybe it's the way he was brought up but I actually like that he's made that way, the perfect leveller for me because I'm so much the opposite. While I feel like I get over the hurdles and gain real strength from being emotional, he shows how equally important it can be to show a measured response. I believe in encouraging men to be open about their emotions but it's equally important that no one should feel pressured to go down that route if they don't want to.

Put Mum and Dad together and they give me so much. Mum nurtures my emotional side while Dad keeps me on an even keel. He understands I'm emotional, that I might want to cry, but he will also make me see there are other ways of approaching a problem. Together they have showed me that emotion and reason can work together. It isn't a choice between the two. Barry and Yvonne are so different yet together they work. I go up to their house every day and every single time I see the same thing – an incredible steadiness and sturdiness between them. For me, that daily visit gives me perspective on life. Even just sitting there having breakfast gives me such a positive balance. When I'm going through a tough time, for instance, Mum will remind me that life is there to be embraced.

'You've been through enough,' she'll tell me. 'Enjoy it. Forget waiting for a rainy day, get out there and enjoy it now.'

My dad will say something similar but in a different, more cautious way. Either way, they have given me balance, a great belief that what I am doing is right. They are my grounding. It's one of the reasons why, aside from that short spell in London, I've never moved away. I would simply miss them too much, but also, more selfishly, I find their advice so valuable. If I lost that physical closeness to them, I would feel lost. Everything I have been through, whether it be rugby or my personal life, my mum and dad have always been my sounding board. I have always known there is somewhere I can go if I feel I want to shut the world away. I look around their house sometimes and think how far I have come when nothing around me has changed. Whatever changes on the outside, my mum and dad always tried to keep the same safe and secure environment within their four walls. As crazy as life can get, it's so special to come back to something that is the same as it always has been, delivering a clear perspective on what I am doing; how I am going to find a way out of whatever mess I have landed myself in. The sense of calm allows me to do that.

I sometimes wonder what I would have done without this space, if I was one of the many people who don't grow up with stable and caring parents like my mum and dad. Who don't have a door they can walk through where the chaos is left behind outside. Maybe they don't have a roof over their head, full stop. So many people have nowhere to go and I find that a tragedy. It's really hard for me to imagine that, to think how I would have coped without my parents and their house as a bolthole.

As a kid, I was really close to my mum's mother and father too. Mervyn and Eileen lived opposite us so I could literally walk out of my mum and dad's house, cross the road, click open the gate and I'd be there. We even went on holiday together like families would in the old days – my mum and dad, my brothers, Nan and Grandad, and my auntie Denise, the youngest of my mother's sisters. Grandad was a real proud hard worker and liked to go down the pub for a pint or to play snooker. Nan, meanwhile, was really glamorous. She would do herself up just to be in the house. Together, they doted on all their grandchildren but, because of my success in rugby, I had a bit of a special place with them.

Looking back now, I can't help but think I did them a massive disservice by not telling them I was gay. They came from a generation that I thought just wouldn't understand. Sadly, they both died before I came out. It remains a regret. The truth was, nothing could have surprised them. I now know that not only wouldn't they have judged me but actually they would have embraced me. Instead, I got so hung-up on imagined generational differences that I felt I would only hurt them – and I could never hurt them. I believe, though, that they knew anyway.

Grandparents are different to your mum and dad, you can be a slightly different person around them, speak differently, get away with things that would be a no-no at home. I was with them so much I can't help but think that meant I wasn't so defensive as I was elsewhere, I wasn't working so hard to hide the reality of what I was dealing with. I have this feeling they understood. They respected my privacy by not pushing but I can totally picture them having conversations with me in a very non-judgemental and very caring way. Think about it, these were people who had had to keep evolving. They'd come through the Second World War, surely thinking that was the end of the toughest of times. Except life doesn't work like that and their generation wasn't lucky enough ever to have much more than a constant diet of hard work and scraping to put food on the table, and that's without the other challenges that inevitably pop up along the way. My nan and grandad somehow just got through everything and they would have dealt with anything I brought along in exactly the same way. Everyone in the family still refers to it as their house, even though it was sold years ago. They are still nearby, buried in Sarn Cemetery. Nan died of horrible, awful cancer. Mervyn, it turned out, had cancer at the same time but kept it to himself because he didn't want to cause more worry. He died not long after my nan, at home because he didn't want to die in hospital. It was a broken heart and not the cancer that killed him, without a shadow of a doubt. Like my mother and father, he and Eileen were inseparable, together every moment they could be, despite being completely different. When the time came, he didn't want to live without my nan. As much as that is sad, there is also something pure and beautiful about such devotion.

The sense of community my street gave me means a gated house in some fashionable city suburb can never be for me. Even if I could afford one, I've never felt the need to live in a mansion. When coronavirus struck, I got stick on Twitter – 'It's all right for you in your massive house surrounded by luxuries.' It made me laugh as I banged my head on the door frame into my little kitchen. Flash isn't what I represent. My history is what I represent. My past, my family, the environment in which I grew up is the dominant part of who I am. I was brought up in my mum and dad's house. My mum was born and brought up in the one across the road. My dad in a valley a few miles away. I don't want to move on from that. I'm really proud I can be a representation of my family, the same as they are a representation of me. The fact they nurtured me to be successful, not just in sport but in life, is a shining acknowledgement of their parenting skills.

I am proud of my real world. I've got through my hardest times precisely because I have remained dead centre in it. In the real world, you have to fight for things. In the real world you have choices to make about your own moral dignity, you have to work hard to achieve, you have to understand the value of everything. Move into a big house behind gates and a high wall and it's tempting to think that everybody on the other side is your enemy. Never for one minute have I felt like that.

Just as the first coronavirus lockdown was lifting, when I was waiting to move into my new house and was back at my mum and dad's (again), I went out for a run. My route took me the couple of miles down into Bridgend, past the rugby club and back up to the house. It was beautiful. Men and women, all different ages, were shouting 'Alfie! Heh, Alfie, butt!' as I ran past. I plodded every step with the biggest smile on my face. It was just the loveliest thing to go on a run round this place that has been my home for so many years and for everyone to be so normal about seeing me knocking around. It felt like a homecoming. I've been to quite a few awards dos and fancy dinners now, and I've been lucky enough to travel to some amazing places, but nothing could ever make me feel better than the normality I experienced on that run that day. I wanted to capture that feeling, wrap it up and carry it with me to show other people how good just being one more member of a community feels, the same as anyone else. The minor challenge of a four-mile run had delivered more than I could have ever imagined.

My parents' house has all sorts of mementos of my career displayed – trophies, shirts, awards. My hundredth cap for Wales sits alongside an award from Stonewall from when I came out as gay. I think I get more out of the fact that my mum so cherishes those items than the fact I won them in the first place. She's proud of me and I love her for keeping all these souvenirs. I don't have anything displayed in our house, though. The only thing is my Pride of Sport Award tucked on a shelf and that's only because Stephen insisted. If it was up to me there'd be nothing. I find showing off awards a little bit cringeworthy. I can't think of anything worse than someone spotting something in my house and saying, 'Oh, I didn't know you won that,' and then I'd have to explain what exactly I was given it for.

Flash isn't a characteristic you generally see in Welsh people. We have a mutual unwritten, unsaid understanding of hardship, of what people have had to go through to get to where they are. Few have had it easy. All along the way there will have been obstacles. It's why, certainly when I was a kid, you respected your kit, wherever it had come from. I would rather not have had a pair of rugby boots from Woolworths but equally I knew that was all Mum could afford. There are other rugby nations where having the best gear will be more expected, not as appreciated. When I started making inroads into the sport, I would end up having extra kit that I had been given. I didn't want to hold on to it for no reason or disrespect it and so I would give it to the kids on my street. If I had too much, which is often the case when you move into the game proper, I wanted people to use it, appreciate it, understand its value, rather than just let it sit in a cupboard.

Wherever I played in Wales, whatever we achieved as a team, or as individuals, it was always understood how hard someone else had worked for us to enjoy the privilege of being out on that field. I did feel there were times with English teams when that was not the case because players had potentially been brought up with more of a sense of entitlement and expectancy. If someone has expected something from the year dot and always been given it, how do they ever understand the value of things?

Like most people who are from where I am, I was taught from day one not just to value every single thing given to me but also everything I earned. You work for everything you get. In the communities of South Wales, opportunities are thin on the ground. They don't come round once a day. Chances are they don't come round once a year. Like the generations who came before, you grab whatever's there and then you try your very damnedest to make it work. From the day we left school, neither me nor my brothers have ever been out of jobs. We've always known the importance of work, for financial reasons and also for the sense of belonging. Work is what good people do. They work hard and they enjoy their lives. All through my life, even as a rugby player when I was getting paid well compared to other people, I have always made sure I feel a sense of justification for my money. I don't want anything for free.

It gives me great comfort that I don't just have a mum and dad who really support me but I have my two brothers as well. I think our parents brought up the three of us with complete equality. There was a long period when we were kids where we all played rugby on a Saturday. They would go to one place, watch Steve for twenty minutes, jump in the car and drive however many miles to where Richard was playing, watch him for twenty minutes, and then be off again to watch me playing the final twenty minutes somewhere else. They followed us around religiously to make sure we all had an equivalent amount of their attention. And that's without mentioning all the other sports we did as well. Growing up, and even now, we have always had an equal share of our parents' love, attention and advice whenever we have needed it. Though my brothers might not agree! They call me 'Golden Bollocks'. Walk in our parents' house, they joke, and you wouldn't even realise they had two other children. It's just full of photos of me and my achievements.

My brothers are no different to anyone else. They have had troubles in their lives as well as successes, ups and downs like us all, and my parents have always been equally supportive, even if it meant creating for themselves a massive logistical headache. I am aware also that my public profile has caused them some real problems at times, perhaps when they've been stood at a bar and someone, not knowing a family member is two feet away, has started saying something crude or unpleasant, or just plain lies, about me. They've had to confront people because of it.

'You don't know anything about him. He's my brother. Shut up.'

People in pubs, as with social media, say things they don't really mean, because the target of their vitriol isn't actually there. It can be a comment that's thrown away and, in their mind, has no ramifications. But no one ever knows who's standing two feet away. I know my brothers have heard so much over the years. Everything I've gone through, whether it be behind closed doors or in the spotlight, they have gone through as well. That's hard. If I walked into a pub and somebody was talking about my brother, I'm not sure how I would react, but they have experienced a lot of that and the way they have dealt with it is a credit to them.

My family has gone through a lot of things that have put us under the microscope. People think it is easier to deal with if you are not the one in focus. That's wrong. If you are under the microscope and nobody can see you, like my brothers, and my parents, then that is hard. They see all the reports on the television, the articles in the newspapers, but nobody knows they are part of the situation. Somehow, they have had to find a coping mechanism.

It's funny to think me and my brothers grew up beating holy shit out of each other. I learned a lot from those scraps. I'm a terrible fighter but I can absolutely take a beating! In decrepit middle age, we all look roughly the same size. As kids, though, they were always physically bigger than me, not just because they were older, but because I was, and still am, naturally very skinny. My brothers were bulky, I was a bag of bones. The result, in terms of physical prowess, was that they were always ahead of me. Until he was fifteen, Steve, who is five years older than me, absolutely battered me. My middle brother Richard, who is eighteen months older and the most intelligent of us three, beat the hell out of me as well. Whether it's normal or not, we grew up absolutely hating each other. And then as soon as we became adults we created this really close, supportive family unit. It's at that point you start to realise that life is more important than fighting, working out who's the strongest.

I'm really proud of my brothers and what they've achieved. Even though I spent the first fifteen years of my life being smacked around, I knew deep down that I really admired them, the same as I knew that had they ever seen me getting some stick in the street they would have been straight over to stand up for me.

I replicated everything they did. My brothers did rugby, I did rugby. My brothers did running, I did running. My brothers did karate, I did karate. I never realised it at the time but what they gave me was a blueprint for how to manoeuvre my way through different periods of growing up, what to do and what not to do, depending on my character, my strengths and weaknesses, and how much I desired one thing over another.

I have always been fascinated by other people. I would watch the kids in the street growing up, what they did, the choices they made, but with two older brothers I didn't need to step out of the house to satisfy my habit of people-watching. They provided plenty of opportunity – how they interacted differently according to who they were with, the paths they chose, how they decided to live their lives. I saw my potential played out in front of me in two different forms and I also saw how supportive my parents were of any decision they made. If one chose one route one day and then woke up the next and wanted to head in a different direction, they wouldn't bat an eyelid. It was never, 'Oh, for Christ's sake!' When we were teenagers, they would much rather we explored opportunities. If we didn't like what we found, fine. Better than ignoring the option and then later having regrets. I feel very lucky that Mum and Dad let us make our own mistakes.

Obviously, there were limits but they knew that ultimately, if we were to find happiness and fulfilment, strength and confidence in ourselves – we had to find our own way in life.

Both Richard and Steve were good rugby players but both chose an alternative route to mine. Steve's love of the game was overtaken by other interests, in particular girlfriends and going out! I saw that as a warning of how easily I too could be distracted by other areas and so, while I would go on to love a few drinks and a night out, rugby was always my main focus. Steve would have no regrets on the rugby front. He went on to excel in other areas of life. Richard, meanwhile, was naturally intelligent. While he loved rugby, he had to make a decision – stick with the sport, which was only in the foothills of professionalism, and take the risk of getting smashed up every weekend, or find a good career to support himself and, when they came along, his family. His brain gave him other opportunities. I'm proud of my brothers and proud that my brothers are proud of me. There's another thing – I'm strong enough to batter the shit out of them now!

It wasn't just my brothers who had a big impact on me growing up. Ours was a really social house with friends and family in and out the front door all the time. Between them they intrigued me, inspired me, and gave me so much. Maybe it's a working-class thing to be interested in other people, not to make everything about yourself. One of my biggest fears is that people might think I am only bothered about myself, that they may misunderstand or misinterpret what I am about, because for me life is so massively about other people. I'm intrigued how they get hurt, what offends them, what makes them laugh, what makes them cry.

I was never one of those teenagers cut off from real life, spending every hour in my room, especially as my life increasingly revolved around rugby, which meant I saw my surroundings and the people in it in their entirety. The game was more than a muddy field and a ball, it was the glue that held entire communities together. The club in Pencoed where I started off and grew up at remains as dear to me now as it was then. It gave not just me but my mum and dad really good friends. For a small town or village, a sports club creates money, solidarity and camaraderie, which is why it's so sad to see clubs disappear from the landscape as the grassroots game is deemed less and less relevant. A lot of people in Sarn would take the half-mile stroll to watch a great little club called Tondu. Does that happen now? Well, a few will still go along, but to a lot of others rugby clubs are no longer the heartbeat of the community. It's a shame, and one which could be addressed to some degree by an injection of money into the grassroots game. I hate to think how many talented young players will never realise their ambitions because they no longer have a team close enough for them to walk or bike to. I hate also to think how many kids of whatever ability are missing out on friendships that last for life. It hurts me that when I drive round Bridgend I never see kids playing rugby or football on a patch of grass. Lack of participation breeds apathy. If kids do show an interest in football or rugby, so often they'll just go and watch

Cardiff City or Cardiff Blues. I'd have watched any team play rugby anywhere.

It's not the fixture list on the wall that provides the strength and value of a sports club, it's the fact that it's somewhere you can go and, no matter what your personality, your shyness, your bravado, automatically find a group of friends, maybe a side of yourself you never even knew existed. Initially, I was really quiet in that environment. I felt down about my spots and hated the colour of my hair and the size of my ears. Some of the boys at Pencoed were actually the ones who had flicked me with the towels at the swimming baths. But the atmosphere of the club made me feel like I had a part to play. Rugby was more of a reason to be at the club rather than a purpose in itself. Before too long, I had totally come out of myself. I always seemed to be the one getting in trouble, the one who was the joker, the one who would go along with a dare. Thinking about it, I'm not actually sure that much has changed!

There was another factor. In my younger years, I felt I wasn't really that talented but I could be part of a successful team while being pretty shit. At Pencoed, I was in a side that went round destroying opponents. My role in that was pretty much just standing on the sidelines – I never had a chance to play. But I was still part of this winning group. I could go in the changing rooms after the match, jump up and down and celebrate. On the rare occasions the team lost, I shared the frustration, the disappointment. As a kid who was quite insecure about himself, to be able to feel like part of something without having actually to contribute anything was both uplifting and empowering. If sport is all about feeling you're worth something, then that's exactly what I got from it. It was truly joyous to feel like I really belonged somewhere, that I'd found my safe place. When I did then start to play, to improve, to contribute, to become truly part of the side, that was another level again.

What I found at Pencoed put to bed any last idea of pursuing an individual sport. I did all sorts growing up – swimming, judo, athletics, tennis, the lot – but I found lone sports never quite delivered what I wanted. More than anything, I needed a shared experience. If you have twenty-three people celebrating a victory, it is so much better than celebrating on your own. Equally, twenty-three people commiserating over a loss makes it much easier to deal with than the overarching despair of 'Nobody else knows what this feels like.'

I'm not saying every minute was idyllic. Like any kid, I didn't always want to go. I had a little phase at around twelve years old when I just didn't fancy it, even sabotaging my mum and dad's alarm clock in the early hours of one Sunday morning, sneaking into their room and changing the time. It didn't work, of course. When 7am came round, I could hear them getting up as normal. But otherwise, playing rugby at Pencoed was always massively important to me and still has a hugely positive impact on my life.

I have a great friend, Harry, from my time at Pencoed. We were down there all the time from the age of eight to eighteen. At that point, he went off and did his thing and I went off and did mine but he remains one of my best mates. All because we played rugby together. Sports clubs provide social cohesion for young people, a group of trusted friends, a sense of purpose. When me and Harry meet up now, we'll spend a few minutes talking about our lives but you can bet within ten minutes we'll be banging on about all the crazy stuff we did back then. We still have Pencoed reunions and, as much as I might stick out a bit because of my rugby career, I know I am no different to so many other people in that room who owe the person they became to that rugby club.

People say to me, 'You are a hero, a trailblazer, an inspiration.' I don't know who I am, but whoever it is I'm like this because I've been brought up properly. I've been surrounded by inspirational people – my mum, my dad, my brothers and the rest of my family. It's nice to hear if people find the work I do meaningful but I am always aware that if I'd not found rugby, not had a strong family set-up, it could well have been a different story. It's from both I learned the majority of my life skills. I have met enough people whose childhood was disrupted to see that it causes a scar that is hard to heal.

It saddens me that so many kids with so much to offer are written off because of their background. They feel they don't matter so they become reckless in their attitude to themselves. If family is absent then community needs to take over but the reality is that it takes a lot of good, strong people, commitment and potentially money to make that happen. We should never be defeatist, however. There are lots of people out there, doing amazing work, allowing young people to experience a different side to life and see there is another way. Sport has to be part of that process. Clubs, now more than ever, need to be part of their community, from the tiniest village rugby club right up to the biggest Premier League football team.

For those denied stability, sport can be their family. It can be their security, the place they go back to again and again. It can be their refuge from every crisis and their centre of celebration. Their council house in Sarn.

CHAPTER 22

LOVED

'Why didn't you marry a pop star or a film actor?' Stephen used to ask me.

'Because I love you,' I'd tell him. 'If I married a pop star and went round in a private jet having holidays in God knows where, it wouldn't be me. I love you. I love your morals. I love everything about you and me.'

That was Stephen's insecurities coming to the surface but I could say exactly the same to him. 'Why didn't you marry someone who is less accident prone? Who offers peace and solitude? Just you and them?' And for his part, he would tell me that he too wants me for exactly the way I am.

Stephen works with kids who have been excluded from mainstream education, helping them acquire new skills. I met him at his college when I was doing some work with schools, helping young people to find their way in life. I'm terrible at introductions. I get really embarrassed and never know what to say. The way I see it, if I say to people, 'Hi, I'm Gareth,' they're often thinking, 'I'm not stupid! I know who you are!' and if I don't say who I am they think I'm an arrogant so-and-so who just assumes everyone in the world knows my face. Stephen, meanwhile, is shy as anything, and so between us the fact that we spoke at all is a minor miracle.

Our quirks of personality meant getting to know each other better was really awkward for a long while but I have no qualms in saying that I fell in love with Stephen straight away. From that first minute, I sensed I was in the presence of someone very special, who I knew had the kindest heart in existence.

Of course, this is me, so there had to be a complication. Stephen hadn't come out when I met him. He hadn't even told his mum and dad – understandable considering they are in their eighties. Telling anyone you are gay can be difficult but especially so those from a very different generation. It made me laugh when Stephen told me how he had yet to come out and I considered what lay ahead in terms of us accompanying him on his journey – 'I've done this once! I don't want to have to do it again!' But I was glad I was there, to be alongside him as he went through that process made our relationship somehow even more special and his family have been so generous and welcoming to me in every way.

The strength I hope I gave him then pales into insignificance in comparison to the strength he has given me. Few consider what Stephen has gone through, on the merry-go-round that often seems to be my life! When I told him I was going to come out as HIV positive he was, as ever, massively supportive. But while he never said it, I picked up that he was absolutely petrified for me in terms of the stigma and abuse my revelation might generate. I, meanwhile, was worrying for Stephen, dragging him into new and potentially rocky terrain. People on the outside see only the person who has the virus; family and friends are invisible. But Stephen has his mum and dad and two brothers. He has his lovely daughter, Anna. We had to sit with her in the car and tell her that her stepfather has HIV. Anna, as ever, was brilliant, but those kinds of conversations are never easy. Stephen had to reassure all those close to him that he wasn't going to contract HIV, that I wasn't going to die and that no one was in danger if they came to stay with us.

Before any of that happened, of course, he had to come to terms with my condition himself. This was an entirely new world to him. He knew nothing about HIV. But at no point did he ever judge me because Stephen never judges anyone. Instead he trusts people, which creates a gateway to openness. It is why he is so good at what he does. He has a personality which envelops rather than pushes people away. If ever I want to just be, I just sit down with Stephen and feel my worries melt away – important for someone as capable as me at creating confusion in their life. Even when I'm doing what I love I am still perfectly capable of unloading a whole heap of mental chaos all over the table.

A lot of that comes from over-analysing. It's a habit I certainly don't share with Stephen. He has such a simple clarity on the world. He just gets on with the life we've created. That's not to say he doesn't worry about me, it's just that he's really clever at hiding it away. When it comes to me taking on a major hurdle, he will only let on afterwards how he was feeling. At the time he's too busy putting his efforts and energy into caring and supporting. So completely unselfish is he that he puts any need for assurance on his part completely to one side.

My learning to swim for the Ironman is a case in point. Stephen, I found out after the event, was petrified of me going into the sea. While my mum will always make her position clear if she thinks I am being reckless – 'What do you think you're doing?!' – Stephen is usually outwardly calm, while inwardly terrified. I know him well enough to know what's happening in his head now but he's the best I've ever seen at concealing his fears. Only the visible sense of relief when something I've involved myself in is finally over could ever give him away. In that way, he is the axis on which my life swings back and forth. He makes me feel safe and secure, somehow grounded even when I'm involved in one high-profile or potentially pressurised situation or another. There are times when I'll be riddled with apprehension about something happening the next day and I'll say to Stephen, 'What's going to happen tomorrow if it all goes wrong?'

'I don't know,' he'll reply. 'I wish I could give you an answer but whatever it is, we'll wake up in the morning and find out.'

And that's the best answer he could give me because I know then he's not bullshitting me and pretending. Too often we just want someone to justify our actions – to tell us everything is going to be great. Steve keeps it simple. He could go through a million different scenarios, enough to make my head spin, but instead we'll have a two-minute conversation. He won't tell me what I want to hear any more than he'll tell me what I don't.

While I'm constantly fretting, always trying to prepare for the future, Steve lives in the moment. He gets up in the morning, does what needs to be done and goes to bed. I love that. Only the other day I was feeling down, consumed by what I want to achieve over the next couple of years. The only thing on Steve's radar was how the house should be decorated for Christmas. I took immense comfort and inspiration from that. OK, sometimes it's really annoying to be with someone so centred! But it's really calming too. Immediately I saw how pointless this internal discussion over my future really was. Who knows what the next fortnight will bring, let alone the next two years? I put down my list and instead we went to Homebase and bought all sorts of Christmas paraphernalia – baubles, lights, trees, the lot. It made me feel so much better, comforted and warm.

For his part, Steve understands that a part of me thrives on the pressure I put on myself. If I don't have anything to worry about, I'll have to find something to worry about. I lay in bed awake for months worrying about my HIV documentary going out and then after it was broadcast I lay in bed awake for several more months feeling weird because I no longer had anything to worry about. Worry and fear has become so much a part of who I am that I feel odd when it isn't around. It motivates me. I worry that if it isn't there I won't be driven to fight for anything. I will completely relax and that will be the end of it. That side of me can't be easy to live with but Stephen gets it completely. He knows my character inside out and so it's another discussion we never need to have.

If fear and vulnerability consume me, Stephen will be there to drag me back into a better place mentally. He saw me through the bleakest moments of being blackmailed and then being pressurised by the newspapers. There have been more times than I care to remember when I have been sat, head in hands in despair, or struggled through a day in a fog of fear and self-doubt, only for him to grab hold of me and magic me back towards something resembling normality. 'Magic' is exactly the right word because it is a gift almost beyond explanation. Stephen is the best person I have ever met for understanding precisely what someone needs to bring them through their difficulties. I can walk through the door feeling down and dejected and within ten minutes I'll be barely able to breathe for laughing. I'll be leaning against a wall genuinely wondering, 'How the hell did that happen? How has he managed to do that?' At other times he knows if I just need to sit down and cry, to get everything out of my system. When I've finished, he will reassure me, as he has so many times before, that whatever doubts I might have, however insecure I might feel, he is here for me forever. The light that never stops shining, always there to show me the path I need to be travelling, my constant companion on that journey.

I've often thought that there must have been times when he wondered just what exactly he'd let himself in for on that journey and yet he has never indicated that in any way, shape or form. Never has he once pushed me to withdraw a little more from the spotlight – something he would have every right to do when you consider the rollercoaster he's hitched himself to. Thankfully, Stephen knows that it's the dips in the track that make you a stronger person, make you look at the world in a different way, make you have empathy with other people. It would be counter to everything me and Stephen think for me to pull down the shutters and stop campaigning. It would be selfish in the extreme for me to blithely expect someone else to take up the cause because I have found personal happiness. And Stephen is so emotionally selfless that he would never think that way.

Stephen's been the biggest part of some of the proudest moments in my life, but at the same time he'll never be the one on the starting line cheering, never be the one in the camera shot. Stephen would never court publicity. One exception to Steve's reluctance to be in the spotlight was recently when I appeared on a BBC cookery show. They filmed us at our house and on the nearby beach with the dog, in so doing really normalising our marriage. I know it's not a big deal to have two men living together but I still felt that to see this on a cooking show, on BBC1, in primetime, really brings it into the mainstream. It felt liberating to talk about that element of my life. I'm very open personally but I'd never been quite this open. It all came back to a happy, balanced home life with two men who have gone through their own troubles and are now so thankful to have found each other.

People in TV now seem to understand I'm not a curiosity, not someone who is defined by his sexuality, or a virus, I am just an everyday person. I have been through the mill – but then hasn't everyone? I love having that freedom to be me. I don't aspire to be known as anything other than a 'nice guy', someone who is proud of what he represents, but acts in a decent and honest way and genuinely wants to help.

It was really important to me that I married Stephen, that we showed both ourselves and the world our strength in that way. I'd been crashing on to the rocks for years and then along came this amazing human being who provided an anchor. He made me feel like whatever happened in my life, he would always be there. I would never again drift off into stormy waters – he would never let it happen.

Our wedding was one of the greatest days of my life, one that I thought would never happen because, after the turmoil I had been through, I genuinely believed I would never find a life partner, especially with my HIV lingering in the background. But in the end I found Stephen and for that I will always be grateful. That day, at the Great House Hotel just down the road in Bridgend, will always be a treasured memory. All Stephen's family, all my family, all our closest friends. Absolutely lush.

There was a moment that day when I felt I stood, as I have so often done before, outside myself. It was as if I was looking down on what was going on. Yes, I could see a wedding, dozens of people celebrating a moment of immense happiness, me among them, but more than that I could see a bridge being built to a future, one where loneliness, so often my companion in the past, would be banished forever. I was going to spend the rest of my life with someone I loved.

It was then I understood the real power of human emotion, the ability it has to drive out negativity and, at its heart, deliver togetherness.

I looked again at that scene unfolding below me and realised in Stephen I had finally found it – the source of all strength.

EPILOGUE

Here I am in the tattooist's chair. I'd have been sat in it a whole lot earlier if it hadn't been for coronavirus but finally I am having my HIV tattoo. It will, like so many of the others I have, reflect an often traumatic but ultimately liberating mental journey; the design, therefore, is something I have dwelt upon for a long time.

It involves a skull being inked – a lot more painfully than I ever imagined – on to one of my kneecaps. This joint, while shot to pieces by rugby, somehow supported me through the Ironman. The skull is dark, ghoulish and threatening, representing the imminent death I believed awaited me. Beneath it is a pair of wings, signifying the freedom I actually found. The dead man coming back to life. The crown that adorns the skull's head, meanwhile, shows myself as someone willing to lead from the front, wanting to take the campaign against discrimination and misinformation forward, highlighting and celebrating people's truth, never asking people to do something I won't.

It is so important for me to carry this image on my body. Before the tattoo gun starts its scream, I genuinely feel I am missing part of who I am. As the picture takes shape, however, I feel myself filled more and more with the essential truth of change. Yes, the life that has gone matters, but not as much as the life to come.

The three hours fly past. I can see Stephen waiting outside in the car. It is another moment where I cannot help but think how far I have travelled. This whole journey started with a tiny needle prick, one which I believed marked the end of my life. Now, as I hold the tissue to my arm, several thousand more tiny needle pricks mark my journey to a wholly different mindset.

I say this carefully, because I have heard people who have had far more drastic life changes than I have say something similar, but I can't help feeling that HIV has given me an outlook on life that has helped me appreciate it so much more. I look to my future now with a real determination to make the best of whatever time I've got left, not just for me, but for others.

To be a gay man, there are those who judge you as weak. To be a gay man and have HIV, there are those who judge you as even weaker. But actually both have given me strength I never thought imaginable. They have given me confidence in who I am. HIV in particular has made me open up, yes, to you the reader, but also to myself. In doing so, it has given me a real sense of liberation.

Am I stronger for having HIV?

Yes.

In every way – STRONGER.

ACKNOWLEDGEMENTS

Something happened during the writing of this book. I came to understand myself in a way I never truly have before.

There has been an undoubted therapeutic element to the process. Thinking deeply about the way my life has panned out, about discrimination and prejudice, and the incredible people I have met along the way, has made me feel mentally uncluttered in a way I haven't always been used to. As I carry forward my campaigning, it is a feeling I would like to maintain.

I would like to thank those in the HIV 'community' who have spoken so honestly and openly and done so much to educate people, spread a positive message, and remove stigma. For helping me and so many others on our journey, from the bottom of my heart, thank you.

I would like also to thank my ghostwriter John Woodhouse, one of life's great listeners, for making it so easy for me to talk honestly and openly, and taking the time and effort to understand me as a human being. I have come out the other end of the process feeling more awareness of myself than I ever thought possible. I hope reading my book will help others find the strength to better understand themselves too.

Last, but very much not least, I want to thank all those closest to me who have guided me again through difficult times. You all know who you are. Words cannot adequately express my gratitude. I love you all.

Oh, and Boyo – thanks, mate, for the walks.